The Language of Science

The Collected Works of M. A. K. Halliday

Volume 1: *On Grammar*

Volume 2: *Linguistic Studies of Text and Discourse*

Volume 3: *On Language and Linguistics*

Volume 4: *The Language of Early Childhood*

Volume 5: *The Language of Science*

Volume 6: *Computational and Quantitative Studies*

Volume 7: *Studies in English Language*

Volume 8: *Studies in Chinese Language*

Volume 9: *Language and Education*

Volume 10: *Language and Society*

Volume 5 in the Collected Works of M. A. K. Halliday

The Language of Science

M. A. K. Halliday

Edited by Jonathan J. Webster

continuum
LONDON • NEW YORK

Continuum

The Tower Building, 11 York Road, London SE1 7NX

80 Maiden Lane, Suite 704, New York, NY 10038

First published 2004

This paperback edition published 2006

British Library Cataloguing-in-Publication Data

A catalogue record for this book is available from the British Library.

ISBN 0–8264–5871–8 (hardback)

ISBN 0–8264–8827–7 (paperback)

Library of Congress Cataloguing-in-Publication Data

A catalog record for this book is available from the Library of Congress.

Typeset by YHT Ltd, London

Printed and bound in Great Britain by MPG Books Ltd, Bodmin, Cornwall

CONTENTS

Preface   vii

Acknowledgements   ix

Introduction: How Big is a Language?
On the Power of Language   xi

PART ONE GRAMMATICAL METAPHOR   1

Editor's Introduction   3

1 Language and the Reshaping of Human
  Experience   7

2 Language and Knowledge: the
  'Unpacking' of Text   24

3 Things and Relations:
  Regrammaticizing Experience as   49
  Technical Knowledge

4 The Grammatical Construction of
  Scientific Knowledge: the Framing of
  the English Clause   102

PART TWO SCIENTIFIC ENGLISH   135

Editor's Introduction   137

5 On the Language of Physical Science   140

6 Some Grammatical Problems in
   Scientific English   159

7 On the Grammar of Scientific English   181

8 Writing Science: Literacy and
   Discursive Power   199

   Bibliography   227

   Index   237

PREFACE

ἐν ἀρχη ἦν λογος

The rate of glass crack growth depends on the magnitude of the applied stress.
'The fracturing of glass', *Scientific American*, December 1987

What about this quote identifies it to the reader as the discourse of science? How did these features evolve into what we recognize as scientific English? In the papers included in this volume, *The Language of Science*, the fifth in the series of his Collected Works, Professor Halliday looks at the language of science from various perspectives, from the historical to the developmental, as a language teacher and as a linguist.

This volume, however, is much more than a volume of papers on scientific language. It is about that most fundamental ability of humankind, the ability to theorize about ourselves and our world. It is about how we move from commonsense theories of everyday experience to technical and scientific theories of knowledge. It is about how our ways of meaning are evolving, from the congruent to the metaphorical, from the clausal to the nominal.

And God said ... With an utterance, the world came into existence. The clausal origin of the universe, as told in Genesis, mirrors our own use of language to construe reality, and transform experience into meaning. Such is the reality-generating power of grammar, that it enables us to define 'the basic experience of being human'.

Over the course of history, as the need arose for more powerful and abstract theories of experience, humankind has relied on the power of language 'to reconstrue commonsense reality into one that imposed regularities on experience and brought the environment more within our power to control'. Aptly titled *How Big is a Language? On the Power of Language*, Professor Halliday's introduction to this volume and the next makes clear that the source of that power lies in its potential for grammatical metaphor.

Grammatical metaphor, which is explored in detail in the first section of this volume, involves the junction of category meanings, not simply word meanings. Examples of grammatical metaphor include *length*, which is 'a junction of (the quality) "long" and the category meaning of a noun, which is "entity" or "thing"', and *motion*, which is 'a junction of the (the process) "move" and the category meaning, again of a noun'. With grammatical metaphor, the scientist can make the world stand still, or turn it into one consisting only of things, or even create new, virtual realities.

In the second section of this volume, Professor Halliday discusses how the features of scientific English have developed over time, evolving to meet the needs of the experts, giving them enormous power over the environment, but at the risk of alienating learners and turning science into 'the prerogative of an elite'. What can the language educator do to help those who have been shut out of scientific discourse? The language educator can only help the learner, if (s)he understands how the discourse works. Halliday makes a strong case for adopting the 'paradigmatic-functional' design of systemic grammar to accomplish this task.

Scientific discourse foregrounds things at the expense of qualities, processes and relations. Grammatical metaphor in scientific discourse is described as 'a steady drift towards things; and the prototype of a thing is a concrete object'. Thus he notes 'the interesting paradox: the most abstract theorizing is achieved by modeling everything on the concrete'. The nominalizing grammar of science results in a discourse that is ultimately just about things. The discourse becomes that which it creates.

και ὁ λογος γαρ ἐγενετο

ACKNOWLEDGEMENTS

We are grateful to the original publishers for permission to reprint the articles and chapters in this volume. Original publication details are provided below, and also at the beginning of each chapter.

'Language and the reshaping of human experience' from *International Symposium on Critical Discourse Analysis*, Athens, 15–16 December 1995. Speech delivered at the official ceremony for M. A. K. Halliday at the National and Kapodistrian University of Athens, Doctor honoris causa of the Faculty of English Studies, School of Philosophy, on 14 December 1995. The speech also appears as No. 44 in Vol. 31 (Athens, 2002) of the *Official Speeches*, (period 1 September 1995–31 August 1997) Part A, 1995–6, pp. 1261–76.

'Language and knowledge: the "unpacking" of text', from *Text in Education and Society*, edited by Desmond Allison, Lionel Wee, Bao Zhiming and Sunita Anne Abraham, Singapore: Singapore University Press and World Scientific, 1998. Reprinted by permission of National University of Singapore and World Scientific.

'Things and relations: regrammaticizing experience as technical knowledge', from *Reading Science: Critical and Functional Perspectives on Discourses of Science*, edited by James R. Martin and Robert Veel, London: Routledge, 1998. Reprinted by permission of Routledge.

Appendix 1, Chapter 3 from *General Microbiology*, 5th edition, edited by Roger Y. Stanier, John L. Ingraham, Mark L. Wheelis and Page R. Painter, Basingstoke and London: Macmillan Education, 1987.

'The grammatical construction of scientific knowledge: the framing of the English clause', from *Incommensurability and Translation: Kuhnian Perspectives on Scientific Communication and Theory*

Change, edited by Rema Rossini Favretti, Giorgio Sandri and Roberto Scazzieri, Cheltenham: Edward Elgar, 1999.

'On the language of physical science', from *Registers of Written English: Situational Factors and Linguistic Features*, edited by Mohsen Ghadessy, London: Pinter, 1988. Reprinted by permission of the Continuum International Publishing Group Ltd.

'Some grammatical problems in scientific English', from *Symposium in Education*, Society of Pakistani English Language Teachers, Karachi: SPELT, 1989.

'On the grammar of scientific English', from *Grammatica: studi interlinguistici*, edited by Carol Taylor Torsello, Padova: Unipress, 1997.

'Writing science: literacy and discursive power' from *Writing Science: Literacy and Discursive Power*, M. A. K. Halliday and James Martin, London: RoutledgeFalmer, 1993. Reprinted by permission of RoutledgeFalmer.

INTRODUCTION: HOW BIG IS A LANGUAGE? ON THE POWER OF LANGUAGE

1

In a paper appearing in the first volume of this series (Chapter 15) I had raised the question, how big is a grammar; the same question was brought up again in Volume 3 (Chapter 18), reformulated this time as 'how big is a language?' I asked this question because I wanted to foreground the power that a language has for making meaning. It seems to me rather paradoxical that, while so much is written about the creative effects of language (these used to be seen more as positive effects, as in literary stylistics; now they are usually presented as negative, e.g. in critical discourse analysis), descriptions of language don't give this sense of its power. If anything, they stress its limitations, so that it becomes hard to understand how these effects are achieved. Somewhere I commented, in reacting to the now familiar motif that political authority is maintained and legitimized through language, that the language of power depends on the power of language; so surely as linguists we should try to bring this out.

Back in the 1950s, as a language teacher, I was already struggling with this anxiety – that we weren't helping those learning a language to appreciate the nature of their task. I wanted to foreground the paradigmatic dimension, whereby a language appears as a meaning-making resource and meaning can be presented as choice. This paradigmatic principle had been established in semiotics by Saussure, whose concept of value, and of terms in a system, showed up paradigmatic organization as the most abstract dimension of meaning (1966, Part 2, Chapters 3–5, pp. 107–27 [French original 1915]).

The best exposition of Saussure's theoretical ideas is Paul Thibault's *Re-reading Saussure* (1997); see especially Part 4, pp. 163–207. The Saussurean project had been carried forward by Hjelmslev, at the level of a comprehensive general theory (1961 [Danish original 1943]); and more selectively by Firth, who made explicit the interaction between paradigmatic and syntagmatic organization, modelling these in the mutually defining categories of system and structure. Firth's formulation is worth quoting:

> The first principle of analysis is to distinguish between *structure* and *system*. . . .
>
> Structure consists of elements in interior syntagmatic relation and these elements have their places in an order of mutual expectancy. . . .
>
> Systems of commutable terms or units are set up to state the paradigmatic value of the elements.
>
> (Firth 1957)

Thus Firth introduced his category of **system** in theorizing paradigmatic relations; and it was this that I tried to follow in my own work. But I wanted to investigate systems in their association with one another, and at the same time to free the system from any constraints of structure (that is, to locate each system in its paradigmatic environment, irrespective of how it happened to be realized structurally); so I took the system out of its context in the structure–system cycle and 'thickened' it to form networks of interrelated systems. Matthiessen (2000) and Butt (2001) trace the history of the system network representation of the paradigmatic dimension in language. The system network enables the analyst to represent sets of paradigmatic options in their own terms, as they intersect with each other. The network, as Butt (2000) observes, is a form of argumentation, one which projects the view of a language as an open-ended semogenic resource.

What I was trying to suggest, in raising the question of how big is a language, was that when we do represent the grammar paradigmatically we get a sense of the scope of its total potential for meaning. The network is open-ended in delicacy: there is no point at which we can stop and say that no further distinctions can be made. But if we extend the systemic description to some point where it is still well within the limits of what speakers of a language can recognize as significantly different meanings, we have some idea of the scale of the options available. I gave the example of the English verbal group, bringing out between 50,000 and 100,000 variants for just one lexical verb, provided it had a passive as well as an active voice.

I included in the tally systems whose terms are realized prosodically, by tone and location of tonic prominence; these will not appear in written form, at any rate not in a text composed in normal orthography, and they are not systems of the verbal group as such but systems of the information unit (realized as a tone group) and hence most typically mapped into a clause; these added significantly to the total – but they have to figure somewhere in the overall account of the grammar. And on the other hand some further distinctions were left out. In any case, the aim was not to establish an exact quantitative value, which would be impossible, but to give an idea of the order of magnitude of a characteristic grammatical paradigm. It takes only thirty independent binary choices to yield a paradigm of a billion options; and while grammatical systems are not typically independent, every language has a very large number of them. Systemic grammars of English in computational form now have between one and two thousand.

It is not this aspect of the 'how big?' question that is being explored in this volume and Volume 6. But let me add one more point about the system network form of representation. The network is, as I have said, a theoretical model of the paradigm: it theorizes a language as a meaning potential – or better, perhaps, as a meaning potential potential: that is, a system that has the potential to create a meaning potential. Clearly, then, the interdependence of the systems that make up a network is of critical importance to determining its overall power. But this can only be established empirically, on the basis of an extensive body of natural text. Such bodies of data are now available, in the form of a computerized corpus. So far, parsing and pattern-matching software, though it has become highly sophisticated, has still not reached the level where the necessary analysis can be carried out mechanically on a big enough scale; one needs to process the grammar of tens of millions of clauses. But Matthiessen has been building up an archive of texts which he has analysed 'manually' for a number of selected features, and investigating the degree of dependence among different grammatical systems. He has examined the frequency profiles of some primary systems of English grammar, such as those of transitivity and mood; and in what he stresses is an 'interim report' (in press) he offers a provisional finding concerning patterns of systemic interdependence. Leaving aside cases where one system is fully dependent on another (such that the two are formally – though not functionally – equivalent to a single system), Matthiessen finds that the degree of mutual conditioning between systems depends first and foremost on their metafunctional relationship. Systems within the same meta-functional component of the grammar affect each others' probabilities significantly more than do systems from different metafunctions. This important finding (with Matthiessen again stressing its provisional nature) gives substance to the metafunctional hypothesis: not only pointing up the fact that the grammar is organized along metafunctional lines, but also suggesting that it is this that provides the framework for the balanced interplay of information and redundancy in the grammar as a whole. Where different **kinds** of meaning are combined, the level of information is very high.

Matthiessen's investigation of the conditioning of probabilities between systems raises in turn the question of the probability profiles of the systems themselves. This is taken up in some papers appearing in the next volume (Volume 6). The suggestion made there is that major (primary) grammatical systems tend towards one or other of two quantitative profiles: either the terms are roughly equiprobable, or they are skewed by about one order of magnitude. (This is the formulation for binary systems such as singular/plural or positive/negative.) If this kind of regularity turned out to be valid, it would mean that mutual conditioning of systems would be a noticeable and significant feature of the grammar. A great deal of work is needed to explore this aspect of the meaning potential of a language. But clearly the quantitative properties of systems in lexicogrammar are an important ingredient in language's semogenic power. To cite a familiar example used by Halliday and Matthiessen (1999), if a shift in the frequency patterns of one major grammatical system can open up a new domain, in the way that future tense in weather forecasting creates a virtual reality in which the future is the unmarked time, this shows that the meaning potential that inheres in the system of tense is not just a simple choice among three possibilities. It is a much richer resource which carries within it a notable reality-generating power.

2

The papers brought together in Volumes 5 and 6 are organized around this same basic issue: that of 'how big is a language?', interpreted as the question of its power. This cannot be assessed in any straightforwardly quantitative terms, such as the number of possibilities arrived at by combining all the options in a network representation of the lexicogrammar. These papers are concerned rather with ways in which the meaning potential gets extended beyond the set of selection expressions generated by a grammatical network. Volume 6 focuses on the notion of a language as a probabilistic system (using "system" here in its wider sense – Hjelmslevian rather than Firthian – to refer to a language as a whole); the basic proposition is that a system (back to its technical sense!) is made up not simply of 'either *m* or *n*' but of 'either *m* or *n* with a certain probability attached'. In that case, local variants of these global probabilities constitute an additional semogenic resource. If for example the global system of *polarity* is formed out of 'positive 0.9/ negative 0.1', while some local variants show negative as equal in frequency to positive, or even significantly more frequent than positive, then the overall meaning potential of the *polarity* system is much more than that of a simple opposition. Register variation as constituted by the resetting of grammatical probabilities is just as meaningful as would be variation marked by a categorical shift into a different inventory of words and structures.

This leads in to the question of the language of science, which is the topic of the current volume. There is of course no single register of science; there are numerous scientific discourses, not only covering diverse disciplines and sub-disciplines but also, and more significantly, different participants in the processes of science: specialist articles (including abstracts), textbooks, science for lay readers and listeners and so on. These have in common the function that they are extending someone's knowledge in some technical domain: the audiences being addressed may be anywhere from high level professionals to complete novices, but the text is organized so as to tell them something that they don't already know, with "telling" covering a range of interpersonal attitudes from a tentative suggestion to an aggressive attempt to persuade.

If we look into the history of the discourses of technology and science, we find new strategies evolving: new ways of organizing the grammar as a resource for making meaning. I think the best way of characterizing these strategies, in very general terms, is that they are grounded in the processes of *metaphor*. Not that metaphor in itself was anything new; metaphor is a feature of every language, and in fact it is a potential that became built into language in the course of its evolution, from the moment when the content plane became 'deconstrued' into the two strata of semantics and lexicogrammar (as happens in the life history of the individual child; cf. Part 2 of Volume 4, and also Painter 1984, Oldenburg-Torr 1997). Once that has taken place, any relationship of form and meaning can be 'decoupled' and replaced by a new 'cross-coupling' in which the meaning is now represented by a different form; only, it is no longer the same meaning, because some fusion has taken place, a 'semantic junction' in which the meaning of the original form has left its mark.

This is the critical characteristic of metaphor. When for example *an inflexible will* is relexicalized as *an iron will*, a new meaning is construed which is a junction of the congruent senses of these two lexical items, 'which cannot be deflected' and '(made of) a rigid metal'. The simile form, *a will like iron*, provides the link between the congruent and the metaphorical modes of meaning. Of course, this particular example has been around for a very long time; it is now fully coded in the language, not construed afresh on each occasion. But this is the essential nature of the metaphoric process.

The step that was taken when languages began to evolve technical forms of discourse was simply to move this strategy across from lexis into grammar. This probably started, or at least first reached a significant scale, with nominalization: decoupling 'qualities' and 'processes' from their congruent realizations as adjectives and verbs, and recoupling both these meanings with nouns. The cross-coupling here is not between words (lexical items) but between grammatical classes. It was already happening long ago, in the classical languages (Chinese, Greek, Sanskrit) of the Bronze and Early Iron Ages; but we can illustrate from English, with words such as *length* and *motion*. These show the same phenomenon of semantic junction; but it is a junction of category meanings, not of word meanings:

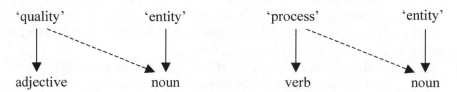

Thus, the word *length* expresses a complex meaning that is a junction of (the quality) 'long' and the category meaning of a noun, which is 'entity' or 'thing'. Likewise *motion* expresses a complex meaning that is a junction of (the process) 'move' and the category meaning, again, of a noun. It seemed natural to refer to this as "grammatical metaphor", to show both its relationship to, and its distinctness from, metaphor in its familiar, lexical guise.

The potential for metaphor, which arises once language evolves to become stratified (though to put it like that makes it sound too much like a by-product, whereas metaphor is an inherent part of the stratification process), is a major contributor to the overall power of language. But it is especially grammatical metaphor, because of the breadth and generality of its application, that has the most significant effect. Grammatical metaphor creates virtual phenomena – virtual entities, virtual processes – which exist solely on the semiotic plane; this makes them extremely powerful abstract tools for thinking with.

Thus what grammatical metaphor does is to increase the power that a language has for **theorizing**. All use of language embodies theory; as I have said in various earlier contexts, the grammar of every language contains a theory of human experience: it categorizes the elements of our experience into basic phenomenal types, construing these into configurations of various kinds, and these configurations in turn into logical sequences. For much of human history, no doubt, this was the only model of reality; and it remains the model of reality into which human children are first inducted. But as some human groups became settled, developing writing systems and technical competences, so their theory of experience became more abstract and more powerful – and more and more the product of conscious design. Grammatical metaphor reconstrued the human environment, transforming the commonsense picture of the world into one that imposed regularities on experience and brought the environment more within our power to control. This reconstrued version of reality is the one our children have to master as they work their way through the obstacle course of the educational process. It is presented most clearly in the discourse of the natural sciences, which is where it evolved. This is the theme of the papers in the present volume.

3

There is obviously no way of measuring the size of a language – that is, assigning it some kind of overall quantitative value. Some things can be counted: the number of distinct syllables, for example [this is discussed in a subsequent volume of papers on the Chinese language]; and possibly, though with rather less accuracy, the number of distinct morphemes. It is also possible to calculate the output of a system network, meaning the number of selection expressions generated by it, and the information carried by any one system based on the relative probabilities of its terms; combining these two would then give a measure of the information contained in the total network. It may turn out to be worthwhile doing such calculations, once we have enough reliable corpus-based data on relative frequencies. But it is doubtful – though interesting to think about – what kind of interpretation one would put on the result. As I put it earlier, while the meaning potential of a language at any one moment in space-time is limited, its meaning potential **potential** is unlimited. In that perspective, a language is indefinitely large.

So is asking this question just playing a game, like searching for the longest word when we were children? (In my primary school the longest word in English was said to be *antidisestablishmentarianism*, which we triumphantly capped by adding *pseudo-* at the beginning.) As I said at the beginning, I first thought of this question of size when I was working as a language teacher, teaching a foreign language to adult beginners. I was not thinking of longest words or longest sentences, of course, but of the nature of the learner's task: how did one construct a course, a project of designed learning, to open up the huge meaning potential (not that I had that notion at the time) that the learner was attempting to attain? I had no clear concept of the relation between text and system (i.e. of instantiation); but I have always tended to think of language paradigmatically, relating what was said to what might have been said but was not, and tried to use current practices like "structure drill" as windows on to a wider world of meaning. It was in this perspective that the question of 'how big?' presented itself: as a way of thinking about the task faced by someone studying a foreign language.

When I moved over to working with teachers of English as a mother tongue (at a time when it was coming to be accepted that there was a significant component of language learning in all school subjects – "language across the curriculum" was the new conception), the question became, if anything, even more critical. It was in this context that I began the intensive study of the language development of a child, which I formulated to myself as the process of 'learning how to mean'. I tried to track the remarkable expansion of the child's meaning potential through the first three years of life (see Volume 4; and also the growth modelling of important parts of the same data in the form of 'shadow' networks by Joy Phillips).

There was no question that the child's language was getting bigger all the time.

Given this developmental perspective, the phenomenon of grammatical metaphor contextualizes itself, so to speak, as part of the overall process of extending the power of language. It is in school, in the course of their institutionalized education, that children will start to expand their meaning potential along metaphoric lines. This takes place in stages. The initial move into, or in the direction of, grammatical metaphor takes place in the primary school, with the introduction of abstract technical terms; these relate first to language itself, with the move into the written channel (which then very quickly becomes the default channel for further educational learning), and to numerical operations of measuring and calculating. But here we see the origin of the split between the two cultures, which continues to distort so much of our educational practice. In the move towards science and mathematics, the metaphoric foundations of terms like *length* and *addition* are strengthened and built upon, so that by the fifth and sixth years of primary school the learner has become versed in this mode of meaning and can begin to cope with discourse that is grounded in grammatical metaphor. But the treatment of language remains at a very unsophisticated level, or else is abandoned altogether; the development of writing skills is expected to take place without the benefit of any technical knowledge, and if grammar continues to be mentioned at all it is only in the context of rules of good behaviour. At the beginning of secondary school, textbooks in mathematics and science are already assuming a highly elaborated, technical level of knowledge; whereas the treatment of language is primitive and naive, and often also apologetic in its presentation, as if serious technical discourse about language was something obscene, or else invading the private terrain of the individual. Such, at least, is the way it has seemed to me in the English-speaking contexts with which I am familiar.

But it is only in the secondary school, with its technical, discipline-based forms of knowledge, that the student will be learning through forms of discourse where the predominating mode is the metaphoric one. This reflects the level of maturity of the learner: it is only when approaching adolescence that children can cope with this level of semiotic complexity. (It is no use asking whether the difficulty for younger learners lies in the content or in the mode of expression, because the two are simply aspects of the same thing: the "content" is the construction of the grammar. When grammatical metaphor occurs in other contexts, interpersonal or non-technical ideational, it can still cause problems; but it is found to be more accessible and may help to bridge the distance to the fully metaphoric discourse of the scientific disciplines.)

Grammatical metaphor adds a new dimension to the expanding meaning potential. It is not simply adding new features and new systems to the network; rather, it is 'thickening' the processes of meaning by creating another plane of semiotic reality, where theories can be construed out of 'virtual' phenomena which exist solely on the semiotic plane. In that respect it provides an essential component in the construction of scientific knowledge. By the same token, metaphor in general — but in particular, because of its ability to irradiate the entire discourse, metaphor in the grammar — is a major source of the energy that constitutes the power of language.

4

Thus, what began for me as an enterprise in language education, trying to find the source of the difficulties faced by learners of science, turned first of all into an excursion into history, as I tried to follow back the grammatical styles of scientific writing in English through the preceding centuries. I did not concern myself with the genres of scientific discourse; not, obviously, because I thought them unimportant but because they had already been studied and described by others much more thoroughly than I would have been able to attempt. It was intriguing to see how the metaphoric grammar evolved, from Newton to the present day, as more of the clause got co-opted into the metaphoric code and the density of metaphor steadily increased. Sadly for personal reasons I was unable to finish a book that I was writing, bringing together (under the deliberately ambiguous title *Language and Learning*) the educational and the historical aspects of the picture; it remains one of the (all too many!) unfinished projects of a rather disorganized life.[1]

Meanwhile I came to think of grammatical metaphor from another angle, namely that of its central role in (as I have been putting it here) extending the power of language. In this respect, tying it too closely to the language of science may turn out to have been misleading. Metaphor, as I have tried to make clear, is a feature of all post-infancy language: once the "content plane" has been deconstrued into (what we call) a stratum of lexicogrammar and a stratum of semantics, any connections between the two can be decoupled and new 'cross-couplings' established, resulting by what I have been calling "semantic junction" in new constructions of meaning. Whether there was a time when this kind of cross-coupling happened only with individual lexical items, not grammatical classes, I do not know; in any case languages differ greatly in what they grammaticalize, and how they do it, so it is not easy to formulate the question in sufficiently abstract terms. But it seemed to me that the wholesale transformation of discourse into syndromes of grammatical metaphor (such as those I am using now) was a recent feature and was associated with the theorizing of knowledge which transformed technology into science; it was then, by virtue of its esoteric nature and accompanying prestige, borrowed into other discourses as a vehicle of power. This history may be wrong – it may simply reflect my own way in when coming to explore the phenomenon twenty-five years ago. But the point is that it is **motivated** in the discourses of science, because of its massive potential for creating new knowledge; whereas elsewhere, say in bureaucratic discourse, its function is a **ritual** one – motivated because of its association with power, but having no semogenic potential (creating no new edifices of meaning) in the context in which it is occurring.

As in all the other volumes, most of the papers collected here began as single invited lectures or as chapters of books. This explains why material gets repeated: the background has to be made explicit on each occasion. It also explains why many of the chapter titles are rather too general: they began as titles of abstracts which had to be submitted long before the paper itself came to be written! But at the same time, I tried to use each occasion as an opportunity for going further into the topic; I hope that the parts do add up to a reasonably coherent whole. And I hope that my own writing, while it relies on grammatical metaphor in both its two main functions (technicality and rationality; see Chapter 3), is not so saturated with it that it brings on a bout of semiotic indigestion. I try to avoid this by reading what I write aloud; but for that to be effective it would have to be addressed to an audience other than myself, and that is rather too much to inflict on one's relatives and friends.

5

It is perhaps not too fanciful to suggest that the chapters in Volume 6 also fall within the scope of this same motif, the power of language. They cover two related aspects of language as system and process.

One is the representation of a language in computational form, and the use of a computer to operationalize the relation between system and text (text generation and parsing). The other is the quantitative study of text data as compiled in a computerized corpus. Both fall within the domain of computational linguistics; more importantly, following the paradigmatic principle both theorize the grammatical system as a network of connections that generate instances of text.

To put these papers in some kind of chronological sequence, I will switch into the narrative mode, with apologies for the consequent prominence of first person themes. The story starts with machine translation. I had first read about this in, I think, 1950, just as I came to know Jeff Ellis and Trevor Hill and we began to follow up our shared interest in the development of national languages in newly decolonized countries. UNESCO had then produced a significant report which stressed the advantages of education in the mother tongue, and it seemed to me that machine translation would make it possible to produce the necessary teaching materials cheaply and quickly. I applied for a position in one of the early projects but was turned down – the task was seen as one for computer engineers, not for linguists!

In 1956 Margaret Masterman invited me to join the Cambridge Language Research Unit, which she had set up to investigate machine translation from a theoretical standpoint; the other founder members were A. F. Parker-Rhodes and R. H. Richens. Using test sentences from three languages (English, Chinese and Italian), we worked on the representation of grammatical structures; but I failed to persuade my colleagues that we ought also to represent the underlying grammatical systems. (See Jacqueline Léon 2000 for an account of the history of the C.L.R.U.)

At University College London in the 1960s I started a research project in the grammar of scientific English (DSIR/OSTI Programme in the Linguistic Properties of Scientific English), with Rodney Huddleston as chief investigator. He, Richard Hudson and Eugene Winter undertook a large-scale analysis of scientific texts, with the aid of Alick Henrici as programmer. Henrici was the first to implement some components of systemic grammar in a computer, forming paradigms from a network and operating on the structural output. (See Huddleston et al. 1968; Henrici 1981.)

Meanwhile I had been counting (manually) occurrences of a number of grammatical features in four varieties (registers) of English texts, noting the first 2,000 occurrences of each system (tense, polarity, etc.). I was interested in the information and redundancy of grammatical systems. The view that prevailed among linguists was that information theory had nothing of interest to offer to linguistics; but that was because they were not thinking paradigmatically. Information can only be a property of a system, not of a structure. A paper I wrote on this topic in 1968 got lost; but the reason I selected two thousand as the number of occurrences to be counted was that I wanted 200 instances of the less frequent term – as the bottom line, so to speak – and I had noticed in my first rough tryouts that if a binary system was skew (like positive/negative polarity) the relative frequency of the two terms seemed to tend towards one order of magnitude.

It was not until 1992 that I was able to return to the study of grammatical probabilities. Meanwhile in 1980 – the third of my encounters with computational linguistics, which seemed to take place at roughly twelve-year intervals – I had the good fortune to meet William Mann of the University of Southern California, who was inaugurating a project in text generation and invited me to write the initial grammar for it. By this time computers had evolved to the point where they were now a valuable resource for linguistic research, and this would provide for the first time an opportunity for testing the basic mechanism of a systemic grammar. Christian Matthiessen joined the project and over a number of years extended the scope of the grammar and worked with Bill Mann in exploring strategies for controlling the grammar 'from above'. By the end of the project there were about a thousand systems in the total grammatical network. (See Mann and Matthiessen 1991.)

In 1992 I worked for some months in John Sinclair's groundbreaking COBUILD corpus research project, and collaboration with Zoe James produced what I think was the first large-scale quantitative study of grammatical systems, covering one and a half million clauses of running text. That work with Zoe is one reason why 1992 stands out for me as an exciting year. The other is meeting Michio Sugeno, then professor at the Tokyo Institute of Technology, who was reading up systemic theory because it seemed to him to offer the kind of approach to language that he was seeking in order to test and develop his ideas on 'intelligent computing' – the keynote being that, if computers were to move forward significantly in the future, they would have to learn to mean like human beings. This resonated well with the project that Christian and I had been pursuing at odd moments ever since 1985, and which eventually emerged in 1999 as the book *Construing Experience through Meaning*. Sugeno called his own project "computing with words"; I suggested that perhaps "computing with meanings" would be more apt.

The chapters in Volume 6 have been chosen and arranged so as to bring out the motif of computational and quantitative methods as a way in to a deeper understanding of language. I think that this sort of work is still only just beginning, and will in time have a significant impact on our theoretical knowledge of semiotic systems.

Notes

1. But one for which I feel more than usually delinquent. I had been invited as a Lee Kwan Yew Distinguished Visitor by the National University of Singapore; with the understanding that, having given a series of lectures, I would write them up as a book for the University Press. I tried to rewrite the lectures, much too ambitiously, but had to put the project aside on two occasions, owing to illness in my family, and after that, never managed to complete it. I feel very aware of this failure to honour what I regarded as an important commitment.

PART ONE

GRAMMATICAL METAPHOR

EDITOR'S INTRODUCTION

This first part of this volume, *Grammatical Metaphor*, contains four papers, all published since the mid–nineties, in which Professor M. A. K. Halliday sets out to 'problematize the issue of a special grammar for the languages of science' (Chapter 4, *The grammatical construction of scientific knowledge: the framing of the English clause*). What we come to realize is that, in fact, 'Science has no beginning; it is simply the continuation of the grammar's theorizing of ourselves and our relations with our environment.' Humankind is forever 'theorizing' about ourselves and the world around us. To understand something we must first turn it into meaning, only then can we internalize or know it. To transform our experience into meaning, we need language. Be it commonsense or scientific knowledge, no matter whether it concern our 'taken for granted reality' or some phenomena far removed from the experiences of daily life, there can be no theorizing without language, or more specifically, without the semogenic power of the grammar.

'The categories and relations of our commonsense world are not given to us readymade'; rather, as Professor Halliday explains, 'we construe them grammatically, using grammatical energy to theorize – to select among the indefinitely many ways in which experience could be "parsed" and made to make sense' (Chapter 4). But while we acknowledge it to be the same grammatical power at work in common-sense and scientific theorizing, nevertheless, we must recognize that '[a] scientific theory is a dedicated and partially designed semiotic subsystem which reconstrues certain aspects of components of human experience in a different way, in the course of opening them up to be observed, investigated and explained'

3

(Chapter 3, *Things and relations: regrammaticizing experience as technical knowledge*). In the discourse of science, the clausal world of the mother tongue, in which 'experience is construed as an interplay between happenings (which are transitory) and entities (which persist)' (Chapter 1, *Language and the reshaping of human experience*), is reconstrued as 'a semiotic universe made of things' (Chapter 2, *Language and knowledge: the 'unpacking' of text*).

This reshaping of experience is accomplished over 'three successive waves of theoretical energy' (Chapter 2), which Halliday describes as follows: **generalization**, i.e. from proper noun to common noun, making possible our commonsense theories of knowledge; **abstractness**, i.e. from concrete categories to abstract ones, making it possible to retheorize in 'uncommonsense' terms; and **metaphor**, i.e. from congruent construals to metaphorical ones, allowing us to retheorize over again, in the form of our technical and scientific theories of knowledge. Each wave takes us 'one step further away from ordinary experience', but at the same time each step may be thought of as having 'enlarged the meaning potential by adding a new dimension to the total model'.

The power of metaphor is inherent in the nature of language; it is 'a concomitant of a higher–order stratified semiotic – once the brain splits content into semantics and grammar, it can match them up in more than one way' (Chapter 4). Metaphor in the grammatical sense – grammatical metaphor – allows 'the wholesale recasting of the relationship between the grammar and the semantics' (Chapter 1). Halliday gives the example of calling 'move' *motion*. It is more than just turning a verb into a noun. Rather, the category meanings of noun and verb have been combined together to form a new type of element. While nothing in the real world has changed, repeating the metaphorical process over and over again with hundreds if not thousands of words gradually reshapes our experience of the world, 'making it noun-like (stable in time) while it is observed, experimented with, measured and reasoned about' (Chapter 1).

Grammatical metaphor is '[a] critical feature of the grammar through which the discourse of science evolved' (Chapter 1). Elaborating this point in Chapter 4, Halliday writes,

> Scientific discourse rests on combining theoretical technicality with reasoned argument; and each of these relies on the same metaphorical resource within the grammar. Semantically, each relies on the grammar's power of condensing extended meanings in a highly structured, nominalized form. In the latter, it is a **textual** condensation, in which

stretches of preceding matter are condensed instantially, to serve as elements – typically thematic elements – in the ongoing construal of information [...] In the case of technicality, however, the condensation is **ideational**: it is a paradigmatic process, in which the metaphoric entity is distilled from numerous sources of related semantic input.

There are parallels to be found between the evolution of the language of science and the development of the individual human. Generalization occurs in the transition from child tongue to mother tongue (ages 1–2 years). Between ages 4 to 6 years, children begin to 'construe entities that have no perceptual correlate'; they can handle abstraction. It is also around this age that children in literate cultures begin to 'recast their language into a new form, as written language'. Writing, as Halliday notes, is more than just a new medium, it changes the way we mean (Chapter 1). The ability to grasp the move from congruent to metaphorical comes later, around the age of puberty, between ages 9 to 13.

'Thus we have two histories,' writes Halliday in Chapter 4, 'both change, over time, in the same direction: from the congruent to the metaphorical, building up new meanings through repeated instances of semantic junction' (Chapter 4). The writings of Galileo and Newton reveal evidence of significant innovations which have since 'infiltrated more or less every register of our standard written language' (Chapter 1). The evolution of a new form of discourse begins 'the process whereby our experience will be reconstrued. It is a long process, stretching phylogenetically from the iron age to the present age of information science, and ontogenetically from initial literacy to adulthood; and in the course of this process, knowledge becomes designed, systemic and technical' (Chapter 4).

Also, in Chapter 4, Professor Halliday notes certain problematic features of scientific/educational discourse: 'namely its exclusiveness and ritualistic power'. More generally, 'It is just possible that a semiotic which foregrounds things at the expense of processes and relations – precisely because we are not aware that it is doing so – may be dysfunctional for the relations between ourselves as a species and our environment, and even for our interactions one with another.'

If, as noted at the outset, science has no beginning, then it has no end. In the transition to an 'information society on a global scale', Professor Halliday asks, 'Will our grammars go on evolving towards yet another reshaping of experience?' (Chapter 1). As information technology causes the disjunction between the written and spoken language to break down, will the grammar move towards a new synthesis of the clausal and nominal modes? 'Whatever the "information society" will actually look like in the next two or three generations' (Chapter 1), Professor Halliday concludes,

> I am confident of one thing: that the new forms of human experience, no matter how much they differ from those we recognize today (which are already very different from those that I grew up with), will still be being construed, exchanged, contested and transmitted by means of language.

Chapter One

LANGUAGE AND THE RESHAPING OF HUMAN EXPERIENCE (1995)

Those of us who work in universities are fortunate in that in our research we can usually choose our own point of departure: we can fix the boundaries of what we are investigating, and we can decide on the perspective in which we want to locate it. This is not to say that universities are 'ivory towers'; in my experience, academics are more anxious than most people to be relevant and useful to their community (which is not to say they always manage to succeed!). But if they are to make their contribution to knowledge and, via knowledge, to people's lives, they have to be allowed to theorize: if you want to apply principles to practice of any kind you have to have principles to apply, and that means developing a theory. And in order to develop a theory, you have to be able to determine the content, and the approach. As my teacher, J. R. Firth, used to say, if you are a linguist, then language is what you say it is; you are not called upon to define it in simple terms – indeed it is far too complex a phenomenon to be defined at all; and you are certainly not bound by any commonsense notions of what language is (still less by moralistic conceptions of what it ought to be!).

But while scholars must be free to delimit their own objects of study, and to adopt their own ways of approaching and theorizing

'Language and the reshaping of human experience' from *International Symposium on Critical Discourse Analysis*, Athens, 15–16 December 1995. Speech delivered at the official ceremony for M. A. K. Halliday at the National and Kapodistrian University of Athens, Doctor honoris causa of the Faculty of English Studies, School of Philosophy, on 14 December 1995. The speech also appears as No. 44 in Vol. 31 (Athens, 2002) of the *Official Speeches*, (period 1 September 1995–31 August 1997) Part A, 1995–6, pp. 1261–76.

those objects, they also have to face the consequences: that the phenomena they see around them may look very different from the commonsense phenomena that make up daily life. What linguists mean by language is not the same thing as what language means to everybody else. It is the same set of phenomena that we are talking about, more or less; but placed in a different light, and so having different properties and different possibilities. For me, as a grammarian, a 'language' is a resource for making meaning – a semogenic system, together with the processes which instantiate the system in the form of text (spoken and written discourse); and 'meaning' is understood in functional terms – in relation to the social contexts in which language has evolved with the human species.

This is different from the ordinary commonsense perception of what language is – and certainly of what grammar is: the anomaly in this case is glaringly clear. But it is in fact a double anomaly. What do we mean by the "commonsense" perception of language? We usually mean the ideas about language that we learnt in school – especially in primary school, when we were being taught to read and to write. It is there that we first learn about grammar: grammar is a set of rules, arbitrary rules of behaviour that we have to follow or else we will be punished for breaking them. Then later on, as we go through secondary school, we learn that only certain kinds of language are pure (every literate culture has its Katharevousa!), that a very few instances of text carry value (usually literary texts from the past), and the rest – the spoken, the dialectal and so on – is inferior stuff, lacking in elegance or beauty, and so hopelessly illogical that it needs philosophers to come along and tidy it up.

It would be hard to construct any picture of language that is more in conflict with our theoretical models than this one. But notice that this picture that we get from our schooling does not, in fact, match up with our "commonsense" experience of language. It is more like the popular view of evolution that causes so much trouble to neuroscientists and geneticists. Richard Dawkins, in his book *The Extended Phenotype* (1982), describes the misunderstandings of natural selection caused by notions such as 'survival of the fittest' – this again begins in primary school, when children read in books about dinosaurs that "some learnt to swim, some learnt to fly" and so on. But the situation regarding language is even more anomalous, because children have been working hard at their language since the first few months of life; they have a very rich and accurate perception of what kind of a resource language is and what they can expect to achieve with it. Only, their perception of language is 'unconscious' – that is, it is below the level of consciousness where they can reflect on it and pay attention to it. If these early insights could be made accessible, they would match much more closely a linguist's notion of a socially responsible and practically useful account of human language. If we could somehow recapture and reflect on our earliest engagements with language, without their being refracted through the classroom discourses of our primary school (and don't blame the teachers, who are only passing on the received wisdom of the culture!), we should have a clearer sense of how (in the wording of my title) language is responsible for shaping human experience.

When you were about one year old, you began learning your mother tongue in earnest. But at the same time as you learnt it, you were also using it in order to learn: using language to build up a picture of the phenomenal world that you experienced around you and inside your own body. Your experience was being "construed" for you by language (where **construe** means 'construct semiotically'). To put this another way, your experience was being transformed into meaning; and this transformation was effected by the grammar – the grammatical systems of your language, and the words and structures through which these systems are realized.

The grammar of every natural language is a theory of human experience: a theory that we hold unconsciously, but that is all the more potent for that very reason. The grammar breaks down the continuum of experience into *figures*, each figure representing a 'happening' of some kind; and it does this by means of the clause: you will hear small children saying things like (from my own records) *tiny bird flew away*, *that tree got no leaf on*, *put butter on toast*, and so on. It also analyses each figure into different types of *elements*: the happening itself, like *flew*, *got*, *put* and so on; and the various participating entities and circumstantial elements that surround it: *tiny bird*, *that tree*, *butter*, *away*, *on toast* – these are the grammar's verbal, nominal and other primary classes. And thirdly it joins the figures into *sequences* by means of various logical semantic relations such as time and cause; e.g. *but* in *That tree got leaf on but that tree got no leaf on*. Grammar is able to do all this precisely because it is also doing something else at the same time: as well as construing our experience, it is also enacting our interpersonal relationships – sharing experiences with others, giving orders, making offers and so on. To put this in technical grammatical terms: every clause is a complex structure embodying both transitivity and mood. This is a very powerful semogenic resource, which we all learnt to control very early – some time during the second year of life.

It is customary in western thinking to relegate language to a subordinate status, that of (at best) reflecting, or (at worst) obscuring and distorting, the reality of the world we live in. We are brought up to believe that the categories of our environment, the regularities we observe within it, are objective features existing independently of ourselves and of the way we talk about them. We assume there are 'natural classes': that the meanings construed in the grammar – the word meanings, and the meanings of grammatical categories – are given to us by the very nature of things. If we reject this view – as I think we must – it is tempting then to go to the opposite extreme: to assert that there are no natural classes at all, and that what we encounter in our environment is a random flux of happening in which there are no regular proportionalities and the grammar has to impose order by inventing categories of its own. Neither of these extremes is satisfactory. Rather, our environment as we experience it is bristling with analogies: everything that happens is in some way like something else. The problem is, most things are like many other things in many different ways. What the grammar does is to sort these out: to give priority to some subset of the possible dimensions along which phenomena can be perceived as being alike.

We see this selective recognition most obviously in vocabulary. Think of any lexical set in everyday English, like *tree / shrub / bush / hedge*, or *hot / warm / mild / tepid / cool / chilly / cold*, or *car / van / truck / lorry / coach / bus*, or *jumping / hopping / skipping / prancing / leaping*: these are not clearly distinct perceptual categories; they are constructs of the language, and as everyone who learns a foreign language knows they do not correspond from one language to another. At the same time, they are not arbitrary: they all construe some aspect of perceptual or at least experiential likeness. These lexical examples illustrate rather specific domains of experience: growing plants, temperatures and so on. But there are some variables so general in scope that we meet them in almost every figure we construct; and these tend to get organized systemically rather than lexically. For example: every happening has some address in time, either relative to now or relative to some other happening or state of affairs. Here again the grammar has to **construe** the experience; this time it does so in the form of grammatical systems. But the same principle holds good: the grammar selects certain analogies, certain kinds of likeness, to be construed as regular proportions, like tense in English, where there is a regular proportionality such that *went : goes : will go ::: said : says : will say ::: ran : runs : will run* and so on. Again each language does this in its own distinctive way.

What the grammar does is to construct a semiotic flow – a flow of meaning – that is analogous to the flow of events that constitutes human experience; in such a way that, when this semiotic flow is superimposed on experience it operates selectively as a grid. This gives depth, dimensionality to our perspective, so that certain regularities are made to stand out. I used the wording "grammar transforms experience into meaning"; and it is this that constitutes what we call "understanding". To understand something is to transform it into meaning; and the outcome of this transformation is what we refer to as 'knowing', or – in reified terms – as 'knowledge'. Understanding, and knowing, are semiotic processes – processes of the development of meaning in the brain of every individual; and the powerhouse for such processes is the grammar.

This semogenic power in the grammar depends on selection. The grammar selects patterns that have experiential value, and construes them into a multidimensional semantic space. And since these various patterns, the different dimensions that constitute a semantic space, often contradict each other and conflict with each other, the grammar of every language is based on compromise. The only way of construing the incredibly complex interactions between human beings and their environment – let alone those between one human being and another – is to evolve a system that is highly elastic: that has a great deal of 'play' in it, that celebrates indeterminacy, and that is optimally functional as a whole even if none of its parts ever seems to be entirely optimal when taken by itself.

This system, language, has evolved – along with the human species: it's the *sapiens* in *homo sapiens*. We cannot observe language evolving. But we can, and we do, all the time, observe the epigenetic processes whereby language develops in the individual. We are all familiar with the – often very explicit – efforts made by children in matching up their meanings to those of their elders round about; and these older, wiser folk (parents, big brothers and sisters and so on) join in the game: 'no, that's not a bus; it's a van', 'that's not blue, it's green' and so on. Since all semantic categories are inherently fuzzy sets – not just those construed lexically, but even the apparently clearcut grammatical ones like positive/negative or singular/plural (consider an English clause like *not everybody believes*

11

that, do they?: is that positive or negative? is it singular or plural?) – there is always going to be some semantic drift across the genera- tions. But when children learn a mother tongue, they are shaping their own experience as individuals according to the accumulated experience of the human species, as already construed for them by the grammar. The grammar defines for them the basic experience of being human; with lots of local variations, but shaping, as a whole, the form of their commonsense knowledge: their knowledge of the ecosocial system that is their environment, and of their own place, and their own identity, within it.

And then, when all this has just become taken for granted, it has to change. Once our children reach the age of around five, in the literate cultures of Europe and elsewhere, we (the adults) decide that they (the children) need to recast their language into a new form, namely as written language; we put them into school, and teach them to read, and to write. We think of writing, in this case, as just a new kind of channel, a new medium: children already know the fundamentals of language; they're now going to learn to process language visually, in order to gain access to books and magazines and forms and public notices and all the other trappings of our written culture. If we think of literacy as in any way changing their language, we usually mean by this a change of dialect: it is a means of inducting them into the standard form of the language. We don't think of it as changing the way they mean.

But why do we teach them writing at just this age (one of the few things about which all literate cultures seem to agree)? We put them into school to get them out of the house and off the street: that's the popular answer. But the real reason is a more subtle one. Children of around four to six years old are just reaching the stage, in their language development, when they can handle meanings that are abstract: they can construe entities that have no perceptual correlate, like *worth* and *clue* and *habit* and *intend* and *price*; and this has two important consequences. First, it means that they can cope with abstract symbols, like letters or characters, and the abstract concepts that go with them (including the critical distinction between writing and drawing); so they can now master this new medium. Secondly, it means that they can cope with abstract categories, and so are ready to explore new forms of knowledge. In other words they are ready for a reshaping of their previous experience.

Let me give you an example of what I mean. When my son was small, he used to play with the neighbour's cat, which was friendly but rather wary, as cats are with small children. On one occasion he turned to me and said "Cats have no other way to stop children from hitting them; so they bite". He was just under three and a half years old. Some years later, in primary school, he was reading his science textbook. One page was headed: "Animal Protection"; and underneath this heading it said "Most animals have natural enemies that prey upon them. ... Animals protect themselves in many ways. Some animals ... protect themselves with bites and stings." Now Nigel had worked out this explanation – why animals bite – for himself (no doubt in dialogic contexts; commonsense knowledge is dialogic knowledge) at the age of 3½; it was now being presented back to him, five or six years later, monologically – and in a different grammar. I don't mean that the grammar was more formal; in that respect, in fact, there was no significant difference. What differed was the grammar's shaping of the experience. It was now a general fact, not just about cats but one relating to a wider, systemic class to which cats belong, namely animals; and biting, in turn, was part of a wider, systemic class of behavioural and other properties which included stinging, running fast, having certain colouring and so on. But even more drastic than these generalizations is the way the grammar has reconstrued the essential nature of the experience. It has taken the wording *protect themselves* (as a verb) and reworded it as a noun *protection*; and this is then classified as *animal protection*, implying a possible typology of protections of different kinds. (Notice by the way how ambiguous this expression *animal protection* is if you take it by itself: does it mean 'how people protect animals', 'how people protect themselves from animals', 'how animals protect people', 'how animals protect themselves', or even 'how people use animals to protect themselves'? – there are at least five plausible interpretations!) Similarly the meaning 'bite' has been worded as the noun *bites*. In other words, the grammar has replaced the names of happenings with the names of things.

From the child's point of view, this is a new way of seeing the world. He would have said *by biting and stinging*, not *with bites and stings*; after all, biting and stinging is something you do, or at least something you have done to you if you don't watch out, it is not some object that is being used as a tool. In the child's grammar, happening is construed by verbs; whereas nouns construe things – things that take part in happening, certainly, but not happenings as such. Why is this? – it is not because of any prior cause or grand principle of design, but simply because that is the way that grammar evolved. It is important I think to make this point explicit, to avoid any false assumptions about cause and effect. People often ask: does human experience determine the form of grammar, or does the form of grammar determine human experience? The answer has to be: neither – or, what comes to the same thing: both. The form taken by grammars, with their nouns, verbs and the rest, is shaped by human experience; just as, at the same time, the form taken by human experience, with its happenings, things, qualities and circumstances, is also shaped by the grammar. There is just one process taking place here, not two. In the evolutionary history of homo sapiens, this is how our experience was transformed into meaning. And this is the kind of pattern – the 'world view', if you like – that is first construed by children, the way their semantic space is organized and deployed. A verb means happening; a noun means an entity – a thing; and both typically have some correlates in the world of perceptions. We call this mode of meaning the **congruent** mode of the grammar; and it is this congruent pattern that lies behind the wealth of commonsense knowledge that children lay down in the first few years of life.

But if grammar can construe experience in this way, it can also reconstrue it in other terms. Having once established that biting and stinging, and protecting, are forms of happening and doing – that is, having construed them congruently as verbs – we can then say "but there may be some experiential value, some payoff, in treating them 'as if' they were some kind of abstract entity or thing". Note that we don't need to say this, in so many words; we can simply mean it, so to speak, by reconstruing them, in incongruent fashion, as nouns. If we do this, we have enlarged our total meaning potential: we have enriched the model of experience by creating a new semiotic category that is both happening and entity at the same time. So the child is beginning to explore a new way of understanding and of knowing; we can call it "written knowledge" – or better (since although it was associated with writing it doesn't actually depend on being written down) "educational knowledge".

At this point, we might want to ask why. If our species was well enough served by the congruent shaping of experience in which grammar evolved, why reshape it in a different form – one which seems to blur the very distinctions on which the commonsense knowledge depends? In the west, of course, it was the ancient Greeks who started it, as they started so many other things, when they used the grammar in precisely this way to create abstract entities out of qualities and events: 'virtual' objects like *motion* and *change* and *addition* and *depth* and *proportion*. They were exploiting the grammar's potential for turning words of other classes – verbs and adjectives – into nouns. What is the advantage of this? Our everyday world, the world of commonsense knowledge, is a mixed construction – a mixture of objects and events: there are the happenings, of doing, making, changing, moving, saying, thinking, being, which we construe in the grammar as verbs; and there are the people and the other creatures and the objects of various kinds that take part in all these different happenings, and these we construe in the grammar as nouns. A typical figure is a happening with one or two entities taking part, like *cats bite children*. The grammatical mode is the clausal one: the figure is construed in the grammar as a clause. But if we want to systematize our knowledge, we may have to transform it along the way. The problem with happenings is that they are transitory – they don't last; so it is hard to assign fixed properties to them and to organize them into classificatory schemes. If our knowledge is to be organized systematically (especially if this depends on being able to measure things), we need phenomena that are stable: that persist through time, and can readily be grouped into classes. The most stable elements are the entities, the kinds of phenomena that are realized congruently in the grammar as nouns.

Now this is where the grammar reveals its power. Grammatical classes are not immutable; the grammar can always turn one class of word into another (note that there may or may not be a change of form; what matters is the change of syntactic function). It is already part of our commonsense experience that events can have entities that are derived from them, for example with the sense of 'the person who performs an action': so from the verb *make* we can derive the noun *maker*. But we can also draw on this same nominalizing power to turn the event itself into an entity: we can talk about a *making* (the making of modern Europe, for example), or a *creation*. Here the grammar is reconstruing a happening as if it was a kind of thing. This is what happens when from verbs we create nouns like *motion* and *drift* and *change*; and similarly when we turn adjectives into nouns like *depth*, *size*, *speed* and so on. Once these other phenomena have taken on the feature of 'entity' we can measure them, generalize about them, and classify them. So, for example, when we turn *move* into *motion* we can say things like *all motion is relative to some fixed point*; we can set up *laws of motion*, and discuss problems like that of *perpetual motion*; we can classify *motion* as

15

linear, rotary, periodic, parabolic, contrary, parallel and the like. Not because the word *motion* is a noun, but because in making it a noun we have transformed 'moving' from a happening into a phenomenon of a different kind: one that is at once both a happening and a thing.

We could do this because the category of thing, or 'entity' (that which is congruently construed by the grammatical class "noun"), is not a class of phenomena in the real world; it is a class of meanings. The grammar has construed this category in the first place; so when it reconstrues it, in a different form, what results is a new type of element, one that combines the category meanings of noun and verb. By calling 'move' *motion*, we have not changed anything in the real world; but we have changed the nature of our experience of the world. Of course, there is not much impact from just one single word; but when the same thing happens with hundreds and indeed thousands of words this does reshape our experience as a whole. And this, in the long run, can open the way to changes in the material world: to the appearance of things like trains and cars and aeroplanes which had not existed before. All scientific and technological progress consists in the interplay of the material and the semiotic: neither of the two drives the other, but equally neither can proceed alone.

So as our children go through primary school they are in some sense recapitulating semiotically the historical experience of a culture moving into the iron age. They have already built up one model of reality, in the everyday grammar of the mother tongue; now, they are rebuilding, reshaping it, as it had been reshaped as part of a major change in the human condition: one which took place more or less simultaneously across much of the Eurasian continent. It is not a total reconstruction, of course; the model still rests on the same semiotic foundations. But the edifice is being very substantially altered. In Thomas Kuhn's interpretation, the two are no longer fully commensurable.

Needless to say, this is not the end of the story. The reshaping is still going on. But before I trace it one step further let me first problematize the theoretical notion of grammar itself. How is it that grammar has this semogenic energy: that it has the power (or, if you prefer, that through grammar we have the power) to create, and then to recreate, meaning? Where does grammar emerge, in the evolution of the human species and in the development of an individual human being? Evolutionary biologists have been saying for some time that the brain of mammals evolved as the ecological relationship of the organism to its environment became more and more complex; as linguists, we can agree with this, but add to it 'and as the social relationship of one organism to another also became more and more complex'. Gerald Edelman, perhaps the leading neuroscientist working in this field, in his theory of neural Darwinism traces the evolution of consciousness from its origins (probably in the warming of the blood, the endothermic principle) through two stages: "primary consciousness", with selective recognition of experience based on biological value, and "higher-order consciousness", extending to self-consciousness, memory, and the ability to apprehend the future. Higher-order consciousness seems to have evolved only in homo sapiens. Now I think we can show that higher-order consciousness is semiotic consciousness – that is, the ability to mean, or to transform into meaning; and that the critical element in higher-order consciousness is grammar. But it is a form of consciousness that develops, in the individual human organism, only after infancy. Human infants, in the first year of life, first develop primary consciousness; they do construct a system of meaning (what I described, in *Learning How to Mean*, as "protolanguage"), but this is not yet a 'language' in the adult sense. Why? – because it has no grammar. The elements of infant speech are pure signs, content-expression pairs analogous to a cat's miaow or the danger warnings signalled by an ape. (I am not belittling these creatures, or their abilities; I am simply locating them in an evolutionary perspective.) For the human child, this primary semiotic serves as their proto-language in the sense that it is there they first learn how to mean; but they then replace it, in the second year of life, by the higher-order semiotic system which we call "language". And language, unlike the protolanguage, has a grammar in it.

Children take this step very quickly, leaping over what must have occupied hundreds of generations of evolutionary time. I shall have to try to describe this leap in metaphorical terms. What the child does is to deconstruct (or rather, deconstrue) the two faces of the sign, the content and the expression, and insert a new, purely abstract stratum of organization in between. This new, interpolated stratum is the grammar. You can watch – or rather, listen to – this happening if you observe carefully a child's transition from proto-language to mother tongue. The culmination of this transition is language as we know it: a stratified semiotic system consisting of a semantics, a grammar, and a phonology. The phonology is the system of expression, where language interfaces with the human body, through the organs of articulation and of hearing. The semantics is the system of meanings, where language interfaces with the whole of human experience. But the grammar interfaces only with these two interfaces (this is what I meant by calling it "purely abstract" just now); it does not interface directly with either surface of the material world. Because of this freedom it can adapt readily to changes in the ecosocial environment (Jay Lemke 1993 has shown how this adaptation can take place): both local changes in the ongoing context of situation and global changes in the background context of the culture.

Thus major historical shifts in the human condition – the shift into settlement, that into iron age technology – take place at once both materially and semiotically: the different construal of experience in the grammar is inseparable from the different nature of experience itself. And this means that further semiotic shifts may always take place. We now meet with another instance of the reshaping of experience by the grammar: that which accompanied (and, likewise, formed an essential part of) the transition into the modern, "scientific" age which we associate with the European Renaissance. If we look at the writings of the founders of modern science – Galileo's Italian, or the English of Isaac Newton – we find there that the grammar is evolving some further significant innovations; and now, some ten generations later, these have infiltrated more or less every register of our standard written languages. We are all familiar with the sort of wordings that are characteristic of today's scientific discourse, like

> *Osmotic tolerance is accomplished in bacteria by an adjustment of the internal osmolarity.*

But these same features are regularly present in much of the written discourse that impinges on us all the time: not just in science but in non-technical contexts as well – particularly those concerned with establishing and maintaining prestige or power. My airline told me that

> *Failure to reconfirm will result in the cancellation of your reservations.*

The managing director of a business corporation apologizes because

> *We did not translate respectable revenue growth into earnings improvement.*

And a financial consultant advises that

A successful blending of asset replacement with remanufacture is possible . . . [to] ensure that viability exists.

Military strategy requires that

Manoeuvre and logistic planning and execution must anticipate . . . the vulnerabilities that deep attack helps create.

And in the driving cab of the locomotive

Strength was needed to meet driver safety requirements in the event of missile impact.

– that is, the glass must be strong so that the driver remained safe even if it was struck by a stone.

We know where schoolchildren encounter this metaphorical kind of grammar. This is the language of the specialized disciplines – of knowledge that is technical and grounded in some theory (the theory may or may not be explicitly affirmed). Just as the first reshaping of experience took place when they moved into primary school, so this second reshaping coincides with another educational transition: the move from primary to secondary school. The critical feature of grammar through which the discourse of science evolved is one which children cannot fully apprehend until they reach their middle school years, around the age of puberty. This is the phenomenon of grammatical metaphor. While the first phase of educational knowledge, that associated with writing, depends on abstractness, this later phase, that of technical knowledge, the discourse of the specialized disciplines, depends on metaphor: metaphor in the grammatical sense, the wholesale recasting of the relationship between the grammar and the semantics. Instead of

If a fire burns more intensely it gives off more smoke

we now say

Fire intensity has a profound effect on smoke injection.

We have already seen the beginnings of this transformation: some abstract terms like *motion, speed, proportion* are already metaphorical in origin, since they involve reconstruing processes or qualities as nouns: treating them as if they were kinds of things. So this second reshaping of experience is exploiting a resource that had already begun to be available with the first. But now it is no longer a matter of creating technical terms; the metaphor takes over the entire discourse – because it provides the means for developing a sustained

19

argument, the sort of logical progression that goes with experimental science. The grammatical metaphor allows any observation, or series of observations, to be restated in summary form – compressed, as it were, and packaged by the grammar – so that it serves as the starting point for a further step in the reasoning: some theoretical conclusion can be drawn from it. Here is an example from a microbiology text:

> When a *solution* of any substance (*solute*) is separated from a *solute-free solvent* by a membrane that is freely permeable to solvent molecules, but not to molecules of the solute, the solvent tends to be drawn through the membrane into the solution, thus diluting it. Movement of the solvent across the membrane can be prevented by applying a certain hydrostatic pressure to the solution.

Note the expression *movement of the solvent across the membrane*, where the grammatical metaphor 'packages' the preceding assertion to function as point of origin for the next.

In sentences like these, the metaphoric recording involves more or less the whole of the grammar. Qualities become nouns; happenings become nouns or adjectives; and logical relations become verbs. It seems that only entities stay as they are; but their status too may be affected, as will be seen when we analyse the grammar in functional terms: in *movement of the solvent across the membrane* the active entity *solvent* is still a noun; but instead of functioning as an active element in the figure it is functioning as possessor of another noun *movement* – and this is not an entity at all but a happening that has itself become metaphorized. In other words, the original things often disappear, becoming mere modifiers of these metaphoric nouns – as happened with *fire* and *smoke* in *fire intensity has a profound effect on smoke injection*. It is not unusual to find sentences in which every element has been functionally transposed into something other than its congruent form.

Given that the grammatical processes taking place here at this third stage are so complex and varied, can we see anything like a general pattern emerging, in the way experience is being reshaped? I think perhaps we can. While the language of the primary school contained among its abstract terms a number of nouns derived from verbs or adjectives whereby happenings and qualities were reified as general principles (like *motion, force, multiplication* and so on), with the technical language of the sciences and other disciplines – the classroom "subjects" of the secondary school curriculum – this process of grammatical metaphor has been elaborated to such an extent that the reality it projects is of quite a different order. In place of the mixed, clausal world of the mother tongue, in which experience is construed as an interplay between happenings (which are transitory) and entities (which persist), our technological world is one that consists almost entirely of things – the only 'happenings' in it are the relations we set up between one 'thing' and another. Thus in each of the following examples we find two processes, both construed as nominal groups; they are then being said to be related, one to the other, by a logical relationship that is construed as (or includes within its construal) a verbal group [this logical relator is shown in italic]:

> fire intensity *has a profound effect on* smoke injection
> the conducting capacity *depends on* the width of the channel
> lung cancer death rates *are associated with* increased smoking
> rapid changes in the rate of evolution *are caused by* external events
> increased responsiveness *may be reflected in* feeding behaviour

This sort of discourse has served well for the natural sciences, where it was important to construe a world of 'things', including virtual entities that could be brought into existence as and when the discourse required them; some of these virtual entities then remain in existence as theoretical constructs, while others function locally in the argument and then disappear. Symbolically, this kind of discourse is holding the world still, making it noun-like (stable in time) while it is observed, experimented with, measured and reasoned about.

But this sort of synoptic vision is less relevant to other realms of our experience; and it may be positively obstructive in certain contexts, when it becomes a means of obscuring the critical issues and a vehicle for maintaining the *status quo ante* of power. We see extreme cases of this obfuscation in the language of military strategy, where instead of *weapons that kill more people* the planners now demand *weapons of greater lethality* (and, as we saw, *manoeuvre and logistic planning and execution must anticipate by many hours the vulnerabilities that deep attack helps create*). Such discourse seems not so much to construct reality as to construct unreality.

What I have been suggesting is that, if we compare the two histories, the evolutionary history of the linguistic system and the developmental history of the learning of language by children, we find that the two are related epigenetically: that is, the development of the child's power of meaning follows the evolutionary trajectory of the grammar – in a way that is analogous to the epigenetic biological development of the organism. But I want to make it clear that the analogy is only partial: semiotic systems are not the same as biological systems; and one fundamental distinction is that the grammar retains the features of all its earlier historical moments. Children do not give up the commonsense grammar when they move into educational knowledge; nor does the clausal mode disappear from the system when the nominal mode takes over. Thus when experience is reshaped, the significance of this reshaping lies in the impact between the new form and the congruent forms in which it was construed in the first place.

Now that we are (we are told) undergoing yet another upheaval – the transition to an "information society on a global scale" (though I am not sure how truly 'global' it is, or even how truly 'informative'), will our grammars go on evolving towards yet a further reshaping of experience? During the "modern" period, since the invention of printing, there has been a fairly wide gulf between written and spoken language. These features that I have been talking about, which you have probably been thinking to yourselves are just typically English, are in fact features only of written English – the kind of English used in contexts that are associated with writing (like my present talk). In other words, they are features of a "standard language". They did not appear in the unwritten English dialects; on the other hand, they will also be found in standard written French, and German, and Italian, and Russian, and Chinese – and no doubt Greek as well. But this disjunction between the written and the spoken languages is now, with information technology, breaking down; the next phase may well be one where the grammar moves towards a new synthesis of the clausal and the nominal modes. This sort of language is also likely to be favoured in the context of "intelligent computing", as envisaged by the leading Japanese scholar in this field, Michio Sugeno. In Sugeno's view, computers have to be taught to function more like human beings – by using informal everyday language rather than formal languages or special registers. This is certainly a more promising notion than the opposite approach, still fairly prevalent, according to which the human brain is an information processing device and the way to improve its performance is to make it operate more like a computer.

One of the many responsibilities that a university bears is that of monitoring the way in which human knowledge is organized: embodying this in its own organizational structure, anticipating the

22

trends of the future, and giving guidance to the community as a whole – particularly to schools and educational authorities. I wanted to suggest where the study of language might be located in the overall structure of knowledge in the period we are now moving into. As I said at the beginning, a grammar – the system of words and structures at the core of every natural language – is itself a theory, although one that we are not usually aware that we hold: a theory about ourselves and our relations to each other and to our environment. The study of language – of language in general, and of the particular languages that are valued in the context of our culture – has a central place in the institutional framing of knowledge. This has always been true, at any moment in history; but I think it is becoming more true, and more urgent, now that so much of our energy is spent in exchanging information. Information can take many forms: it is not always made of language, though prototypically it is; but, more critically, in whatever form it comes it always depends on the fact that those who are processing and receiving information already have grammar. Whatever the "information society" will actually look like in the next two or three generations I am confident of one thing: that the new forms of human experience, no matter how much they differ from those we recognize today (which are already very different from those that I grew up with), will still be being construed, exchanged, contested and transmitted by means of language.

Chapter Two

LANGUAGE AND KNOWLEDGE:
THE 'UNPACKING' OF TEXT (1998)

1

As I was planning this paper, I noticed that, in the title of our conference, *text* appeared in inverted commas ("scare quotes", as they are called these days), whereas *unpacking* did not. My topic was very close to the conference theme; but I wanted to problematize, not the text, but the unpacking. So I hope you will excuse me, first for appropriating the wording the organizers had thoughtfully provided – and secondly for changing it, transferring the scare quotes from the *text* to the *unpacking*. What this means is that I shall take the concept of "text" for granted: but I shall treat 'unpacking' as something that needs to be unpacked.

My own "text" – in the other sense: that which is to be the topic for exegesis – could be the first paragraph of the original conference description:

> Developing cognitive processes, building knowledge of the world and of self takes place through overt exploration of meaning. One of the chief ways of doing this is through formal education where the learner moves from the world of common-sense knowledge, which is typically spoken 'text', to the world of educational knowledge, which is typically 'text' written down. The purpose of this conference is to explore how language, in the way it is put together, allows the development of common-sense and educational knowledge and also how this exploration of 'text', both oral and written, can play a

---

★ Editors' note: Professor Halliday delivered this paper in his keynote speech at the 1996 conference entitled 'Language and Knowledge: The Unpacking of "Text"'.

significant part in shaping the social system and defining the individual's access to, and participation in social processes.

What happens, linguistically, as a child moves from common-sense knowledge to educational knowledge? From one point of view, the picture seems fairly clear; for some years now linguists have been accumulating detailed information about children's language development, from infancy through to primary and secondary schooling – although there is still much remaining to be found out, even in relation to English, perhaps the most thoroughly investigated language of all. But while I do want to be reminding you of some features that will be familiar enough, such as increasing nominalisation, I shall try to look at such features from the point of view of what they mean: asking what changes take place in the child's potential for meaning, and so looking at language development as the development of the semogenic, or meaning-creating, resource.

I shall make the assumption that all forms of human knowledge are capable of being construed as text. Knowledge is prototypically made of language. Once you have language – whether 'you' as species, or 'you' as individual – then you have the power of *transforming experience into meaning*. But, by the same token as you are enabled to do this, you are also constrained to do it; you have not internalised an experience until you have transformed it into meaning. And once you have done that, it has the potential for being worded – it can now be transformed into text. Since it is the lexicogrammar that has transformed experience into meaning in the first place, this experience already exists as 'virtual' text. But experience comes to be construed in very different ways, as children mature – as they move from home and family, via neighbourhood and peer group, into primary school and then beyond.

The perspective I am adopting here is that of a continuous developmental progression, from birth through infancy and childhood, then via primary and secondary schooling, through adolescence and into maturity (for research in early language development, based on case studies, see Halliday 1975, 1978, 1979, 1983, 1984b (all in 2004), Oldenburg-Torr 1990, Painter 1984, 1989; for case studies of language development and learning in childhood, Derewianka 1995, Painter 1993; for large-scale research in conversation between mothers and three-year-old children, Hasan 1991, 1992, Hasan and Cloran 1990; for language education and children's language experience in school, Martin 1989, 1993, Halliday and

Martin 1993, Part 2, Martin, Wignell, Eggins and Rothery l988). Let me at this point just highlight certain aspects of this developmental progression. We see how, in early infancy, linguistic and biological maturation proceed together. When babies first sit upright, and so view the world as landscape, they begin to develop a small inventory of differentiated signs with which to explore and to control it; and when they learn to crawl around, so that their relationship to the environment is constantly changing, they expand this into a semiotic system, the **protolanguage** – small sets of contrasting signs in distinct functional contexts. In the process, they become able to separate the 'self', semiotically, from the environment by which the self is defined: this is the level of primary consciousness, which humans share with all "higher" animals (perhaps all those which control their body temperatures; cf. Edelman 1992). Then, when children learn to stand up and move around on two legs, combining perspective with mobility, their infant protolanguage develops further, becoming 'language' in the sense that we know it. This is Edelman's "higher order consciousness", and it is in its developed form unique to homo sapiens – as far as we know, although current work now going on in primatology, such as that in Atlanta (Benson & Greaves 2004), should make it clear how far other apes have moved in the same direction. Critical to this post-infancy language is that it is **stratified**: it has an additional level of semiotic, a lexicogrammar, that is absent from the infant protolanguage. Higher order consciousness is consciousness that is built on grammar.

Moving from infancy to childhood enlarges the horizons, both materially and semiotically at the same time. And this enlargement takes place on two fronts. One is interpersonal: the enlargement of the sphere of social control, from the small 'meaning group' of the infant towards the 'speech fellowships' of adult life. The other is ideational: the enlargement of the experiential domain, from the small world of the infant towards the unbounded world that lies beyond. When we talk of 'building knowledge of the world and of the self', we usually think in terms only of the second form – of language as knowledge, rather than of language as interaction and control; but both are involved at every point, and new ways of meaning, new textual resources, tend to develop in interpersonal contexts first, even if their eventual functional load is mainly experiential. To give a brief example: the evidence shows that children first develop logical conditions ('if . . . then' relations) in the context of threats, warnings and promises, where the interpersonal element predominates, rather than in ideational contexts of reasoning about the world.

As children move through these ever enlarging spheres, the nature of their text changes. They learn new ways of meaning. We tend to think of this first and foremost as adding new words; that of course they are doing all the time – but then so are we, as adults: this is a steady process, one that goes on throughout our lives. But there are also critical moments, periods of more rapid change; and these tend to be brought about in the grammar. Thus, as well as moving into new semantic domains, and refining the grid – the *delicacy* – of those already entered, both of which are relatively steady and gradual developments, children pass through three, more catastrophic changes, in which the grammar comes to be radically transformed. The first is the move from protolanguage to language, already referred to, when the grammar is first laid down in the second year of life. The second is the move from everyday spoken grammar to the grammar of literacy, when we take them and put them into school around age five; and the third is the move from the grammar of written language to that of the language of the subject disciplines, when we move them out of primary into secondary school. If we want to characterize these in terms of knowledge, then the three critical moments are the moves into commonsense knowledge (age 1–2), into educational knowledge (age 4–6) and into technical knowledge (age 9–13, childhood to adolescence). Each of these moves is enacted through a critical progression:

1) generalization: from 'proper' to 'common' terms (individual to general);
2) abstractness: from concrete to abstract elements;
3) metaphor: from congruent to metaphorical construals.

The first enables the child to *construe* experience (to transform it into meaning, as I put it earlier); while the second and third successively *reconstrue* experience in an increasingly theoretical mode. Again modelling this in systemic terms while *elaborating* the meaning potential (refining the grid) and *extending* the meaning potential into new domains are relatively steady processes; *enhancing* the meaning potential involves shifting the gears, moving on to a higher plane where what is known has to be reconstituted in a deeper, long-term perspective. In terms of a concept that has been used in evolutionary theory, language development takes the form of "punctuated equilibrium": periods of relatively steady growth, with moments of rapid change from time to time; and each such punctuation requires some 'packing' of the text.

Let me make explicit what I am talking about. Consider the following pairs of example sentences:

(1a) Strength was needed to meet driver safety requirements in the event of missile impact.
(1b) The material needed to be strong enough for the driver to be safe if it got impacted by a missile.

(2a) Fire intensity has a profound effect on smoke injection.
(2b) The more intense the fire, the more smoke it injects (into the atmosphere).

(3a) The goal of evolution is to optimize the mutual adaption of species.
(3b) Species evolve in order to adapt to each other as well as possible.

(4a) Failure to reconfirm will result in the cancellation of your reservations.
(4b) If you fail to reconfirm your reservations will be cancelled.

(5a) We did not translate respectable revenue growth into earnings improvement.
(5b) Although our revenues grew respectably we were not able to improve our earnings.

Those lettered (a) are typical specimens of adult written English, such as we come across every day of our lives; highly metaphorical, even if not particularly technical. In those lettered (b), I have unpacked them into a more congruent, less metaphorical form. I will have to explain, of course, in what sense they had first been "packed" – in other words, I need to unpack the metaphor of packing. In part, perhaps, I could explain it as meaning 'packaged': the wording seems to have been more elegantly wrapped – which is why it is not noticeably shorter; the implication that 'packing' means reducing in size is actually rather wide of the mark. And yet, in spite of this, there is a sense in which such instances have been condensed, or compacted: more meaning has somehow been 'packed' into the text. If we want a physical metaphor, the (a) versions seem to be considerably more dense. It is as if, when we move from common-sense knowledge into literate and then into technical knowledge, the semantic density of the text has to increase. And this makes quite considerable demands on one's powers of language.

2

Let us look at a fairly densely packed sentence of English writing and consider what might happen if we started to unpack it. This conference is on the theory of knowledge; so here is a sentence from a book about marxism, taken from a passage that is dealing specifically with the marxist theory of knowledge. I used it several years ago in a class I was giving on semantics (and cf. Halliday and Matthiessen 1999). I said to the class: here is a learned sentence, addressed to an adult readership; let us 'unpack' it by seeing how we might put it across to younger people, preserving as much of the meaning as we can. I chose a sentence that did not require a high degree of **technical** knowledge, for obvious reasons; and I assumed that it would be intelligible, as it stood, to an educated adult of voting age (18 years). I asked the class to imagine themselves making this same observation but addressing it, successively, to children of younger age, going down in steps of three years of age at a time: to a fifteen-year-old, a twelve-year-old and so on. The original sentence was:

> The truest confirmation of the accuracy of our knowledge is the effectiveness of our actions.

Naturally, many variations in wording were suggested; the following represent my idealised versions accommodating the principles that I found lay behind the various rewordings:

> The best proof that our knowledge is accurate is the fact that our actions are effective. (15)
> What best proves that we know something accurately is the fact that we can act effectively. (12)
> We can prove that we know exactly what's happening by seeing that what we do is working. (9)
> How can you be sure that you really know what's going on? You do something, and then you see that it works. Like growing plants: you water them, and then they grow. (6)
> Look – wasn't it good that we watered that philodendron? See how well it's growing! (3)

What exactly have we done here? Looking at these synoptically, we have produced a paradigm of agnate forms that are (from top to

29

bottom) less metaphorical, less abstract and less general – or, to put these in positive terms, more congruent, more concrete and more specific. Looking at them dynamically, we have reconstituted the history of the text. Now, there are three possible dimensions of history that we could recognise as lying behind the original sentence:

1) evolutionary: according to the evolution of the forms of discourse in the language (going back through the centuries of English: C20 – C19 – C18 – C17 – . . .);
2) developmental: according to the development of the forms of discourse by a child (going back through the ages of the receiver; 18 years – 15 years – 12 years – 9 years – . . .);
3) unfolding: according to the unfolding of the forms of discourse in the text (going back from conclusion through reasoned argument through observation to first premises and introduction).

I chose the second, the ontogenetic, because that was most readily accessible to a thought experiment. The aim was to keep as close as possible to the original; this is not as easy as it sounds, because the more 'packed' a piece of text is, the more ambiguous it becomes, so that as you unpack it you are constantly having to make choices. For example, does *the effectiveness of our actions* correspond to *(the fact) that our actions are effective*, to *whether our actions are effective or not*, or to *how effective our actions are*? I chose the first of these three possibilities; and on this basis we arrived at the paradigm:

the accuracy of our knowledge (18)
(that) our knowledge is accurate (15)
(that) we know something accurately (12)
(that) we know exactly what's happening (9)

We can then relate these analytically in the grammar, along a scale of metaphoric to congruent (note that this is not a fourth dimension of history; it is a 'metahistory' of the other three). Of course, we **must** be able to do this, because all these different wordings coexist in the language potential (the *system*) of the adult; the earlier construals do not disappear, they remain in place as the system develops and expands. Likewise:

the truest confirmation (18)
the best proof (15)
what best proves (12)
what can best prove (9)

There is of course some lexical unwrapping: *accurately – exactly, confirm – prove – be sure*; but the main work is being done in the realm of the grammar. Figure 2.1 gives a brief summary of some of the grammatical variation.

[18] clause: Value + *be* + Token (both nominal)	lexical density: 6/1 = 6
n.gp.1: Deictic + Epithet + Thing + Qualifier	[of + [De + Th +Qu [of + [De + Th]]]]
[12] 1 clause: Value + *be* + Token (both clausal)	lexical density: 12/3 = 4
el.1 (nexus): [[Sayer + Process ‖ Senser + Process + Phenomenon + Manner]]	
[6] 2 clause complexes, each of 3 clauses	lexical density: 6/6 = 1
c.c.l: $\alpha'\beta$ ($\alpha'\beta$)	c.c.2: 1 $'2(\alpha'\beta)$

Figure 2.1 Some grammatical variation among text variants displaying different degrees of 'packing'

If we now take this text down to the grammatical potential of a six-year-old we have to do more work so as to make it concrete:

you can be sure you know what's happening (because) you do something and then you see that it works;

after which you give an example:

– like growing plants: you water them, and they grow.

The **example** cannot of course be derived systemically from the grammar of the preceding text! But making it concrete in this way suggests how it might be made accessible to our three-year-old:

Look – wasn't it good that we watered that philodendron? See how well it's growing!

The three-year-old cannot yet construe the abstract meanings of *you do something and then you see that it works*.

Before leaving the ontogenetic trail, let us just take another sentence, one that might very naturally be said to the three-year-old:

Look – it must be raining! People have got their umbrellas open.

We can now repack this step by step going up the age range instead of down.

31

How can you tell that it's raining? You can see that people have got their umbrellas open. (6)

We can prove that there's rain falling by seeing that people's umbrellas are open. (9)

What best proves that it's rainy weather is the fact that the umbrellas have been extended. (12)

The best proof that the weather is pluvious is the fact that the umbrellas are extended. (15)

The truest confirmation of the pluviosity of the weather is the extendedness of the umbrellas. (18 up)

3

Thus there is a systematic link between the extent of packing in a text and the semiotic maturation of the text-user (or, unpacking this, between how far a text is packed and how old the user is). As I noted earlier, the construct of generalization, abstractness, metaphor corresponds to the three critical moments in child language development:

+ generalisation: from child tongue to mother tongue, age 1–2
+ abstractness: from common-sense (grammar) to literate, age 4–7
+ metaphor: from congruent (grammar) to metaphorical, age 9–13

(cf. Painter 1984, 1993, Derewianka 1995, Halliday 1975, 1999, 2004). In moving from infant protolanguage to post-infancy language, children construe *classes*, with "common" nouns, verbs and so on as distinct from "proper" names (the proper name is transitional from the non-referential protolanguage to the category-referring mother tongue). At first, these common terms construe concrete, perceptual phenomena; but from around the age of four these start to extend to phenomena that are not directly accessible to the senses. Since reading and writing depend on being able to process abstract entities, this means that children of this age can now become literate; and they can move from commonsense to educational forms of knowledge, coping with terms such as *movement* (name of a process), *length* (name of a quality), *circle* (name of a form), *metre* (unit of measurement). Then, the further critical step by which they cross the frontier from literate to technical knowledge, taken essentially at puberty, is the move into metaphor: metaphor in the grammatical sense, the replacement of one grammatical class by another, of which the prototypical example is nominalization (but see below!). Thus the packing of text represents – and enables – the progressive construction of knowledge, from commonsense through literate to technical; it is the opening up of the individual's meaning potential through new forms of semogenic power.

Note that packing is not the same thing as increasing complexity. Let me return briefly to Figure 2.1: which of these forms are we going to say is the most complex? In terms of lexical density, and the internal structure of the nominal groups, clearly the complexity increases as the text 'matures' (with the age of the user). But in terms of the structure of the sentence (the *clause complex*, in systemic terms), the complexity actually **decreases**. The wording addressed to the six-year-old consists of two complexes of three clauses each (which might easily be combined into a single clause complex with six clauses in it: *you can be sure you know what's going on because you do something and then you see that it works*), involving both hypotaxis and parataxis and both expansion and projection. We recognise this pattern as a phenomenon of the difference between speech and writing: as the text is packed it becomes more 'written'. Written technical discourse, in particular, is characterised by rather simple clause and sentence structures: each sentence typically one clause, that clause consisting of just one or two nominal groups (one of them perhaps 'governed' by a preposition), propped up by a verbal group, usually a relational process and most typically the verb *be*. The nominal groups, on the other hand, may be enormously long and complex – since all the lexical material is compressed into these one or two groups. I have referred to these two complementary types of complexity as "lexical density" and "grammatical intricacy" (Halliday 1987a): density measured as the number of lexical words per clause, intricacy as the length and depth of the tactic structures whereby clauses come together to make up a clause complex. We can see how, as the text is progressively 'packed' from the six-year-old version to that of the adult, the *density* is tending to increase (a mean value of around 1–2 in casual speech and around 6–10 in technical writing is typical of many samples that I have counted), while the *intricacy* correspondingly decreases. It is this combination of two associated features that characterises the variation that is familiar to us under the label of nominal and clausal styles (note that the opposition is not between nominal and **verbal**, it is between nominal and **clausal**).

4

To get a sense of the grammatical gradation that links these two different "styles", we might consider another paradigm of agnate wordings:

1 Glass cracks more quickly the harder you press on it.
2 Cracks in glass grow faster the more pressure is put on.
3 Glass crack growth is faster if greater stress is applied.
4 The rate of glass crack growth depends on the magnitude of the applied stress.
5 Glass crack growth rate is associated with applied stress magnitude.

(The original version, which is the fourth one in the set, is taken from Michalske and Bunker, 'The fracturing of glass', *Scientific American*, December 1987.) I have taken the original and produced four rewordings; these are ranged in order from most congruent to most metaphorical. We could give an informal semantic gloss on each of these variants, by treating it as if it was congruent: that is, on the presumption that (a) a clause nexus realises a **sequence**, a clause realises a **figure** and an element of clause structure realises an **element**, and (b) of the types of element, nominal groups realise **participants**, verbal groups realise **processes**, and adverbial groups or prepositional phrases realise **circumstances**. Thus, version (1) would be a sequence of two figures; the first figure consists of three elements, a process *crack*, a participant *glass* and a circumstance *more quickly*; the second figure has four elements, a process *press*, a participant *you*, a participant *it* ('glass') introduced as a circumstance *on it*, and a circumstance *harder*; and the two figures are bound together by the conjunction of the two circumstantial adverbs in comparative form (*more quickly, harder*), each accompanied by (what in modern English appears as) the definite article *the*. (This could have been construed congruently by a conjunction such as *if* or *when*.)

By contrast, version (5) would be a single figure consisting of three elements, a process *is associated*, a participant *glass crack growth rate*, and a participant *applied stress magnitude* introduced circumstantially by *with*. The participants have now become both complex and abstract. They are complex because each is construed as a 'thing' having a string of hyponymic classifiers, e.g. *rate, growth rate* ('kind of rate'), *crack growth rate* ('kind of growth rate') and so on. They are abstract because *rate, magnitude, growth . . .* are the names of qualities ('how fast') or processes ('growing'). Furthermore the process, instead of 'cracking' or 'pressing on', is now one of 'causing or being caused by', which we could also characterize as being abstract. We could then perhaps summarize the semantic progression of these five variants as follows:

(1) thing a undergoes process b in manner c to the extent that in manner x person w does action y to thing a
(2) (complex) thing b-in-a acquires property d in manner c to the extent that (abstract) thing xy has process z done to it
(3) (complex abstract) thing abc has attribute c under condition that (abstract) thing xy has process z done to it
(4) (complex abstract) thing c-of-abd is caused by (complex abstract) thing zyx
(5) (complex abstract) thing $abcd$ causes / is caused by (complex abstract) thing zyx

Here is another set of agnate expressions (clause complexes/ clauses), illustrating the same kind of gradation but glossed in grammatical terms so as to bring out the small steps by which this movement between the most clausal and the most nominal con- stitutes a 'packing' of the text. The original is taken from Stanier et al. 1987, p. 205.

1 Osmolarity increases, so putrescine is rapidly excreted.
(clause nexus: paratactic)
2 Because osmolarity increases, putrescine is rapidly excreted.
(clause nexus: hypotactic)
3 That osmolarity increases means that putrescine is rapidly excreted.
(clause: two rankshifted clauses, finite)
4 Osmolarity increasing leads to putrescine being rapidly excreted.
(clause: two rankshifted clauses, nonfinite)
5 Increasing of osmolarity causes rapid excreting of putrescine.
(clause: two nominal groups, verb as Head)
6 Increase of osmolarity causes rapid excretion of putrescine.
(clause: two nominal groups, mass noun as Head)
7 Increases of osmolarity cause rapid excretions of putrescine.
(clause: two nominal groups, count noun as Head)

However, to represent this packing and unpacking simply in terms of an opposition between nominal and clausal styles is not ultimately very helpful. In the first place, it is not quite accurate: it is valid in the sense that there is a shift between the nominal group and the clause as the structural unit that carries the main lexical loading; but it is not the case that everything in the 'nominal' variant gets nominalised. The logical relationship between the two processes (between pressing and cracking, in the first set; between increasing and excreting, in the second) in fact ends up as a verb, *is associated with*, *causes*, etc. In the second place, this way of characterising the distinction tells us nothing about any variation in meaning among the different versions; it suggests that they are stylistic alternatives which somehow leave the meaning exactly as it was. But surely that is not the way it seems to us as we read the sets of agnate variants. We know that their meaning is in some sense very different. Even if we can represent all the variants in the same ***experiential*** terms, in some such way as in Figure 2.2, this is not at all saying that they all mean the same thing. There are other respects in which the meaning may be found to differ.

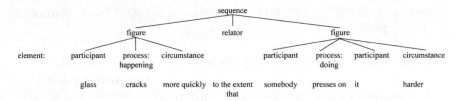

Figure 2.2   Experiential semantic structure underlying all text variants

I have found it helpful to interpret this variation as a form of metaphor: closely analogous to metaphor in its canonical sense, but metaphor that is grammatical rather than lexical (cf. Goatly 1995). What is happening here is a movement between more and less metaphorical forms of wording: between the more congruent (and I will say "congruent" rather than "literal", since I am looking at it from the point of view of **how the meanings are construed** rather than of **what the forms mean** – 'from above' rather than 'from below') – between the more congruent and the more metaphorical wordings. The clausal variant is the one which is more congruent, the nominal variant is the one which is more metaphorical.

Now of course it might be this way round simply because that is how I have chosen to model it; I could have decided to model the nominal variant as the more congruent one. But there is a good reason – three good reasons, in fact – for modelling it the other way. Historically, the clausal variant comes first; and it comes first in all the three dimensions of history I referred to above. It evolves first, in the system of the language; it develops first, in the life of the user (the child); and it unfolds first, in the progression of the text. And this is more than simple precedence in time. The congruent mode of construal is that in which human language first came into being; hence it determines our collective categorisation of the world we live in. It is that in which each child construes his or her personal experience; hence it determines our individual angle on and conception of 'reality'. And it is that in which a text typically starts out – or at least a macro-text, the accumulated literature of some more or less technical discipline; hence it determines our form of argumentation, the construction of theoretical principles from natural and experimental observations. (I have noted this principle at work in Newton's *Opticks*, where each section typically unfolds from a congruent beginning, where Newton recounts his experiments and observations, to a more metaphorical phase in which he reasons from these and builds up his general theory.) Thus the conception of 'congruence' is not an arbitrary one; it captures the inherent directionality of the human semogenic process.

5

In order to illustrate the metaphoric processes that actually take place, let us look in greater detail at one further example:

> Recognition of the tremendous heat resistance of bacterial spores was essential to the development of adequate procedures for sterilisation.

We might try unpacking this as:

> Until <people> recognised that bacterial spores could resist <even> being made tremendously hot they could not develop adequate procedures (?) by which <objects> could be made sterile.

We could of course offer numerous alternative versions; but these will not change the metaphoric quality of the original. Let me enumerate some of the salient features.

(1) There are various instances of nominalization: processes, and

37

qualities, (re)construed as nouns; e.g. *recognition, resistance, development, sterilisation, heat*. But these are not all of the same kind, nor are they all present for the same reasons.

(a) Some are early technical terms from classical times, e.g. *heat*: Greek θερμον, θερμοτης, derived from θερω 'heat up', meaning 'quality of being hot' or 'measurement of how hot'. This is originally created as a **semantic junction**: a quality construed as a thing – that is, by a class of word (noun) that congruently construes things: so it is in origin a complex element having the features of both. It is taken over, already as a technical term, into Latin *calor* and thence into modern European languages such as English. Since it has become a thing, it can be measured (cf. the expression *quantity of heat*, as used for example by John Dalton in the early nineteenth century); it can be a participant, in different participant roles within the clause; and it can be expanded to form taxonomies using the resources of the nominal group: *latent heat*, *radiant heat* and so on.

   In other words, *heat* has become a technical element in a scientific theory; and in the process, the original metaphor has died. It is now a "dead metaphor". And once it is dead, it can no longer be unpacked. The semogenic process that begins with transcategorising an adjective *hot* into a noun *heat*, whereby a new type of complex phenomenon is brought into being (one that is both 'quality' and 'thing'), is now complete; the semantic feature of 'quality' has been transformed, and there has emerged a virtual thing, a thing that exists on a higher, more abstract level, functioning as part of an ordered chain of explanation. (Hence, just as the **relation** of grammatical metaphor is analogous to that of metaphor in its canonical, lexical sense, so also the **process** whereby a metaphor comes into being, lives, and dies, is also analogous. The only difference is that whereas in classical metaphor one **word** takes over from another, in grammatical metaphor one **grammatical class** takes over from another.)

(b) A similar process has taken place with the term *resistance*, except that here the congruent form is a verb, semantically a process; so the semantic junction that takes place is that of **process** construed as thing. This term also has become technicalized – the metaphor is dead: and it appears in a variety of theoretical contexts from electricity to immunology each with its own specialized taxonomic environment.

(c) Such taxonomies are typically construed in English as Classifier +

Thing structures in the nominal group; and here we find these two metaphorical terms combining to form just this structure: *heat resistance*. And once again a semantic junction has taken place. The congruent meaning of this Classifier + Thing structure is 'a kind of', 'a class of'; so *heat resistance* becomes a kind of resistance, analogous (say) to resistance to various kinds of disease or disease-bearing agents (e.g. *phylloxera resistance*, resistance to attack by a particular species of louse); *heat resistance* has thus become a complex technical term on its own. We may note that *heat resistance* is not equivalent to *resists being made hot* − heat-resistant bacteria are not bacteria which resist being heated; they are bacteria which survive even when they **are** heated. This grammatical metaphor is also dead; 'heat resistance' is a complex virtual thing, and the metaphor can no longer be unpacked.

(2) Common to all these instances of grammatical metaphor is the fact that they have become **systemic**. We may contrast, in this respect, the word *recognition*. *Recognition was essential* is agnate to *people had to recognize*; here the metaphor is not systemic − it is, and remains, **instantial**. The context for it is purely discursive: the need to organise the information as 'recognise ... only then could develop', with 'recognise' construed as the Theme, and hence nominalized. This grammatical metaphor is not dead, and can readily be unpacked.

Except in special cases of designed systematic taxonomies, like those of chemistry, and some in medicine, all grammatical metaphors begin as instantial, created in response to the needs of the unfolding discourse. Some of them − the majority, in fact − remain this way, being recreated on each occasion. There is no thing as 'recognition' in the sense in which the word is being used here (there is, of course, in diplomacy, where *recognition* **has** become technicalized). Others become systemic: that is, they become systemic options within the meaning potential of a given register. This is a normal semogenic process within languages as a whole; what creates technical terminology is the combination of two processes: *from instantial to systemic* and *from congruent to metaphorical*.

(3) It would be wrong, however, to equate grammatical metaphor with nominalization. Nominalization is predominant, in the sense that most metaphoric shift is shift into a nominal group. But not all of it is. This is not the sole driving force, even in technical discourse: one that is perhaps equally critical in this context is the experientializing of logical-semantic relationships: that is, reconstruing 'so'

as *cause*, 'then' as *follow* and so on. In this sentence there is a sequence of two processes, 'recognizing' and 'making sterile', with a relator 'only then' (or, in English, 'not until') between them. The congruent construal of this relationship is as a nexus of two clauses joined by a conjunction. We can set up the principle of congruence between semantic and grammatical categories in the following way:

Congruence in rank		Congruence in status (elements)	
semantic	*grammatical*	*semantic*	*grammatical*
sequence	clause nexus	thing (entity)	noun (/nominal group)
figure	clause	quality	adjective (in nominal group)
element	group/phrase	process	verb (/verbal group)
		circumstance (1)	adverb (/adverbial group)
		circumstance (2)	prepositional phrase
		minor process	preposition
		relator	conjunction

The grammatical metaphor thus shifts both the rank and the class status: the sequence, from being a clause nexus, becomes a single clause; and the relator, from being a conjunction, becomes typically a verb – in this instance, there is a further shift whereby the relator is nominalized to become an adjective *essential*. And here again there is a semantic junction: a verb such as *cause, follow, result in* is **both** process **and** relator. It may then become further metaphorised into a noun, such as *cause* or *consequence*; this in turn may become technicalised, the metaphor dies, and the instances can no longer be unpacked.

These are some of the grammatical metaphors contained in that particular sentence. I have discussed them, rather sketchily, case by case, with just passing reference to the general principles involved. A summary of the types of grammatical metaphor I have come across in analysing typical passages of technical discourse in English is given in Figure 2.3 (for a fuller account see Halliday and Matthiessen 1999).

The interesting question that arises is: is there a single principle that we can observe to lie behind these various shifts – a 'general drift' in the direction taken by all the varied types of grammatical metaphor? I think there is; it seems that we can discern a pattern as set out in Figure 2.4, where the arrows numbered 1–10 show the various metaphoric movements that are found to be taking place. The general drift is, in fact, a drift towards the concrete, whereby

Key to figure:	semantic element	grammatical class
	grammatical function	example

1. quality ⇒ entity		adjective ⇒ noun
Epithet = Thing		unstable = instability

2. process ⇒ entity		verb ⇒ noun
(i) Event = Thing		transform = transformation
(ii) Auxiliary = Thing:		
(tense)		will/going to = prospect
(phase)		try to = attempt
(modality)		can/could = possibility, potential

3. circumstances ⇒ entity		preposition ⇒ noun
Minor Process = Thing		with = accompaniment; to = destination

4. relator ⇒ entity		conjunction ⇒ noun
Conjunctive = Thing		so = cause/proof; if = condition

5. process ⇒ quality		verb ⇒ adjective
(i) Event = Epithet		[poverty] is increasing = increasing [poverty]
(ii) Auxiliary =		
(tense)		was/used to = previous
(phase)		begin to = initial
(modality)		must/will [always] = constant

6. circumstance ⇒ quality		adverb/prepositional phrase ⇒ adjective★
(i) Manner = Epithet		[decided] hastily = hasty [decision]
(ii) other = Epithet		[argued] for a long time = lengthy [argument]
(iii) other = Classifier		[cracked] on the surface ⇒ surface [cracks]

7. relator ⇒ quality		conjunction ⇒ adjective
Conjunctive = Epithet		then = subsequent; so = resulting

8. circumstance ⇒ process		*be / go* + preposition ⇒ verb
Minor Process = Process		be about = concern; be instead of = replace

41

9. relator ⇒ process	conjunction ⇒ verb
Conjunctive = Event	then = follow; so = cause; and = complement
10. relator ⇒ circumstance	conjunction ⇒ preposition/-al group
Conjunctive = Minor Process	when = in times of/in . . . times if = under conditions of/under . . . conditions
11. [zero] ⇒ entity	= the phenomenon of . . .
12. [zero] ⇒ process	= . . . occurs/ensues
13. entity ⇒ [expansion]	noun ⇒ [various] (in env. 1, 2 above)
Head = Modifier	the government [decided] = the government's [decision], [a/the decision] of/by the government, [a] government(al) [decision] the government [couldn't decide/was indecisive]= the government's [indecision], [the indecision] of the government, government(al) [indecision]

⋆ or noun; cf. mammal [cells]/mammalian [cells]

Figure 2.3 Typology of grammatical metaphors

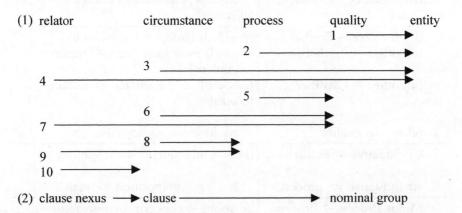

Figure 2.4 The 'general drift' of grammatical metaphor: (1) status, (2) rank

42

each element is reconstrued in the guise of one that lies further towards the pole of stability and persistence through time. Thus, entities are more stable than qualities, and qualities than processes; while logical semantic relators like 'and', 'or', 'but', 'then', 'so', are the least stable – and hence the most complex – of all.

6

Can we then seek to interpret these phenomena of 'packing' and 'unpacking' from the point of view of what they mean? I think a critical notion here is that of **theory**. The grammar of our everyday spoken language, that which a child learns in the first years of life, is itself a theory of human experience: transforming experience into meaning is a theoretical operation. It is also a metaphoric process, since it involves reworking our experience in semiotic terms, creating a semiotic universe in parallel to the material one. The further transformation into what we usually refer to as 'theory' – that is, designed systems of knowledge in science and the humanities – involves rewording within the semiotic (something that we already recognize as 'metaphor'); and in the course of this process the semiotic entities themselves become complex (e.g. *the cause*, where a logical relation has been reconstrued as a process and then further reconstrued as a thing). This **semantic junction** is a meaning-creating operation, since what emerge from it are **new** semiotic entities. Notice however that they are created not by a purely internal semiotic operation but by one involving reconnection with the material: if *a* causes *x*, *b* proves *y*, the new meanings arise not just because *cause* and *prove* are verbs but because of what the category of verb means in the first place: the underlying significance of its function of categorizing certain phenomena as processes – proto-typically, processes that are concrete and can be observed. So a new abstract entity is created at the intersection of 'logical relation' and 'process'. This potential has always been there in the grammar of daily life: every language has its relational processes, and they are critical in the construal of our common-sense theory of experience – especially the verb *be* used in assigning classes to higher classes, e.g. *sparrows, ducks and eagles are all birds*. But in the discourses of technical knowledge these relational processes appear in great numbers: verbs like *represent, constitute, cause, prove, result in, herald, signal, indicate, portend* are central to the whole enterprise of the construction.

Every theory is a system of related meanings; what we think of as a 'scientific' theory is a designed, or semi-designed, system in which the key elements are taxonomies of metaphorical or virtual things – things created by semantic junction between 'process', or 'quality' and the underlying meaning of a noun – as 'entity', especially an entity that is concrete and observable. Hence the importance of nominalizing. This is not a necessary feature of systematic reality construction; Whorf remarked of Hopi, many years ago, that its technical terms were mainly verbs. But it is a feature of all **written** systems of knowledge; and experimental science theorizes the physical world of processes by creating a new world populated largely by virtual entities created at the intersection of 'process' and 'thing'. These become *systemic* things, once the metaphor in them is dead and they can no longer be unpacked. Hence they have the power of entering as participants into the full range of participant roles that the grammar has created for **things**. Their regular formations are in turn supported by the irregulars, the batteries of instantial things, created on the hoof for the flow of information through the discourse. These metaphors are still alive, so they can be unpacked – at least on a clause-by-clause basis: what is lost in this case is not their **technical** status (because they haven't got any) but their contribution to the textual structure of the discourse: the thematic packaging of the information which makes possible the logical progression of the argument. For example:

> When a *solution* of any substance (*solute*) is separated from a *solute-free solvent* by a membrane that is freely permeable to solvent molecules, but not to molecules of the solute, the solvent tends to be drawn through the membrane into the solution, thus diluting it. Movement of the solvent across the membrane can be prevented by applying a certain hydrostatic pressure to the solution. This pressure is defined as *osmotic pressure*. (Stanier et al. 1987, p. 204)

Here *movement of the solvent across the membrane* is an instantial metaphor (note *movement* not *motion*) which can be unpacked as *(that) the solvent moves across the membrane*; this does not affect its ideational meaning, but it destroys its potential for functioning as Theme in the clause which follows.

In any theory, the elements, and the relationships into which they enter, have to become esoteric: virtual, technical objects construed into a self-contained semiotic flow. Experience is transposed on to a higher stratum: we conceive of a theory as 'abstract' because we recognise that it inhabits a different universe. At the same time, there is an unbroken continuity between the theories of everyday common-sense knowledge and those of rarefied scientific knowledge; the frontier between the two is permeable, so that however 'uncommon-sense' much of science is, it is still construed in language, by people who also always retain their commonsense model of the world.

There is in fact an analogue to a designed scientific theory in the discourse of commonsense knowledge. Probably few of my younger colleagues, at least in the English-speaking world, will remember this; but the commonsense theory of experience is a proverb. My grandmother had a proverb for practically any type of situation; she would say things like:

> You'll never make a silk purse out of a sow's ear.
> A fool and his brass are soon parted.
> Take care of the pence, and the pounds'll take care of themselves.
> What's sauce for the goose is sauce for the gander.
> Beggars can't be choosers.
> It never rains but it pours.
> That's the pot calling the kettle black.

and one of her favourites:

> Least said, soonest mended.

– bringing such sayings quite unselfconsciously into her conversation. These were theoretical generalizations about experience; they are **general** truths but, in most cases, construed as **specific** illustrations. But they are discursively contextualized, of course, so that the sort of theory they are propounding (that, for example, a person or object of low value cannot be transformed into one of high value) becomes accessible because it is triggered by some instance already under discussion. Some do depend on grammatical metaphor (e.g. *more haste, less speed*), but on the whole they tend to be congruent; the listener does not have to unpack them but has to move laterally from one instance to another. We can choose to pack them if we wish; we could say *the transformation of inferior raw materials into superior finished products is an impossibility* – and as soon as we do this, contrasting it with *you'll never make a silk purse out of a sow's ear*, we get a sense of what is added, and what is taken away. It would be hard to maintain, I think, that these two were synonymous!

Clearly the semantic distance here is greater than that between packed and unpacked variants such as those I have been discussing, which are systematically related (or **"agnate"**) in the grammar, by grammatical metaphor. We might still want to regard the latter type as experientially synonymous, saying that in some sense they construe the same thesis, or 'state of affairs' (though I think we need to question that also, as a rather too facile assumption); and if that was the whole story, then the packing and unpacking of text would play no part in the construal of knowledge. But even if we accept it, it clearly is not the whole story.

Let me come back for a moment to my account of construing and reconstruing experience as involving the three steps of generalization, abstractness and metaphor. We can look at these as three successive waves of theoretical energy. The move from proper name to common name (generalization) is what makes possible our commonsense theories of knowledge; and the move from concrete categories to abstract ones makes it possible to retheorize this knowledge in 'uncommonsense' terms. In the same way, the move from congruent construals to metaphorical ones allows us to retheorize over again, this time in the form of our technical and scientific theories of knowledge. So 'packing', in the specific sense of this third wave of theoretical energy, is merely an extension of a process that has been going on since language began, in which each step has enlarged the meaning potential by adding a new dimension to the total model. None of them leaves the construal of experience exactly as it was before. Of course, we do not discard the earlier models when we add each new dimension; we may expect to find them all enshrined in the grammatical construction of the text. Consider the following passage taken from James Clerk Maxwell's work on electro-magnetism (1881):

> In this treatise we have avoided making any assumption that electricity is a body or that it is not a body, and we must also avoid any statement which might suggest that, like a body, electricity may receive or emit heat.
>
> We may, however, without any such assumption, make use of the idea of entropy, introduced by Clausius and Rankine into the theory of heat, and extend it to certain thermo-electric phenomena, always remembering that entropy is not a thing but a mere instrument of scientific thought, by which we are enabled to express in a compact and convenient manner the conditions under which heat is emitted or absorbed.

Here, we find a virtual (level 3) entity *entropy*, an abstract (level 2) entity *electricity*, a general (level 1) entity *body*, and a 'proper' (level 0) entity *Clausius*, representing these four different levels of human understanding, all functioning together in a complex edifice of scientific knowledge. Each one inhabits a differently dimensioned space in the overall interpretative act.

7

Each new wave of theoretical energy – each new round of packing, to remain within our own metaphorical domain – takes us one step further away from our ordinary everyday experience. To go from *pussy!* (first calling, then naming, our individual pet) to *cat* (naming the species), we have to have memory; and even more so to get to *cat* as the name of a genus including lions, tigers and so on, since we are unlikely to experience all these together in a collective. To go on from there to the abstract terms **species** or **genus** we have to have a systematic theory; and to go on from there to *gene pool* or *'the selfish gene'* we need a theory of theories, a metatheoretic potential which enables us to project our theories on to new planes of abstraction. We cannot unpack these **systemic** constructs without destroying them; yet if we don't unpack them we produce discourse which is so remote that it has little resonance with daily life. So scientific discourse becomes a discourse of prestige and power, something to be exploited by a technocratic elite that prefers to exclude everyone else from taking part in political processes.

We know that such discourse has given us enormous powers over our physical and biological environment: not by itself, of course, but as the primary semiotic in the dialectic of material and semiotic activity that constitutes the human experience. Without packing the text, it seems, we would never have moved into the machine age, let alone the age of information. All the more important, I think, to be aware of the not-yet-packed, commonsense grammar that lies at the base. In its experiential function, this grammar construes a general typology of experiential categories: processes, qualities, circumstances, relators and things. Some of these category types are less stable than others: processes and qualities are less stable than things, and relators are the least stable of all. We have seen that, in grammatical metaphor, everything shifts in the direction of the concrete: 'packing' the text adds stability and permanence, superimposing on the commonsense construal of experience syndromes of features which collectively serve to establish general principles. In order to stabilize, the grammar creates a semiotic universe made of 'things';

hence the interesting paradox: that the most abstract theorizing is achieved by modelling everything on the concrete. To make 'planets move' into a theoretical term, you turn *move* into a thing, called *motion*, and get the *planets* to function as a class of this thing, namely *planetary motion*. This would not work if *motion* immediately divested itself of the semantic feature of 'process'; but it does not – it begins as a semantic junction of 'thing' and 'process', and then evolves into a more abstract 'thing' in which is distilled a large amount of knowledge that has been accumulated from studying how things move.

But since a text that is highly metaphoric in this sense involves a great number of such 'distilled' terms, by the same token it is likely that, relative to the discourse of commonsense knowledge, it will appear as somewhat ambiguous. Theorizing means generalizing, idealizing out the specifics of this or that particular class of instances; hence in unpacking the metaphors, one is frequently faced with a range of possible congruent forms without any clear principle for preferring one over another. Once you unpack theoretical discourse, it ceases to be theoretical. Inevitably, therefore, a highly technical text has a different meaning for the expert, who processes it without unpacking, from that which it has for the lay person, for whom it may be inaccessible as it stands and ambiguously specific if unpacked. The discourses of science gain their theoretical power precisely because they are not translatable into commonsense terms. It has often been pointed out that scientific principles often contradict what commonsense knowledge leads one to expect; there is bound to be a certain disjunction between the grammar of scientific writings and the commonsense grammar of daily life.

If we 'pack' the text, we turn it into written, standard language; the language of books, written to be read by strangers, people that the writer has never seen or even heard of. Unpacking it brings it back into the family, into the local world of face-to-face encounters. If by 'knowledge' we mean technical knowledge, then it is almost bound to be construed in the form of discourse which is already 'packed'; this is not just a feature of English – it is just as true, for example, of Chinese. But the foundation of human experience, however far that experience may be extended into the mysteries of space and time, ultimately resides in the non-technical construal of local, everyday knowledge, in the typically congruent mode of the local, everyday grammar. Such knowledge does not gain from being packed into a metaphoric format. As my grandmother would have put it, in its own theoretical terms, "Fine words butter no parsnips".

Chapter Three

THINGS AND RELATIONS: REGRAMMATICIZING EXPERIENCE AS TECHNICAL KNOWLEDGE (1998)

1 Questions and assumptions

The question I am asking in this paper is: how does the language of science reconstrue human experience? By **how** I mean both 'in what respects' and 'by what means'. By **the language of science** I mean the various forms of discourse in which the activities of 'doing science' are carried out – but seen as a systemic resource for creating meaning, not as a collection of instances of text. By **reconstrue** I mean 'reconstruct semiotically': that is, replace one semiotic construction by another. I leave open the possibility that, in the end, the question might be dismissed – we might conclude that no such reconstrual takes place; although I have expressly formulated the question so as to suggest that I think it does.

I am concerned specifically with the scientific discourses of English, although it seems that the critical features are present in other languages as well. (Halliday and Martin 1993, Chapter 7 examines scientific writings in Chinese; Biagi 1995 discusses their history in Italian.) My approach is through the grammar, and specifically through systemic functional "grammatics", theorizing the grammar in such a way that it is possible to interpret texts as instantiations of a meaning-creating system and its subsystems. The most general sources for the grammatics are Halliday (1985/94), Martin (1992), Eggins (1994), Matthiessen (1995), Davidse (1991).

'Things and relations: regrammaticizing experience as technical knowledge', from *Reading Science: Critical and Functional Perspectives on Discourses of Science*, edited by James R. Martin and Robert Veel, London: Routledge, 1998. Reprinted by permission of Routledge.

The discussion as a whole takes off from the issues raised in Halliday and Martin (1993); in particular, I hope it will help to clarify the relationship between what appear there as two rather distinct motifs: one that of technicality and categorizing (foregrounded in Martin's chapters), the other that of logicality and reasoning (foregrounded in my own).

I shall make two assumptions about grammar at the start. One is that the grammar of every (natural) language is a theory of human experience. The other is that that is not all that it is. The grammar of a natural language is also an enactment of interpersonal relationships. These two functions, the reflective and the active, are each dependent on the other; and they, in turn, are actualized by a third function, that of creating discourse. Thus grammar brings into being a semiotic mode of activity that models the material mode while being itself a component of what it is modelling (cf. Lemke 1993). This functional framing of the grammar can be summarized as in Figure 3.1. These assumptions constitute the core of the "meta-functional" hypothesis that has evolved over three decades of systemic functional grammatics and will not be elaborated further here.

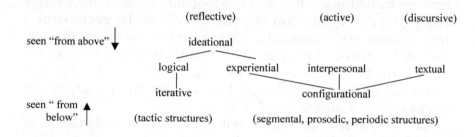

Figure 3.1   The metafunctional framing of the grammar

2 Grammar as theory of experience

When one talks about the grammar as a theory of human experience one is, obviously, focusing on the ideational metafunction; and since this is the aspect of grammar that is almost always given greatest prominence I want to reject, explicitly, the suggestion that it has some kind of priority. Neither historically nor functionally is ideational meaning more basic or more potent than the other components of human semiosis. To say this is not simply to give value to the interpersonal and textual domains. Grammar evolved in the human species, and develops in the human brain, as a form of consciousness in which each instance – each act of meaning – simultaneously both construes (some portion of) experience and enacts (some portion of) the social process. Typically these take place below the level of our (adult) awareness and attention; but when we focus our attention we become aware first of all of the grammar's representational power – its potential for referring to perceptual phenomena; and theories of meaning have usually fixated on that. This potential is critical to the present argument; for that reason, especially, it is important to put it in perspective. In our construction of meaning, the representational has no priority over the other, conative and expressive (to use terms derived from Bühler (1934)) semantic domains. The most abstruse scientific theory becomes actualized only in taking at the same time the form of a social act (Lemke 1990a, 1995).

What the grammar does, in its ideational guise, is to transform human experience into meaning. The grammar construes a universe of things and relations, imposing categories on our perceptions of phenomena; in other words, it sets up a *theory* of experience, modelling the immensely complex interaction between the human organism and its environment. In mainstream C20 philosophy of language this has been interpreted as a largely passive process of correspondence, whereby the grammar fulfils its experiential role by recognizing patterns – forms of likeness among different phenomena – that are 'given' in the material world, so that a lexicogrammatical category (a lexical item, or a term in a grammatical system) simply reflects, or codifies, something that is already there. But, as Ellis (1993) points out, this notion is mistaken. In fact there are no such natural classes; or (what amounts to the same thing) there are indefinitely many of them: that is, indefinitely many ways in which the phenomena of our experience can be seen to be related to one another. What the grammar does is to impose a categorization: it treats a certain cluster of phenomena as alike in certain respects, and hence sets this cluster apart from others which it treats as being different.

It is easy to demonstrate this principle with meanings that are construed lexically: it comes down to the question of what phenomena we call by the same name. Of the various objects sticking out of the ground that I can see outside my window, some are *trees*, some are *bushes* and some are *shrubs*; and of the humans that are passing by some are *walking* and some are *running* (and some are *driving* in cars). We can observe small children working hard to construct the category meanings of words in their mother tongue; and we become aware of the problem for ourselves when we learn a language that is culturally distant from our own. But the more pervasive categories of our experience are those that are construed grammatically, since they provide us with a general foundation for understanding our environment and ourselves.

In the most general terms, the grammar construes experience as **process**, in the form of a grammatical **unit**, a **clause**. Each process, in turn, is construed as a **configuration**, in the form of a grammatical **structure**; the components of this configuration are (1) the process itself, (2) certain entities that participate in the process, and (3) various circumstantial elements that are associated with it; these are construed in the form of grammatical **classes**, the verbal, the nominal, and some more or less distinct third type. Then, one process may be construed as being related to another, by some form of grammatical **conjunction**.

The way things are is the way our grammar tells us that they are. In the normal course of events we do not problematize this construal; it is our 'taken for granted reality', and we do not reflect on why the grammar theorizes experience the way it does or whether it could have been done in some other way. If we do reflect, we are likely still to appeal to a sense of what is natural. We might reason that, as long as to our perceptions things stay just as they are, we do not 'experience' them; experience begins when the organism becomes aware of some change taking place in its environment (or in itself). Hence the grammar construes experience around the category of 'process': a process typically represents some sort of change, of which staying the same – not changing – becomes just the limiting case.

But sorting out a **process** of change from the **entities** that remain in existence throughout and despite the change (let alone from other phenomena that are seen as circumstantial to it) is already a major enterprise of semiotic construction. If we consider a simple clause such as *the sun was shining on the sea* (immortalized as the first line of *The Walrus and the Carpenter*), a considerable amount of semiotic energy has gone into the grammar's construal of this as a configuration of process 'shine', participating entity 'sun' and circumstance 'on the sea'. Taken purely in its own terms, as a perceptual phenomenon, it would have been simpler to construe it as a single unanalysed whole. It is only when the whole of experience is being construed as an ideational *system* that the analytical model – breaking down a complex perception to recognize likenesses of many different kinds – shows up as infinitely more resourceful and more powerful. (To pursue the same text further, the sun's shining may be attended by other circumstances, *with all his might*; and the sun may participate in other processes than shining, trying *to make the billows smooth and bright*.)

What is significant for the present discussion, however, is not so much the particulars of the experiential model, as it evolved in human grammars; rather, it is the fact that the same evolutionary processes which make it possible to construe experience, by transforming it into meaning in this way, also provide the means with which to challenge the form of the construal. When experience has once been construed, it can be reconstrued in a different light.

3 Stratification and metaphor

It is, I think, acknowledged that human consciousness is the product of natural selection (Edelman 1992) – that there is no need to postulate some mysterious entity called "mind" (itself, as Matthiessen (1993) has shown, the rather one-sided product of the grammar's construing of inner experience) that lies outside the processes of biological history. Neuroscientists have shown that the brain (including the human brain) evolved in the context of the increasingly complex relationship between the organism and its environment; I would just want to add here, since this formulation overprivileges the ideational (cf. Section 1 above), that it also evolved in the context of the increasingly complex social interactions among the organisms forming a group. These evolutionary processes have engendered what Edelman calls 'higher order consciousness', something that appears to be unique to homo sapiens.

Higher order consciousness is semiotic consciousness; it is this which transforms experience into meaning. From my point of view in this paper, with its focus on language, higher order consciousness depends on two critical steps by which language evolved. One I have already introduced: that of functional diversity, or **metafunction**: the principle that 'meaning' is a parallel mode of activity (the semiotic, alongside and in dialectic relation with the material) which

53

simultaneously both construes experience and enacts the social process. The other critical step is stratal organization, or *stratification*.

Primary semiotic systems – those of other species, and the "proto-language" of human infants before they embark on the mother tongue – are not stratified; they are inventories of signs, without a grammar. Such systems cannot create meaning; their contexts are 'given' constructs like 'here I am', 'let's be together', 'I want that' (which we distort, of course, by glossing them in adult language wordings). Language, the semiotic of higher order consciousness, is *stratified*: it has a stratum of lexicogrammar 'in between' the meaning and the expression (Halliday and Martin 1993, Chapter 2). The "signified" part of the original sign has now evolved into a meaning space, within which the meaning potential can be indefinitely expanded (Figure 3.2). Such a system can **create** meaning; its text-forming resources engender a discursive flow which is then modified (rather like the airstream is modified, on the expression plane, by articulation and intonation) so that it becomes at the same time both interactive (dialogic) and representational.

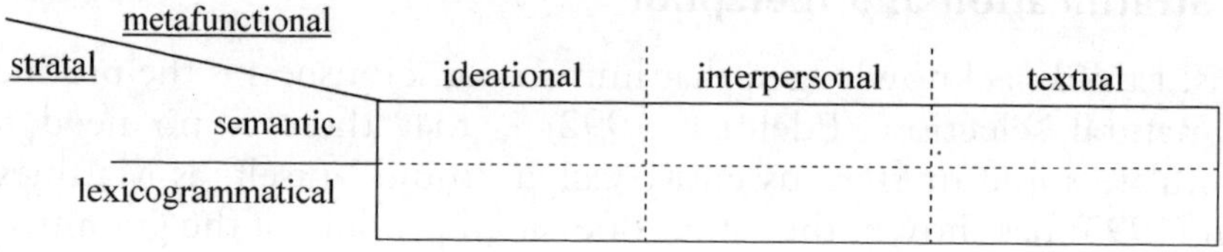

Figure 3.2   The 'meaning space' defined by stratification and metafunction

In the primary semiotic, "content" is formed directly at the interface with the experiential world – hence it is 'given', as described above. In the higher order stratified semiotic, meaning is created across a semiotic space which is defined by the *semantic* stratum (itself interfacing, as before, with the world of experiential phenomena) and the *lexicogrammatical* stratum, a new, purely abstract level of semiotic organization which interfaces only with the two material interfaces. The semiotic energy of the system comes from the lexicogrammar.

This 'thick', dimensional semiotic thus creates meaning on two strata, with a relation of *realization* between them: the semantic, and the lexicogrammatical – analogous to Hjelmslev's "content substance" and "content form" within his "content plane". If we focus now on the ideational function, we can represent the outline of the way experience is construed into meaning in the grammar of English along the following lines:

	semantic		lexicogrammatical
rank:	sequence (of figures)	realized by	clause complex
	figure	"	clause
	element (of figure)	"	group/phrase
types of element:	process	realized by	verbal group
	participating entity	"	nominal group
	circumstance	"	adverbial group or prepositional phrase
	relation	"	conjunction

For example: *the driver drove the bus too rapidly down the hill, so the brakes failed* (Figure 3.3).

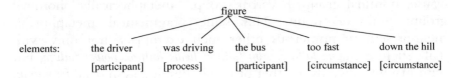

Figure 3.3 Construal of experience

Thus the grammar, in a stratified system, sets up categories and relationships which have the effect of transforming experience into meaning. In creating a formal distinction such as that between verb and noun, the grammar is theorizing about processes: that a distinction can be made, of a very general kind, between two facets: the process itself, and entities that are involved in it.

But, as remarked above, since the grammar has the power of construing, by the same token (that is, by virtue of being stratified) it can also deconstrue, and reconstrue along different lines. Since stratification involves mapping meanings into forms, 'process' into verbal and 'participant' into nominal, it also allows remapping – say, of 'process' into a nominal form: the previous clause could be reworded as a nominal group *the driver's overrapid downhill driving of the bus*. The experience has now been retransformed – in other words, it has undergone a process of metaphor. A stratified system has inherent metaphoric power.

Of course, the initial categorizing of experience is already a kind of metaphorical process, since it involves transforming the material into the semiotic. But, having said that, I will go on to use the term "metaphor" just in its canonical sense, that of transformation **within** the semiotic mode. Traditionally the term is applied only to *lexical* transformations, and it is theorized as "same signifier, different signified" (e.g. *spoonfeed*: "literal meaning" 'feed baby or invalid with small quantities of easily digested food on a spoon'; "metaphorical meaning", 'provide learner with small quantities of carefully chosen instructional materials'). But here I shall be talking about *grammatical* transformations; and I shall theorize these as "same signified, different signifier", for example 'brake + fail' "congruent construal" *the brakes failed* "metaphorical construal" *brake failure*. Notice however that what varies is not the lexical items, which are the same in both cases; it is the grammatical categories, so that the metaphor actually proceeds as follows: 'process + participant' "congruently" clause: nominal group + verbal group, "metaphorically" nominal group: noun + noun. This same grammatical metaphor is then present in numerous other such exemplars: not only with 'fail', such as *engine failure, crop failure, heart failure, power failure*, but with many thousands of other processes besides, as in *cloud formation, bowel movement, tooth decay, tissue growth, particle spin, rainfall* and the like.

If we consider a pair of expressions such as those above:

the driver drove the bus too rapidly down the hill, so the brakes failed

the driver's overrapid downhill driving of the bus resulted in brake failure

it is clear that there is a highly complex relation of grammatical metaphor between the two; a number of transformations are taking place simultaneously: *the driver / the driver's*; *drove / driving*; *the bus / of the bus*; *too rapidly / overrapid*; *down the hill / downhill*; *fail / failure*; *the brakes / brake*; *so / resulted in*). These may be represented diagrammatically as in Figure 3.4.

It will be seen that the metaphorical shift involves two kinds of grammatical movement: one in rank, the other in structural configuration (the latter will be more effectively modelled in terms of grammatical functions, rather than simply in terms of classes). On the one hand, there has been a movement **down in rank**: (1) a (semantic) sequence, congruently construed as a (grammatical) clause

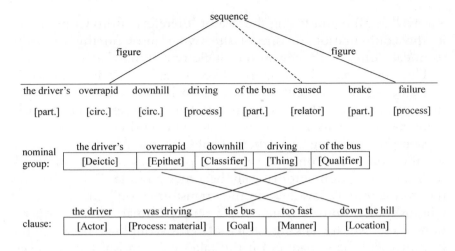

Figure 3.4 Metaphoric reconstrual

complex, is reconstrued as a (grammatical) clause, which congruently construes a (semantic) figure; (2) a figure, congruently
construed as a clause, is reconstrued as a group, which congruently
construes an element in a figure. On the other hand, there has been a
movement **across in function / class**; this is very much more
complex, since it involves (1) reconstruing each configuration of
elements as a whole:

    (i)   'driver + drive + bus + too fast + down hill'
        from clause functioning as primary clause in paratactic clause
        nexus to nominal group functioning as Token in clause

    (ii) 'brake + fail'
        from clause functioning as secondary clause in paratactic
        clause nexus to nominal group functioning as Value in
        clause

and in addition (2) reconstruing each individual element, from a
function in the clause to a function in the nominal group:

(i)	'driver'	from Actor	(in clause)	to Deictic	(in nominal group)
	'drive'	Process		Thing	
	'bus'	Goal		Qualifier	
	'too fast'	Manner		Epithet	
	'down hill'	Location		Classifier	
(ii)	'brake'	Actor		Classifier	
	'fail'	Process		Thing	

– as well as (3) reconstruing the relator 'therefore' from Conjunctive in the configuration of one of the two clauses (in this case, the secondary one) to Process in the single remaining clause.

Thus grammatical metaphor, like metaphor in its traditional, lexical sense, is a realignment between a pair of strata: a remapping of the semantics on to the lexicogrammar; hence the term "reconstrual" being used here to refer to it. It depends entirely on the stratal organization of language; there could be no metaphor without stratification – and once the content plane has become stratified, such transformation automatically becomes possible. (Note that this transformation is distinct from "transformation" in the early Chomskyan grammar, which was a purely formal, syntactic opera-tion. Here we are talking rather of 'cross-coupling' between the grammar and the semantics.) If this takes place in isolated instances, scattered more or less randomly throughout the discourse, it prob-ably has only local significance in the text. But if it becomes a regular, sustained feature of discourses of a particular kind, then certain questions about it seem to arise:

1) What is the payoff? what effect has such reconstrual on the construction of the discourse?
2) What different kinds of metaphorical shift take place, and is there any general principle lying behind them?
3) What are the systemic consequences? To put this in other terms, in what way is "regrammaticizing" experience also 'resemanticizing' it?

I shall try to take each of these questions up in turn.

4 Grammatical metaphor in scientific English

The example discussed in the last section was of course contrived. But it was contrived on the model of what is in many ways the favourite grammatical pattern ('syndrome' of grammatical features) in modern scientific English. In this pattern, (1) a sequence of two figures is construed as a single clause, typically a relational clause of the intensive or circumstantial type (cf. Halliday 1985/94, Chapter 5); (2) each figure is construed as a nominal group, and (3) the logical-semantic (conjunctive) relation between them is construed as a verbal group. Here are some text examples:

rapid changes in the rate of evolution are caused by external events

the thermal losses typical of an insulating system are measured in terms of a quantity called the thermal loss coefficient

the absolute indistinguishability of the electrons in the two atoms gives rise to an 'extra' attractive force between them

this breeding effort was anchored in the American species' resistance to phylloxera

the theoretical program of devising models of atomic nuclei has been complemented by experimental investigations

the growth of attachment between infant and mother signals the first step in the child's capacity to discriminate among people

many failures are preceded by the slow extension of pre-existing cracks

fire intensity has a profound effect on smoke injection

Griffith's energy balance approach to strength and fracture also suggested the importance of surface chemistry in the mechanical behaviour of brittle materials

the model rests on the localized gravitational attraction exerted by rapidly oscillating and extremely massive cloud loops of cosmic string

increased responsiveness may be reflected in feeding behaviour

this acidification was caused mainly by the burning of coal containing high levels of sulphur

Let me put this into the context of the present discussion. I began by observing that a natural language embodies, in its grammar, a theory of human experience. This is a commonsense theory evolving in daily life, and usually remains below the level of attention. A scientific theory differs from this in that it is a dedicated and partially designed semiotic subsystem which reconstrues certain aspects or components of human experience in a different way, in the course of opening them up to be observed, investigated and explained. The problems addressed by modern theories in the physical and biological sciences often involve phenomena that are far removed from the experiences of every day, like human genomes or gravitational waves; but they are still such as to permit an ultimate renewal of connection, and – what is significant here – they derive steadily and unbrokenly from the origins of modern science in the theories of Newton, Galileo and beyond. And when we examine the discourse in which these earlier theories are propounded, the grammatical continuity is very clear. When I first looked into the history of this pattern of reconstrual, I took as two of my principal sources Isaac Newton's *Opticks*, published in English in 1704, and Joseph Priestley's *History and Present State of Electricity* from the middle of the same century (published in 1767). In these texts the features that characterize the grammar of modern scientific writing in English, while they have since become much more highly ela-borated, are already beginning to emerge. Here are two brief examples:

> Now those Colours argue a diverging and separation of the hetero-geneous Rays from one another by means of their unequal Refrac-tions, as in what follows will more fully appear. And, on the contrary, the permanent whiteness argues, that in like Incidences of the Rays there is no such separation of the emerging Rays, and by consequence no inequality of their whole Refractions. (Newton)

> [Some authors] say that, as the dense electric fluid, surrounding two bodies negatively electrified, acts equally on all sides of those bodies, it cannot occasion their repulsion. Is not the repulsion, say they, owing rather to an accumulation of the electric fluid on the surfaces of the two bodies; which accumulation is produced by the attraction of the bodies, and the difficulty the fluid finds in entering them? (Priestley)

These passages already display, in an evolved form, what we have recognized above as grammatical metaphor. This looks at first sight like a loose and rather random assembly of unrelated grammatical effects. Can we make any observations that might suggest whether these writers are exploiting the metaphorical resources of the grammar in such a way as to extend the overall meaning potential – and to extend it in a way which is systematically related to the context in which this is happening, that of the development of forms of discourse for pursuing experimental science?

There seem to be two most general motifs; and they relate to the two features referred to in Section 3 above as properties specific to a semiotic that is stratified: namely, its potential for referring and its potential for expanding. In these discourses, the semiotic power of *referring* is being further exploited so as to create **technical taxo-nomies**: constructs of virtual objects that represent the distillation of experience (typically experience that has itself been enriched by design, in the form of experiment). The semiotic power of *expanding* – relating one process to another by a logical–semantic relation such as time – is being further exploited so as to create *chains of reasoning*: drawing conclusions from observation (often observation of experimental data) and construing a line of argument leading on from one step to the next.

Grammatically, these two discursive processes, which lead out of the daily language into an elaborated language of systematic, theory-modulated knowledge, both depend first and foremost on the same basic resource: the metaphoric transformation of a clausal into a nominal mode of construal. Put like that, this sounds a simple enough operation; but, as we have seen, it actually involves a highly complex series of cross-couplings, culminating in a kind of knight's move within the grammar: down in rank, and sideways in class and function. The two motifs we have identified – technicalizing, and rationalizing – exploit this grammatical potential in rather different ways; although it should be possible to show that, at a more abstract level, they are complementary aspects of an integrated semiotic process.

Appendix text 1 taken from a modern scientific text shows both these motifs at work. The technical terms are generally obvious: there are some that have already been established, like *transport mechanisms* and *catabolic and biosynthetic pathways*; and others that are being introduced here for the first time. Since the book from which the passage is taken is a textbook, new terms are flagged: highlighted in italic type, and sometimes explicitly defined. The use of grammatical metaphor in carrying forward the argument can be seen in sequences such as . . . *until one essential nutrient in the medium falls to a very low value, approaching exhaustion. At this limiting nutrient concentration, . . .*, where the second sentence recapitulates the preceding point but in a grammatical form such that it can serve as the departure point for the next step in the reasoning. I shall draw further illustrations from this text in the later sections of this chapter.

5 Grammatical energy: the semogenic power of nominalization

The nominal group is a powerful resource for making meaning – in English, and in many other languages besides. The main reason for its semogenic power is that it can be expanded to a more or less indefinite extent. In a historical perspective, a "group" is an expanded word; both verbs and nouns get expanded into groups, but while the verbal group expands grammatically, with complex tenses, modalities, phases and the like (processes get elaborated on the temporal dimension), the nominal group expands lexically, by the device known as modification: one noun functions as a kind of keyword, and other words are organized around it, having different functions with respect to this head noun. For example,

one of the	last few	viable	subtropical	rainforests	in Australia
Deictic	Numerative	Epithet	Classifier	Thing	Qualifier

The semantic principle of this expansion, and its significance for discourse, is that it locates the participating entity along certain parameters ranging from the most instantial to the most systemic; in English, this appears as a movement in the pre-modifying segment of the group "from left to right", beginning with the Deictic and ending up with the Classifier. The Deictic element is the one which locates the entity instantially, with respect to the speech situation; the Classifier locates it systemically, by subclassifying; other elements lie on the continuum in between.

The nominal group also accommodates expansion by down-ranked figures (congruently, clauses and phrases). These may be grammaticized as words and fitted in to the pre-modifying schema, as in *a four-legged animal*, where *four-legged* is Classifier; but in their (more) congruent form, as clauses or phrases, they occupy a special place in the group, as the Qualifier: *an animal with four legs* (phrase) / *having four legs* (non-finite clause) / *which has four legs* (finite clause). Such figures are often ambiguous when they occur in a pre-modifying function; contrast the following pair:

four-legged animal	where	four-legged	is Classifier	[lɛgɪd]
long-legged animal	where	long-legged	is Epithet	[lɛgd]

(Here the two are usually pronounced differently, although that is not a typical feature.) If such modifying elements are grammaticized as finite clauses the difference between these two functions is realized as a difference in tense, provided that the process is of a certain type (material, including behavioural, rather than mental/verbal or relational); thus contrast:

our forces need low–flying aircraft: Classifier ... which fly low
hit by a low–flying aircraft: Epithet ... which was/is flying low

Thus the nominal group has, in its grammar, the potential for organizing a large quantity of lexical material into functional configurations, in which lexical items operate either directly (as words) or indirectly (through rankshifted phrases or clauses). This potential that nominal groups have for structural expansion is clearly related to their role in the construal of experience. Congruently, nominal groups construe participants – entities that participate in processes; these are the more stable elements on the experiential scene, which tend to persist through time whereas the processes themselves are evanescent. When leaves have fallen, the leaves are still around; but the falling is no longer in sight. Two things follow. One is that participants are more likely than processes to be subcategorized – to be assigned to classes, and to carry attributes (there are more classes of leaves than classes of falling). The second is that participants are more likely than processes to function as anchorpoint for the figure in which they occur. Given a figure 'fall + leaves', we are more likely to construe it messagewise as 'as for the leaves, (they) were falling' than as 'as for the falling, it was (being done by) leaves'.

When a figure (congruently construed as a clause) is reworded, by grammatical metaphor, in a nominalized form, a considerable amount of energy is released, in terms of the two semantic potentials mentioned above: the potential for referring, and the potential for expanding – that is, for transforming the flux of experience into configurations of semiotic categories, and for building up such configurations into sequences of reasoned argument. These are spelt out more fully in the course of the next two sections.

6 The pay-off: (1) categorizing, taxonomic organization

We have noted that the grammar, in its guise as a theory of experience, construes phenomena into classes. The primary resource for doing this is the vocabulary; a lexical item, like *bird*, constitutes an experiential category, more or less indeterminate at the edges but in explicit paradigmatic contrast with others, e.g. *reptile*, *fish*. The lexis also allows for taxonomizing (constructing classes of classes): *swift*, *magpie*, *owl*, *toucan* are all classes of *bird*. The taxonomic relationship may or may not be made explicit in the word structure; in *swift*, *toucan* it is not, whereas in *blackbird*, *lyrebird* it is.

It is in the nominal group structure that this taxonomizing potential is fully opened up, through the iterative character of modification. Thus, one kind of *toucan* is a *mountain toucan*; one kind of *mountain toucan* is a *grey-breasted mountain toucan*; and so on. Such taxonomies are already a feature of everyday language; the semi-designed registers of technology and science simply take over the same potential and systematize its application (see Wignell, Martin and Eggins 1987/93, for a discussion of folk, expert and scientific taxonomies of living creatures). The prototypical form is of course the categorizing of concrete objects in the perceptual world; and the organizing concept is that of hyponymy, '*a* is a kind of *x*'. The grammar also allows for classes to be intersected; thus an *immature grey-breasted mountain toucan* shares the feature *immature* with a subclass of birds as a whole.

In a taxonomy of this kind, the relationship is one of generality; the superordinate category is more general than its hyponyms. It is not any more abstract: a *bird* is not more abstract than a *grey-breasted mountain toucan*. It is simply a more inclusive set. But at the same time assigning a class to a larger, more general class is a theoretical operation. If it is a feature of the everyday grammar of English that *toucan* is a hyponym of *bird*, along with other lexical items as co-hyponyms, then *bird* is a theoretical construct, in the grammar's overall theorizing of experience. It has a value in people's theory of the living environment. Suppose now that this "folk" taxonomy is reconstrued as an expert or a scientific taxonomy, the category of *bird* is likely to get more explicitly defined, in an attempt to show what is 'in' the category and what is outside it. This is a way of recognizing both its **place** in the taxonomy, and its **value** as a theoretical construct. It has now become what is called a "technical term".

In the course of this process, the meaning may get a new name: so a *bird* becomes an *avis*. *Avis* is, of course, merely the Latin word for 'bird'. But a subtle change has taken place: it has now become a more abstract bird, a link in a chain of explanations of how species evolved. The metaphoric shift into another tongue, one which is both exotic and highly valued, symbolizes the move to a higher, technical status; it is not a necessary feature of technicalization – just relocating the term in a designed theoretical schema would suffice; but it is typical of the technicalizing process in many languages, and very markedly so in scientific English.

To that extent, therefore, this new 'bird' – the *avis* – does function at a somewhat more abstract level. In becoming technicalized, it has also become condensed: it is no longer just the name of a list of members, but embodies certain other semantic features besides. Hence its relationship to one particular specimen no longer appears as one of simple instantiation; when we are woken by the dawn chorus we don't say "Listen to those noisy aves" – or if we did, it would be as a rather self-conscious joke. The noun *avis* still retains the category meaning of a noun; but it has something else besides – some meaning that we might gloss as 'theoretical abstraction'.

But this opens up the possibility of extending the theoretical power of the grammar still further, by technicalizing elements which construe phenomena of other kinds: not only things, but qualities of things, and even processes themselves. Nouns like *length* and *motion* construe 'be(ing) long' and 'mov-e/-ing' as theoretical entities. In doing so, they are exploiting a further resource which has always been part of the grammar of everyday language: that of (not merely categorizing but) transcategorizing – deriving one grammatical category from another. Specifically, they are exploiting the gram-mar's potential for ***nominalizing***: turning verbs and adjectives into nouns, as in these prototypical examples from ancient Greek:*

(1) verb: active (Actor) noun
   'one who / that which ...-s'
      ποιέω make: ποιητής maker

      πράσσω do: πράκτωρ doer

(2) verb: passive (Goal) noun
   'that which is ... -n'
      be made: ποίημα thing made

      be done: πρᾶγμα thing done, deed

(3) verb: middle (Medium) noun
   '...-ing' (abstract)
      make: ποίησις making

      do: πρᾶξις doing, action

(4) adjective: noun of quality / degree
   'being ...; how ...?'
      μέγας big: μέγεθος size; greatness,
      βαθύς deep: βάθος depth; deepness, altitude

* The Greek forms provided the model for scientific terminology in Europe; they were translated into Latin (which was fairly close to Greek both in its grammatical structure and in its semantic organization), and the Latin terms were subsequently borrowed into the modern European languages. In Greek and Latin, transcat-egorization always involved some morphological alternation; the morphology was also borrowed, so that from the late middle ages new terms were typically coined from Latin and Greek resources. (Transcategorizing does not necessarily entail morphological change; in Chinese and Vietnamese, for example, words do not usually change in form when they shift from one class to another – as also in much of the Anglo-Saxon component of English.)

The nouns in (1) and (2) originate as concrete, or at least per-ceivable, 'things'. Type (1) is an entity, typically a person, identified as actor in, or causer of, a process; type (2) is an object coming into being as product or as outcome of a process (it may then develop a more abstract sense; e.g. πρᾶγμα coming to mean something like 'affair'). The nouns in (3) and (4), on the other hand, do not represent entities. Here some process itself (3), or else some quality

(4), is being construed **as if it was** a 'thing': that is, as an ongoing, stable – and hence, in (4) measurable – phenomenon. It is these latter types, (3) and (4), that are particularly potent, because they are reconstruing the process or quality **as a kind of entity** – and hence as something **which can itself participate in other processes**.

In other words, there is no metaphor involved in (1) and (2); these are entities defined by processes, but they do not themselves contain any semantic feature of 'process'. (3) and (4), however, embody a semantic *junction*: (3) contain **both** the feature 'entity', which is the congruent meaning of the grammatical category 'noun', **and** the feature 'process', which is carried over from their original status as verbs. Likewise, (4) combine 'entity' with the feature 'quality' that is present in their adjectival form. Types (3) and (4) provided the semiotic foundation for ancient Greek science and mathematics: qualities transcategorized into vectors and units of measurement, like *length*, *distance*, *straight line*; processes transcategorized into abstract, theoretical 'things' like *motion*, *change*, *growth*.

It is type (3), above all, that opens up the full semogenic potential of metaphoric nominalization in the grammar. A process, such as 'move', is observed, generalized, and then theorized about, so that it becomes a virtual entity 'motion'; as a noun, it now has its own potential (a) for participating in other processes, as in: "The Rays of Light, whether they be very small Bodies projected, or only Motion or Force propagated, are moved in right Lines;" (*Opticks*, p. 268) and (b) for being expanded into a taxonomy, such as *linear motion*, *orbital motion*, *parabolic motion*, *periodic motion*, ... Semantically, *motion* realizes the junction of two features, (i) that of 'process', the category meaning of the congruent form *move*, and (ii) that of 'entity' or 'thing', which is the category meaning of the class 'noun' of *motion*. This kind of semantic junction is what is meant by saying that the meaning of the term is "condensed". But, as Martin has shown, technicality involves more than the condensation of ideational semantic features. The term *motion* is now functioning as a theoretical abstraction, part of a metataxonomy – a theory which has its own taxonomic structure as a (semi-)designed semiotic system (see Lemke 1990a, for scientific theories as semiotic systems). Martin (Halliday and Martin 1993, Chapter 9) refers to this semantic process as *distillation*. We can get a slight sense of the gradual 'distilling' effect of progressive nominalization from a simple morpho–syntactic sequence in English such as moves – is moving – a moving – movement – motion

planets move – the planet is moving – a moving planet – the planet's
   moving – the movement of planets – planetary motion

– culminating perhaps in the Greek *kinesis* (the most distilled terms
in English tend to be those from Greek; cf. *ornitho-* for 'bird' at its
most theoretical level).

The gradual distillation of terms such as these, in ancient Greek
science (κίνησις in the original Greek will serve as example), so that
they became technical abstractions, was the beginning of the evolution of scientific theory in the west. This nominalizing metaphor is
the principle on which all technical terminology is ultimately based.
(The difference between technological and scientific discourse, in
this respect (cf. other chapters in Martin & Veel eds 1998), is that, of
the overall nominalizing potential, technological nomenclatures
depend relatively more heavily on the taxonomizing and less heavily
on the metaphorical; and they also develop taxonomies based on
meronymy (*b* is a part of *y*) – the semantic analogy between meronymy and hyponymy, and the fact that both use the structural
resources of the nominal group, explains the familiar impression we
have that the smaller an object is, the longer its name is likely to be.)

The potential for creating technical language, therefore, is one
aspect of the pay-off derived from metaphoric nominalization. As
Martin (1993 p. 172) expresses it, "Technical language both **compacts** and **changes the nature of** everyday words. ... For the
biologist [marsupials] are warm-blooded mammals that give birth to
live young with no placental attachment and carry the young in a
pouch until they are weaned; and they contrast with the two other
groups of mammals, monotremes (egg-laying) and placentals". This
kind of distillation is a necessary resource for theory building. At the
same time, there is another aspect of the pay-off which we become
aware of in the unfolding of the discourse itself; this is now taken up
in the following section.

7 The pay-off: (2) reasoning, logical progression

The features discussed in the last section (creating technical language
by categorizing, taxonomizing and distilling) depend on the ***ideational*** resources of the nominal group – its potential for expanding
through an iterative pattern of modification. They also depend on

the *systemic* effect of these resources – the terms created are not transient constructs that serve for one moment of discourse and then disappear. They become part of a subsystem within the overall semantic space that constitutes the experiential domain of the grammar.

But technicality by itself would be of little value unless accompanied by a discourse of reasoning: constructing a flow of argument based, in its prototypical form in experimental science, on observation and logical progression. Here is another example from Newton's *Opticks* (pp. 15–16):

> If the Humours of the Eye by old Age decay, so as by shrinking to make the Cornea and Coat of the Crystalline Humour grow flatter than before, the Light will not be refracted enough, and for want of a sufficient Refraction will not converge to the bottom of the Eye but to some place beyond it, and by consequence paint in the bottom of the Eye a confused Picture, and according to the Indistinctness of this Picture the Object will appear confused. This is the reason of the decay of sight in old Men, and shews why their Sight is mended by Spectacles. For those Convex glasses supply the defect of Plumpness in the Eye, and by increasing the Refraction make the Rays converge sooner, so as to convene directly at the bottom of the Eye if the Glass have a due degree of convexity. And the contrary happens in short-sighted Men whose Eyes are too plump.

This passage contains numerous instances of reasoning from one process to another; largely in congruent form, with the processes construed clausally and the logical–semantic relations realized by conjunctions functioning as relator: *if, so as to, for, why, by*. But some of the reasoning depends on a different grammatical resource, illustrated in the following pairs of wordings:

> make . . . grow flatter than before : supply the defect of Plumpness
> will not be refracted enough   : for want of a sufficient Refraction
> paint . . . a confused picture   : according to the Indistinctness of
>   this Picture

In each case, we are first told something in a clausal form; then, when it is brought in again to further the argument, it becomes nominalized, with the process or quality construed metaphorically by a noun functioning as Thing: *defect (of Plumpness), (sufficient) Refraction, Indistinctness (of this Picture)* – other elements being accommodated in the nominal group as its modifiers. Compare this with a modern example (Layzer 1990, p. 61):

If electrons weren't absolutely indistinguishable, two hydrogen atoms would form a much more weakly bound molecule than they actually do. The absolute indistinguishability of the electrons in the two atoms gives rise to an 'extra' attractive force between them.

Here the grammatical metaphor has a discursive function: it carries forward the momentum of the argument.

At the same time as construing instances of human experience the grammar also has to construe itself, by creating a flow of discourse. This is often referred to as "information flow"; but this term – as always! – privileges the ideational meaning, whereas the discursive flow is interpersonal as well as ideational. It is as if the grammar was creating a parallel current of semiosis that interpenetrates with and provides a channel for the mapping of ideational and interpersonal meanings. The metafunctional component of the grammar that engenders this flow of discourse is the *textual* (cf. Martin 1992, especially Chapter 6; Matthiessen 1992, 1995).

Many features contribute to the discursive flow; those that primarily concern us here are those that form part of, or are systemically associated with, the grammar of the clause – because it is there that the explicit mapping of textual and ideational meanings takes place. The two systems involved, in English, are those of theme and information. The *theme* system is a system of the clause, where it sets up a structural pattern that we can interpret as a configuration of the functions Theme and Rheme. The *information* system has its own distinct structural domain, the *information unit*, where it sets up a configuration of the functions Given and New. The management of these two systems is one of the factors that contributes most to the overall effectiveness of a text (Martin 1992, Chapter 6; Hasan and Fries 1995).

(1) The theme system maps the elements of the clause into a pattern of movement from a point of departure, the Theme, to a message, the Rheme. The point of departure may be a consolidation of various elements; the part that is relevant here is its experiential module, defined grammatically as that part which has some function in the transitivity of the clause (semantically, some participant, circumstance or process). This thematic structure, in English, is realized lineally – the Theme comes first; furthermore there is a strong bond between the (textual) system of theme and the (inter-personal) system of mood, such that, if the clause is

declarative, then other things being equal the same element will function both as Subject and as Theme – which means that it will be a nominal of some kind, since only a nominal element can function as Subject. So *those Convex glasses*, in the clause *for those Convex glasses supply the defect of Plumpness in the Eye*, is a typical "unmarked" Theme of this kind.

(2) The information system maps the discourse into a pattern of movement between what is already around, the Given, and what is news, the New. The "Given" is what is being presented in the discourse as recoverable, to be taken as read; while the 'New' is what is being foregrounded for attention. This system is not directly represented in written English because it is realized by patterns of intonation and rhythm, especially the pitch contour of speech; it constructs its own domain, in the form of a ***tone group***, and hence is independent of the grammatical clause – which means that the movement of 'information' (in this technical sense) can vary freely with the thematic movement. However, the two systems are associated: other things being equal, one information unit will be mapped onto one clause – and, within the information unit, the Given will precede the New, so that, in the "unmarked" case, the Theme of a clause is located within the Given portion, and the New, that which is under focus of attention, within the Rheme. What this means is that, typically, a speaker takes as point of departure something that is (or can be presented as being) already familiar to the listener, and puts under focus of attention something that forms part of (and is typically at the culmination of) the message.

It is this pattern of association between the information system and the thematic system which guides the readers – and the writers – of written text. Unless there is some clear indication to the contrary, the default condition will be assumed. (Such counterindication might be lexical – repetition, or synonymic echo, marking a later portion as Given; or grammatical – the predication of the Theme, as in *it was the drummer who stole the show*, marking *the drummer* as New.) The two systems together give a rhythm to the discourse, at this micro level, creating a regular pattern whereby in the unmarked case each clause moves from one peak of prominence to another – but the two prominences are of different kinds. The initial prominence, that of Theme, is the speaker/writer's angle on the message: this is the point from which I am taking off. The culminative prominence, that of New, is still of course assigned by the speaker/writer; but it carries a signal to the listener/reader: this is what you are to attend to. Of course, this underlying discursive rhythm gets modulated all the time by the other meaning-making currents that are flowing along in the grammar, as well as being perturbed by the larger-scale fluctuations – moves in dialogue, shifts of register and the like. But it provides the basic semiotic pulse, not unlike the chest pulse that gets modulated by the sound-making antics of the organs of articulation.

The discourse of experimental science depended on an ordered progression in which not just this or that single element but **any chunk of the argument** could be given prominence in the unfolding of a clause. Let us look again at the example from David Layzer (for the complete paragraph see Appendix text 2). The first part of the paragraph builds up the story that in the quantum world all electrons are alike; and this motif is stated, in a congruent form, as the first step in an illustration of the principle: *if electrons weren't absolutely indistinguishable, two hydrogen atoms* .... The next clause is going to give the reason; so the writer recapitulates – but this time the whole figure 'electrons + indistinguishable' becomes part of a larger motif in which it is functioning simply as point of departure. Previously, this figure occupied a clause on its own; but now it becomes the Theme of another clause, which (like most clauses of written science) is declarative – hence it gets conflated, in typical fashion, with the Subject. Subjects are nominal groups, so the writer uses a nominalizing metaphor: *the absolute indistinguishability of the electrons in the two atoms*. The quality 'indistinguishable' is now construed as a 'thing', *indistinguishability*; and the electrons, previously functioning as Carrier in a Carrier + Attribute clause structure, now appear inside this nominal group, as a postmodifying element *of the electrons*.

Most noticeably it is the Theme that is metaphorized in this way: the writer carries the argument forward by 'packaging' some semantic construct from the discourse to serve as point of departure for a further step. As already noted, there is a strong association between Theme and Given; so such packages are typically condensations of material that has gone before. This may be material that has extended over a long and complex sequence of preceding argument (it is of course impossible to illustrate this without citing large passages of text). It is important to reiterate, however, that the

Theme may not be informationally Given; and in discourse such as that of written science, where the Given / Theme conflation is powerful and highly favoured, considerable effect may be achieved by departing from it. And conversely, considerable confusion may be brought about when such departure is unmotivated and unannounced (cf. Halliday and Martin 1993, Chapter 4; this volume Chapter 7).

But there is also a tendency – a kind of secondary discursive motif – whereby such nominalized packages occur in culminative positions in the clause, where they are Rheme not Theme and hence in strong association with the New. Fries (1992, 1995) refers to this conflation as the "N-Rheme"; this is an important concept for written text because it embodies the culminative principle – that the way the writer ensures that something is read as New is by making it (a part of) the Rheme of a ranking clause. If we look again at the Layzer text: the N-Rheme [*gives rise to*] *an 'extra' attractive force between them* is also a metaphoric nominalization, in this case one based on an established technical term *force*. This is locally New – it is what is called to the reader's attention **in this particular clause**; but it also picks up on what the reader has just been told (it does not add any new content; but it moves up to a higher level of abstraction, expressing 'would otherwise be more weakly bound' in more theoretical terms – compare in this connection, from another source, the clause *solid particles are held together by the strong attraction between them*, where by simply rewording the congruent form of the process as a metaphoric variant in the N-Rheme the writer establishes 'are held together' as a construct within the theory). The first passage cited from Newton [p. 9] also contains a metaphoric nominalization as N-Rheme: (*those colours argue*) *a diverging and separation of the heterogeneous Rays from one another by means of their unequal Refractions*, where 'diverge' and 'separate' are nominalized for the occasion and contrast with *there is no such separation . . . and by consequence no inequality of their Refractions* in the succeeding sentence.

The complex interplay of Theme + Rheme in the clause with Given + New in the information unit constitutes an immensely powerful discursive resource; it is the primary source of energy for the dynamic of scientific and technical argument. The reason it works so powerfully is that it is a structure of the clause: a configuration embodying the system of transitivity, which is the grammar's theory of ***process***. But because it is a clause, the parts which are configured in it are bound to be elements of clause structure; and the defining elements of clause structure are groups and phrases. It is possible to incorporate unreconstructed clauses by means of rank-shift. But, as we saw, the nominal group has the potential for expanding to include all the elements of the (congruent) clause (and the noun, likewise, has the potential for transcategorizing processes and qualities); moreover, unlike a rankshifted clause, a nominal group moves freely within the textual systems of theme and information. This is the payoff of these nominalizing metaphors in the instantial context of the discourse.

8 Unpacking the metaphors; the "favourite clause type"

Let me stay with the Layzer example for one further step. (We should however be aware of the problem of exemplification in a discussion of grammar: in a semiotic system, every instance is unique, with its own particularities, so that any one instance is an example only in respect of certain specific features.) We can 'unpack' the metaphors in the clause in question and produce a more congruent rewording such as the following:

> Because the electrons in the two atoms are absolutely indistinguishable, they attract each other 'extra' strongly.

We now have a clause nexus consisting of two clauses in a hypotactic interdependency. The relationship to the semantics is congruent both in rank and in status; compare Figure 3.3 above. (The grammar puts the relator inside one of the figures, as a conjunction at the beginning of the clause.)

In the metaphoric version, that in the original text, each figure has been nominalized – reworded in the form of wording that congruently construes 'things', with nouns for the quality (*indistinguishability*) and the process (*attraction*). But things do not stand up in the grammar by themselves; they gain entry only as participants, by virtue of being configured with some process. The 'process' here is *gives rise to*. This, however, is the outcome of another metaphoric transformation, whereby the relator (the logical-semantic relationship between the two processes, congruently construed as a conjunction (or cohesive conjunctive; cf. Halliday and Hasan 1976, Chapter 5)), is metaphorized as a verbal group, the form of wording that congruently construes a process. The effect is the same as in the contrived example of the bus driver: *the driver's overrapid downhill driving of the bus resulted in brake failure*.

73

This combination of metaphoric features is what we can regard as the "favourite clause type" of English scientific writing. It is a fuzzy type; but we could perhaps characterize it as follows:

semantic: sequence of two figures, linked by a logical–semantic relation

grammatical

  [congruent]: nexus of two clauses, with Relator / conjunction in secondary clause (optionally also in primary clause)

  [metaphoric]: one clause, 'relational : identifying / intensive, circumstantial or possessive', of three elements:

Identified	+ Process	+ Identifier
nominal group	verbal group	nominal group

There are variant forms (1) with 'relational : attributive' process, where the second nominal group may have adjective as Head; (2) with 'relational : existential' process, with one nominal group only. These have slightly different semantic profiles.

The second nominal group (if present) may be inside a prepositional phrase.

All examples given above in Section 4 are of the canonical type. Examples of the variant types are: (1) *the indistinguishability of electrons is also responsible for the structure of the periodic table*; *a total head range of less than 10 m. was inadequate to account for this variation*; (2) *the phylloxera resistance collapsed*; *rapid bonding occurs*; *viability exists*.

In saying that these are the "favourite clause type", I am not asserting that they are the most frequent (there would be no sensible way of estimating this; at the least, they are certainly very common). But they are the most critical in the semantic load that they carry in developing scientific argument. What is interesting about them is that their clause structure is extremely simple: typically one nominal group plus one verbal group plus a second nominal group or else a prepositional phrase. But packed into this structure there may be a very high density of lexical matter; again, compare the examples cited in Section 4, which have up to thirteen lexical words within this single clause. (The average lexical density for spontaneous spoken English barely exceeds two lexical words per clause.) If the agnate, more congruent variant is always just one nexus of two clauses, then the lexical density will be simply halved. Often, however, the "favourite" has gone through more than one cycle of metaphoric transformation, and the most plausible "congruent" rewording will have three, four or even more clauses in it.

It is clear from all the examples that a great deal more is happening at the rank of the word than simply construing processes and qualities as nouns. We need to look more systematically at grammatical metaphor considered as a stratal phenomenon – that is, as the exploiting of the 'play' that arises at the interfacing of the grammar and the semantics; and to ask what metaphoric processes actually take place there. We noted in Section 3 that grammatical metaphor involves a complex move, both 'down' in rank and 'across' in status (function/class). We have not yet examined the possible range of metaphoric cross-couplings in status. The question that arises is: do all the logically possible shifts take place? or are only certain of those that are possible in principle actually taken up?

9 Types of grammatical metaphor

Let me first return to the congruent pattern – noting that 'congruent' means that pattern of relationships between the semantics and the grammar in which the two strata initially co-evolved (I come to the evidence for this in the next Section). I shall arrange the entries in a different order from that in which they were given in Section 3; and – since we are now looking at processes taking place at word rank – I will express the grammatical realization as a class of word. The categories, as always, are those of English.

Congruence of status (semantic functions with word classes):

semantic function	[construed by]	grammatical class
relator (in sequence)		conjunction
minor process (in circumstance)		preposition
process		verb
quality		adjective
entity ('thing')		noun

The types of grammatical metaphor that I have found in investigating scientific discourse were summarized in Chapter 2 above (Figure 2.3).

The list in Figure 2.3 is not exhaustive; but it includes those that I have identified in the course of analysing instances that seemed to me significant in the unfolding of the text. The entries there are arranged according to the following design:

shift in semantic function	shift in grammatical class
shift in grammatical function	example(s)

For example, the metaphoric transformation of *unstable* to *instability* would represent a shift from 'construed as quality' to 'construed as entity', from 'adjective' to 'noun' and from the typical function (here, in the nominal group) of Epithet to that of Thing. A text example illustrating this pattern was: *diamond is kinetically unstable . . . the kinetic instability of diamond leads to . . .*

It seems that not all possible metaphoric moves actually occur; the ones that do occur can be summarized as in Figure 3.5, where they are set out in terms of semantic function (cf Figure 2.4 above).

Figure 3.5 shows that it is possible to order the semantic functions from left to right in such a way that (i) all possible moves to the right can occur, but (ii) no move can take place to the left. The ordering is:

relator → circumstance → process → quality → entity

What this means is that (1) any semantic element can be construed as if it was an entity (i.e. grammaticized as a noun); (2) a relator, a circumstance or a process can be construed as if it was a quality (i.e. grammaticized as an adjective); (3) a relator or a circumstance can be construed as if it was a process (i.e. grammaticized as a verb); (4) a

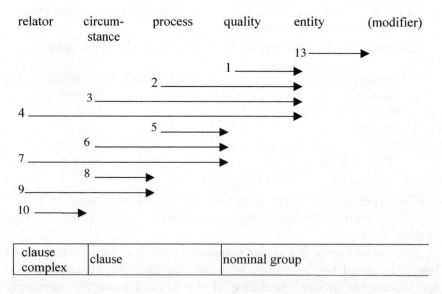

Figure 3.5 The 'general drift' of grammatical metaphor

relator can be construed as if it was a (minor process within a) circumstance (i.e. grammaticized as a preposition, in a prepositional phrase). But not the other way round: entities cannot be construed as if they were processes; and so on.[1]

Here, therefore, we can recognize what we might call a general drift: this is the drift towards 'thinginess'. The direction of metaphor is a move towards the concrete – with nouns, typically the names of **participants** (concrete objects, animals and persons), as the terminal point. The noun is the most metaphorically attractive category: everything else can end up as a noun. This drift towards the concrete is, of course, exactly what one finds to be a feature of metaphor in its traditional, lexicalized sense.

We can now see the close relationship between the two aspects of the metaphorical process: the shift in rank, and the shift in status. Let us try to show these two things happening together; in order to do this, however, we shall have to focus on one single semantic element at a time – otherwise there will be too much happening at once. The figures in the left hand column refer to the numbering in Figure 2.3. I will present two examples: one of the relator 'therefore', the other of the process 'grow, become greater', each of them shifting step by step towards the metaphoric status of a noun.

Example 1: relator 'therefore'.   Congruent rank: clause complex;
                                    congruent status: conjunction

	move in status	move in rank	example
–	relator: conjunction	clause nexus	(*a* happened) so (*x* happened)
10	(minor process in) circum-stance: preposition	clause	(*x* happened) as a result of (happening *a*)
9	process: verb	clause	(happening *x*) resulted from (happening *a*)
7	quality: adjective	nominal group	the resultant (happening of *x*) ...
4	entity: noun	nominal group	the result (of happening *a*) ...

Example 2: process 'grow'.   Congruent rank: clause; congruent status: verb

	move in status	move in rank	example
–	process: verb	clause	(poverty) is increasing
5	quality: adjective	nominal group	increasing (poverty)
2	entity: noun	nominal group	the increase (in poverty)

There is one apparent exception to the drift towards the concrete: this is what I have recognized as type 13, where participants are metaphorized from being nominal groups to being modifiers inside other nominal groups: for example *the driver's driving of the bus*, where the driver has become a possessive Deictic and the bus is inside a prepositional phrase functioning as Qualifier. Two things may be noticed about these. One is that they do not occur alone; they occur only in combination with other metaphorical shifts – whereas others can occur by themselves; e.g. 5(ii) *possible* in *possible enemies* '(creatures) that may be enemies', or perhaps 'enemies that may be around'. The other is that the Thing (the main noun) of the nominal group in which they occur is always itself a metaphoric entity – a transformed quality or process. When the process has been nominalized, the grammar still has to incorporate somehow the displaced participants and circumstances from the congruent figure. If 'failed' in 'brakes + failed' becomes *failure*, what happens to the 'brakes'? The controlling metaphor is that of process to entity; the others are carried along with it, so that the 'brakes' take over some modifying function in the nominal group: Range (in Qualifier), *failure of the brakes*; possessive Deictic, *the brakes' failure*; or, as in the original example, Classifier: *brake failure*. In other words, these 'entities' become expansions of the new nominalized entity. The grammar is exploiting the potential of the nominal group to give functional status to the participating entities (as they would be) in the congruent clause. Thus:

Deictic	Epithet	Classifier	Thing	Qualifier
[congruent]				
the cat's	old	wicker	basket	for sleeping in in winter
the driver's	overrapid	downhill	driving	of the bus
the	natural	buffering	capacity	of the agricultural soils
Griffith's		energy balance	approach	to strength and fracture
[metaphoric]				

One question that arises with these secondary metaphors, if they do occur as the structural consequence of the controlling metaphor of nominalization (rather than as metaphors in their own right), is whether they also entail semantic junction: do they also acquire the congruent semantic features of the categories into which they have shifted? Are *engine failure, heart failure, crop failure, power failure, brake failure* classes of a 'thing' called *failure*? We may note that (since a stratified system has so much play in it) the grammar tends to become play-ful at this point; given the metaphoric progression

the president decreed == the president's decree == the presidential decree

we construct, by analogy,

Ø   the president's pyjamas == the presidential pyjamas

– where the humorous effect of *the presidential pyjamas* shows that there is an anomaly between the function Classifier and the lexical collocation of *president* with *pyjamas*. If *presidential* is not a class of *pyjamas*, this suggests that *engine, heart, crop, power, brake* are not classes of *failure*; an *energy balance approach* is not a class of *approaches*, and so on. It seems that these should be explained as secondary effects, consequential on another metaphoric movement, and that for this reason they do not undergo semantic junction.

10 Syndromes of grammatical metaphor

Lexical metaphor usually presents itself as a simple opposition between two terms; for example, *fruit / result*, where a more concrete, metaphorical expression *the fruit(s) of their efforts* contrasts with a more abstract, "literal" expression *the result(s) of their efforts*. If, as sometimes happens, we are able to set up longer chains this is because they embody a piece of semiotic history in which a metaphor has "died" and a new one has taken over.

In grammatical metaphor, where the shift is not from one lexical item to another but from one grammatical category to another, the situation becomes more complex. As Figure 3.5 brings out, there may be more than one degree of metaphoric displacement; so if, to take the most extreme case (namely type 4), a relator is construed grammatically as a noun, there may well be a number of intermediate steps, as suggested by the example of 'therefore' in Section 9. In any given instance not all of the intermediate manifestations may be plausible; but typically at least some of them are, so that in 'unpacking' a highly complex metaphor we have to choose how far to go. To follow up one of the examples from Section 4,

fire intensity has a profound effect on smoke injection,

we might unpack the metaphor in the word *effect* in any of the following ways (proceeding step by step towards the congruent):

the intensity of a fire profoundly affects (2) the injection of smoke

according to (3) the intensity of a fire more or less smoke is injected

as (4) a fire grows more intense, so (4) more smoke is injected

Again, figures in parenthesis refer to the types of metaphoric shift set out in Figure 2.3: thus, if the verb *affects* was to be taken as the congruent form (that is, if the semantic element was being interpreted as 'process') the metaphoric shift whereby it appears as a noun *effect* would be one of type 2. If on the other hand we interpret it semantically as a relation between processes, congruently construed as a conjunction *as* (... *so*), then the metaphoric shift to the noun *effect* is of type 4.

But since the metaphoric process is taking place in the grammar, any transformation is likely to reverberate throughout the clause, and may affect an entire clause nexus. Almost inevitably one displacement in rank and status will involve a number of others. So grammatical metaphors tend to occur in syndromes: clusters of interrelated transformations that reconfigure the grammatical structure as a whole. The limiting case of such a syndrome is that which was discussed in the previous section in explaining the maverick type 13, whereby a noun is driven out of its functional role as a participant (congruently, as Thing in a nominal group) by a controlling metaphor of type 1 or 2; for example (from sentences cited in Section 4):

the child's capacity ...   (the child is able to ...)
    13   2ii
the burning of coal   (coal was burnt)
    2i   13
the indistinguishability of the electrons   (the electrons are indistinguishable)
    1   13
the American species' resistance to phylloxera   (the American species resisted phylloxera)
    13   2i   13

In other syndromes, however, while a cluster of metaphors is clearly functioning in association, there is no single controlling type and each one could in principle occur alone.

Below is a paragraph of text with the instances of grammatical metaphor marked according to the same notation.

Even though the fracture of glass can be a dramatic event, many failures
                2i   13   11   2i
are preceded by the slow extension of preexisting cracks. A good example
   9   6i   2i 13   7 or 5i
of a slowly spreading crack is often found in the windshield of an
      5i   12
automobile. The extension of a small crack, which may have started from
              2i
the impact of a stone, can be followed day by day as the crack gradually
    2i   13
propagates across the entire windshield. In other cases small, unnoticed
                                         5 i
surface cracks can grow during an incubation period and cause a
 6iii   2i 13   9

catastrophic failure when they reach a critical size. Cracks in glass
  6ii   2i   8   1
can grow at speeds of less than one trillionth of an inch per hour, and
                              1
under these conditions the incubation period can span several years
              4   2i   13   8
before the catastrophic failure is observed. On an atomic scale the slow
        6ii   2i   12   6i
growth of cracks corresponds to the sequential rupturing of interatomic
  2i   13   9   6ii   2i   13   6iii
bonds at rates as low as one bond rupture per hour. The wide range of
    1   13   2i   3
rates over which glass can fracture – varying by 12 orders of magnitude
  1   1
(factors of 10) from the fastest shatter to the slowest creep – makes
                  6i   2i   6i   2i   9
the investigation of crack growth a particularly engaging enterprise.[2]
  2i   13   2i   5i   11

In analysing this passage I have interpreted the elements 'crack' and 'bond' as theoretical entities, and hence considered their wording as nouns to be congruent. If we treat 'crack' and 'bond' as processes, this will necessitate further unpacking; the difference between these two interpretations may be illustrated by reference to one sentence which happens to contain both these terms. The analysis given above corresponds to a congruent version as follows:

> The slow growth of cracks corresponds to the sequential rupturing of
>   [6i   2i   13]   9   [6ii   2i   13
> interatomic bonds at rates as low as one bond rupture per hour.
>   6iii]   1   [13   2i]

Cracks grow slowly – as slowly as when the bonds between the atoms rupture one after another only once an hour.

If 'bond' and 'crack' are treated as metaphoric, the analysis, together with the corresponding congruent rewording, will be as the following:

> The slow growth of cracks corresponds to the sequential rupturing of
>   [6i   2i 13 2i]   9   [6ii   2i   13
> interatomic bonds at rates as low as one bond rupture per hour.
>   6iii   2i]   1   [2i   13 2i]

Glass cracks slowly – as slowly as when one atom stops being bonded to another atom only once every hour.

As is to be expected, given that grammatical metaphor involves two distinct moves in rank (clause nexus to clause; clause to group),

81

the "syndromes" of metaphoric features fall into two groups along these same lines:

(a) Lower rank syndromes: figures reconstrued as if elements (a figure, congruently construed as a clause, is instead reworded as a nominal group, which congruently construes an element)

(b) Higher rank syndromes: sequences reconstrued as if figures (a sequence, congruently construed as a clause nexus, is instead reworded as a clause, which congruently construes a figure)

I will look briefly at each of these in turn.

(a) Lower rank syndromes: figures reconstrued as if elements. These are the clusters of features that co-occur in metaphoric nominal groups (the 'limiting case' of type 13, discussed in Section 9, fall within this group). Here the key metaphors are the nominalizations of qualities (type 1) and processes (type 2); these are then accompanied by transformations of other elements of the figure, either participants (which are already realized as nouns, but change their function from Thing to Deictic, Epithet, Classifier or (part of) Qualifier; hence type 13) or circumstances (type 6). Examples:

indistinguishability of electrons   (electrons are indistinguishable)
       1   13

fire intensity   (how intense fire is)
13   1

the fracture of glass   (glass fractures)
       2i   13

Griffith's approach to ...   (Griffith approached ...)
    13   2i

slow extension   (extend slowly)
  6i   2i

Any given nominal group may of course contain a number of these together:

the sequential rupturing of interatomic bonds
      6ii   2i   13   6iii
       (the bonds between atoms rupture one after another)

the importance of surface chemistry in the mechanical
         1   13 6iii   6iii
behaviour of brittle materials
   2i   13
        (that the chemistry of the surface is important in relation
                      to how materials behave mechanically)

And metaphors of other types may also be involved in these lower rank syndromes:

increased responsiveness   (... becomes more responsive)
   5i   1
feeding behaviour^3 (how ... feed)
  5i   11

the slow extension of preexisting cracks
  6i   2i   13   5i
(cracks which existed before slowly extend)

a consequence of the differing contributions of ...
  7   6i   2i
(because ... contribute different(ial)ly)

(b) Higher rank syndromes: sequences reconstrued as if figures. These were referred to earlier, with illustration from the intemperate bus driver: where a semantic *figure* (congruently construed as a grammatical *clause*) is reconstrued in the grammar as a *group* (which congruently construes a semantic *element*), the *clause* now comes to construe a *sequence*. See Figure 3.6.

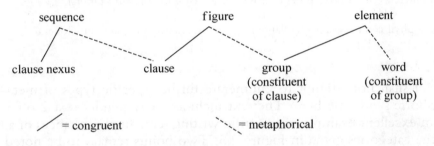

Figure 3.6. Reconstrual of semantic units by grammatical metaphor

In characterizing type (b) in these terms, I am not suggesting that either metaphoric movement **causes** the other. In terms of the discussion in Sections 5–7 above, the lower rank movement (figure as group, and element as constituent of group: type (a) syndromes) is more directly associated with taxonomic categorizing, while the higher rank movement (sequence as clause, and figure as constituent of clause: type (b) syndromes) is more directly associated with logical reasoning. But the metaphoric grammar hangs together as a whole, and there is no reason, either logical or historical, for supposing that any one component is driven by any other.

The grammatical manifestation of this unity of the metaphoric process is what I referred to earlier as the "favourite clause type" of scientific English, which consists of two nominalized processes or qualities (each one a nominal group) joined by a verbalized relator (a verbal group), illustrated in all the examples set out in Section 4. The higher rank syndrome in question can be generalized as [1/2] + 9 + [1/2], where [1], [2] stand for any possible syndrome of type (a); for example,

increased responsiveness may be reflected in feeding behaviour
        [1]   9   [2]
this breeding effort was anchored in the American species' resistance...
        [2]   9   [2]
the rate of glass crack growth depends on the magnitude of the applied stress
        [1]   9   [1]

There is then a secondary type (b) syndrome in which there is only one process, likewise nominalized, and the verbal group simply indicates that it happens, or does not happen; for example,

rapid bonding occurs   (... bond rapidly)
    [2]   12
a difference in osmotic pressure exists   (osmotic pressure differs)
    [1]   12
the phylloxera resistance collapsed   (... ceased to resist phylloxera)
    [2]   12

I shall not attempt to enumerate further specific types of metaphoric syndrome here. The text included as Appendix text 2 offers an excellent example of scientific writing, containing instances of all the categories given in Figure 2.3. Two points remain to be noted. One is that the grammar, in its metaphoric potential, typically accommodates a series of steps intermediate between the most congruent and the most metaphorical. I can perhaps best illustrate this by constructing a paradigm of agnate forms on the basis of a text example:

increases of osmolarity cause rapid excretion of putrescine

1   Osmolarity increases, so putrescine is rapidly excreted.
                                    (clause nexus: paratactic)
2   Because osmolarity increases, putrescine is rapidly excreted.
                                    (clause nexus: hypotactic)
3   That osmolarity increases has the effect that putrescine is rapidly excreted.
                                    (clause: two rankshifted clauses, finite)

4   Osmolarity increasing leads to putrescine being rapidly excreted.
(clause: two rankshifted clauses, non-finite)
5   Increasing of osmolarity causes rapid excreting of putrescine.
(clause: two nominal groups, verb as Head)
6   Increase of osmolarity causes rapid excretion of putrescine.
(clause: two nominal groups, mass noun as Head)
7   Increases of osmolarity cause rapid excretions of putrescine.
(clause: two nominal groups, count noun as Head)

Starting from a rather congruent form of wording I have kept the two processes at more or less the same degree of metaphoricity; in real texts, of course, they will often diverge – compare the clause that concludes the immediately following sentence:

> ionic strength is maintained approximately constant as a result of the excretion of putrescine.

The other point to bring out is that, while I have illustrated this "favourite" syndrome with the generalized category of cause, there are other categories of conjunctive relationship that appear as the verbal element in clauses of this type. Perhaps the most widely encountered are:

complex causal (e.g. *prevent, increase*)
temporal (e.g. *follow*)
identifying (e.g. *be, constitute*)
symbolizing (e.g. *signal, mark*)
projecting, 'cause to know / think' (e.g. *prove, suggest*)
additive (e.g. *complement; accompany*)

I will give a very brief sketch of these, together with examples.
In the "complex causal", the relator 'cause' is fused with some other semantic feature, typically 'negative' ('cause not to') or some quantity or quality ('cause to become more, stronger, etc.'):

> the presence in the medium of the amino acid proline dramatically increases a bacterium's ability to grow in a medium of high osmotic strength

> movement of the solute across the membrane can be prevented by applying a certain hydrostatic pressure to the solution

> osmotic tolerance ... is accomplished in bacteria by an adjustment of the internal osmolarity

The "temporal" relationship construes the two processes as being related in time:

many failures are preceded by the slow extension of existing cracks

In the "identifying" and "symbolizing" types, some Token + Value relationship is set up between the two parts; for example

the most efficient energy-producing mechanism is respiration

the growth of attachment between infant and mother signals the first step in the child's capacity to discriminate amongst people

the ionic strength of a solution is defined by the equation...

the slow growth of cracks corresponds to the sequential rupturing of interatomic bonds at rates as low as one bond rupture per hour

In some instances, taken by themselves, there can be ambiguity between the senses of 'symbolizing' and 'causing':

increased responsiveness may be reflected in feeding behaviour

– where it is left open whether the feeding behaviour is sign or effect. The "projecting" relationship is exemplified by:

Griffith's energy balance approach to strength and fracture also suggested the importance of surface chemistry in the mechanical behaviour of brittle materials

relative osmotic tolerance can be deduced from their relative K^+ contents

Here the prototypical sense is not cause but proof: not 'because *a* happens, *x* happens', but 'because *b* happens, I know that *y* happens' – the intersection of causing and symbolizing. Finally, the "additive" are those which simply conjoin two figures in a relationship of 'and', or sometimes 'but'; e.g.

the theoretical program of devising models of atomic nuclei has been complemented by experimental investigations

the induction of mutations by causing base-pair transitions is to be contrasted with the mechanism of induction of mutations by certain acridine dyes

the inheritance of specific genes is correlated with the inheritance of a specific chromosome

These syndromes of higher and lower rank constitute the syntagmatic dimension of grammatical metaphor. They are of course represented in the description of the grammar as structural configurations in their own right; in presenting them as "syndromes" I am emphasizing their metaphoric status – the fact that they arise from a cross-coupling between the semantics and the grammar, and are significant because, taken as a whole, they manifest a reconstrual of the experiential world.

11 The distillation of technical meaning

In trying to understand how, and why, this reconstrual has taken place, I have postulated two distinct metafunctional environments for grammatical metaphor: one textual – creating reasoned argument through managing the information flow of the discourse, the other ideational – creating ordered taxonomies of abstract technical constructs. I used different, though overlapping, (lexical) metaphors for the two: packaging and compacting for the former, and (following Martin) condensing and distilling for the latter. It is helpful, I think, to recognize these as two distinct contexts for grammatical metaphor, if only because in any given text instance either factor may be present without the other. Thus, many of the wordings that are textually motivated, like *the indistinguishability of the electrons* (following *all electrons ... are indistinguishable*), *movement of the solvent across the membrane* (following *the solvent tends to be drawn through the membrane into the solution*) (and compare Newton's *the permanent whiteness*, which follows *continues ever after to be white*), are not, and do not become, technical terms. They are and remain **instantial** constructs, created for the immediate requirements of the discourse (typically, functioning as Theme, or else as focus of New information). Thus they can always be 'unpacked' – reworded in a more congruent form. Likewise, many occurrences of the terms with a technical status have no motivation in the particular discursive environment; they may be occurring in titles, headings, abstracts, definitions and so on. These are systemic constructs, created for the long-term requirements of the theory; and they **cannot be unpacked** – there is no agnate rewording in a more congruent form. So there seem to be two independent factors at work leading to grammatical metaphor: one textual and instantial, the other ideational and systemic.

But they are not, in fact, as separate as they seem. If we view the discourse of science in the longer term, we can observe the instantial **becoming** the systemic. Technical terms are not, as a rule, created outright, in isolation from the discourse; they emerge discursively, as the "macrotext" of the discipline unfolds. In this respect they are just one manifestation of the general phenomenon whereby instantial effects flow through into the system – because there is no disjunction between system and instance: what we call the "system" of language is simply the potential that evolves over time. Thus any wording that is introduced discursively as a resource for reasoning may gradually become **distilled**; and in the course of this distillation out of successive instances of its occurrence, it becomes a new 'thing', a virtual entity that exists as part of a theory. It now "stands to reason" as a part of our reconstrued experience; it can enter into figures, as a participant; and, as already remarked, it can no longer be unpacked. As a metaphor, it is "dead" – because it has taken on a new, non-metaphoric life of its own.

Since this process – the instantial becoming systemic, compacting turning into distilling, the semantic junction of the two grammatical categories – typically takes place over a long period of text time, it is impossible to illustrate it adequately in a short paper. But writers of scientific textbooks often recapitulate the process as a way of introducing technical terms to the learners; so it is possible to gain some impression of it from an extract such as that in Appendix text 1: for example, the build-up of the term *osmotic tolerance*:

some halophiles ... can tolerate high concentrations of salt

the tolerance of high osmolarity

Osmotic Tolerance. Osmotic tolerance – the ability of an organism to grow in media with widely varying osmolarities – is accomplished in bacteria by an adjustment of the internal osmolarity

Compare the lead-up to *'redox' potential* (which is likewise first introduced as the heading) in the New Scientist text reproduced as Appendix text 3. Compare also Appendix text 1, where we might speculate whether (*electron*) *indistinguishability* could be taking the first steps towards becoming a technical term.

All these processes take place in real time – but in different dimensions of time. I shall distinguish logogenetic, phylogenetic and ontogenetic time. Logogenetic time is the time of unfolding of the text: the history of the instance. I have cited elsewhere the gradual building up of the technical concept of *glass fracture growth rate* in the text on 'The fracturing of glass' (Halliday 1995; this volume, Chapter 4). Martin and his colleagues have documented the construal of technicality in the context of science textbooks (see e.g. Halliday and Martin 1993, Part 2).

Phylogenetic time is the time of evolution of the language, in the particular registers in question (e.g. "scientific English"): the history of the system. In the metaphoric processes taking place in the grammar, these two histories intersect; and it is this that enables us to speak about the ordered relationship between the metaphorical and the congruent. Taken out of time, each of a pair of expressions such as

> the solvent tends to be drawn through the membrane

> movement of the solvent across the membrane

is metaphoric with respect to the other; there is no way of identifying one or other as "congruent" (cf. the bus driver example in Section 3). As soon as we view them historically, however, the picture changes: both instantially and systemically the clausal mode precedes the nominal one. It is this that explains our "intuitive" sense of congruence. Experience is first construed clausally, and only later is it reconstrued in nominalized form. Once again there is a parallel with metaphor in its traditional, lexical guise.

What of the third dimension of history – ontogenetic time? Ontogenetic time is the time of growth and maturation of the user of the language: the history of every human child. And here again the picture is the same: children first construe experience in the clausal form, in the grammar of daily life. For them the nominalizing grammar of scientific discourse demands a massive act of reconstruction, one of the major barriers to the technical, discipline-based knowledge of secondary education.

12 Ontogenetic note

Clare Painter says of young children's speech that 'meaning and lexical class are congruent with one another' (Painter 1993, p. 112). What this means is that, when children first move from their infant protolanguage into the mother tongue, they build up their picture of the world according to the same principles on which the grammar itself evolved. Painter adds that "control of experiential grammatical metaphor is a late development" (1993, p. 111).

The protolanguage has no grammar: there is no stratification of the content plane into a lexicogrammar and a semantics (Halliday 2004 *passim*; Painter 1984). Hence it has no possibility of metaphor, which depends on cross-coupling between the two strata – decoupling, and then recoupling in a different fashion. What distinguishes *language*, in its prototypical sense (that is, post-infancy human language), from infant protolanguage is precisely that it is stratified in this way. We can observe the effect of this early in life when children start constructing discourse; here are two clear examples:

Hal [age 1;8, watching seagulls eating] breàd; eàt; bìrdies.

Nigel [age 1;7, seeing a cat run into a house] blā' miào; rān dòor.

In each case the child in question is able to form a semantic figure but is not yet able to construe it as a grammatical clause. The semantics runs ahead of the grammar – and it stays ahead throughout our lives. Semantically, we can construe a whole book as a single text, whereas grammatically we can create structure only up to the rank of the clause complex, or at most perhaps to something like a paragraph.

But for those units which do fall within the compass of the grammar, as long as the coupling of semantics to grammar remained congruent it would not matter whether we labelled the categories in grammatical or in semantic terms: either (1) semantic or (2) grammatical representations would suffice (see Figure 3.7).

It is only when cross-coupling begins that we cannot avoid theorizing both semantic and lexicogrammatical patterns and keeping them terminologically apart. Painter describes a child's early attempts

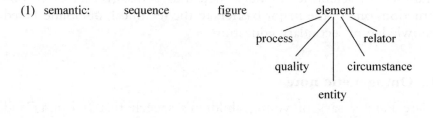

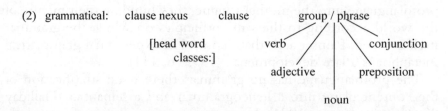

Figure 3.7. Congruence of semantic and grammatical categories

90

to come to terms with this cross–coupling, citing examples such as (1993, p. 136):

Stephen	[4;8, whose father has said that the hired car can't go as fast as the usual one] I thought – I thought all cars could – all cars could go the same – all cars could go the same . . . fast.
Mother:	The same speed.
Stephen:	Yes; same speed.

Beverly Derewianka (1995) provides a detailed and insightful account of one child's language development from childhood to adolescence (ages 4–14), with the development of grammatical metaphor as the central theme. Here is one of her examples of a child (her main subject's younger brother, at age 12) consciously construing metaphoric modes of expression (p. 128):

Stefan:	Mum, is "preservation" a word?
Mother:	Why?
Stefan:	Because I need it for my project. I've written "Mummification was necessary . . ." – you know, to keep the body intact and keep the corpse from decaying. Can I say "mummification was necessary for the preservation of the corpse"?

In the way that educational knowledge is organized, at the present stage of our history, children have to undertake this secondary reconstrual of experience before they can succeed in secondary education. They are initiated into grammatical metaphor in the upper years of primary school; note how *animal protection* and *capacity* are brought in in these examples:

Put a label on each [container] to show two things:

(a) The quantity it holds.
(b) What fraction of a litre in it. [sic]

Put all that measure one litre together. Some will be tall, some short, some rectangular, some cylindrical for milk or drinks, some wine bottles or carafes. But they all contain 1 LITRE. A litre is a litre, whether long, round or square. . . . So all kinds of shapes can be made to have the same capacity.[4]

(Perret and Fiddes 1968/77, p. 71)

ANIMAL PROTECTION. Most animals have natural enemies that prey upon them. To survive, these animals need some protection from their enemies. Animals protect themselves in many ways.

Some animals rely on their great speed to escape from danger. . . . Animals like snakes and spiders protect themselves with bites and stings, some of which are poisonous. These bites and stings can also help the animals capture food.
(R. L. Vickery et al., *The Process Way to Science, Book C*, Sydney: Jacaranda, 1978, p. 85)[5]

Soon after reaching secondary school, they may have to cope with:

Braking distance increases more rapidly at high speeds.

(This is not easy to unpack: one would have to say something like *the faster you're going, the more quickly the time it takes you to stop gets longer*. It recalls the well known footnote on 'acceleration' in Whorf (1941/56, p. 151).)

Derewianka sums up by saying (1995, p. 198) "... grammatical metaphor is intimately involved in the development of experiential meanings and is particularly implicated in the shift from common-sense to uncommonsense". This is in no way to imply, of course, that young children do not engage in logical reasoning – of course they do, from the time they are able to talk at all. Commonsense knowledge is no less dependent on rationality (see especially Hasan 1992). But (whether or not it could have evolved in other grammatical formations) scientific knowledge in fact evolved as a metaphoric reconstrual of experience; and it is this that has determined how it is pursued by those who are 'doing science' and how it is transmitted to those who are learning.

13 Rewording; remeaning?

Young children's world of meaning is organized congruently; this is how they are able to move into it, at one and the same time both construing the grammar and using the grammar to construe their own experience (cf. Wells 1986). The world is, in Edelman's words, an "unlabelled place"; grammar is our way of categorizing it, enabling us to analyse out the elements that are commutable – that you can vary while leaving the remainder constant. This is the significance of the clause (or rather, of the category that is congruently both clause and figure): it is an organic configuration of elements having different, complementary functions with respect to the whole.

Then, as children are approaching adolescence, and as a condition of entry into the world of adult knowledge, children have to reconstrue their clausal grammar in a different, nominalized form. It is this reconstrual that I have been exploring in the present chapter.

Using the concept of **grammatical metaphor** I have tried to set up a taxonomy of types of rewording which would make it possible to examine both the inherent directionality of the reconstrual and the patterns of co-occurrence or "syndromes". This has meant 'unpacking' the metaphors and plotting the types of cross-coupling that occur between the semantic and the lexicogrammatical stratum. Such unpacking is not a unique operation; as in other metatextual activities, such as translation, or error analysis, there will usually be more than one possible route to travel. I have suggested a classification of grammatical metaphor based on the terminal point – the category into which the metaphoric shift takes place; this makes it possible to vary the degree of congruence in the analysis: that is, to decide how far any instance is to be unpacked.

So is the grammatical metaphor simply a rewording, saying the same things in different ways? or is it also a 're-meaning' – saying something different from the congruent form?

It is noticeable how ambiguous the metaphoric variants are. When a figure, which is congruently a clause, is reworded as a nominal group, much of the semantic information becomes hidden. Thus *animal protection* might be the realization of 'how animals are (or should be) protected (by humans)', 'how animals protect themselves', or 'how we protect (or should protect) ourselves from animals'; or even of 'how animals protect other things (such as humans, or the environment in general)'. The slightly less metaphorical wording *the protection of animals* rules out one or two of these; and if we then replace *of* by a true preposition such as *by* or *from* we recover some more semantic information – but only when we reach the congruent, clausal form can we be sure what function animals have in the protecting process. This suggests that the nominal grammar would not have served very well in the primary construal of experience: you have to know the answers before you start.

From this point of view it seems as if there is a loss of meaning potential in the nominal, metaphoric mode of discourse. But this is a misleading impression. There is, certainly, a great deal of neutralization taking place when a figure is reworded as a nominal group; but the result (in almost all cases; there are some exceptions)[6] is not loss of semantic distinction but ambiguity: the different possible meanings are still discrete. This may – indeed it often does – create problems for the learner, who has to guess right, often without realizing there is more than one possible interpretation. (The textbook writer may provide the answer, using the text as a key to metaphorical modes of expression: for example, the heading *Animal Protection* is followed in the first paragraph by the clause *animals protect themselves in many ways*.) But the total semantic range is not reduced. On the contrary: in shifting into the metaphoric mode the grammar actually creates new meanings, by the semantic junction across ranks and across categories.

Let me briefly summarize this part of the argument. Language – every human language – is a stratified system in which the content plane is split into a semantics, interfacing with the world of human experience (and of human social relationships), and a grammar, which is a purely abstract level of organization; the two are coupled through a relation of congruence, but they can be decoupled and recoupled in other ways (which I am calling "grammatical metaphor"). This gives the system indefinitely large semogenic power, because new meaning is created at the intersection of the congruent and the metaphoric categories ("semantic junction").

This potential seems to be exploited particularly at moments of major change in the human condition. We find one such reconstrual of experience in the languages of the iron age cultures of the Eurasian continent (of which classical Greek was one), which evolved discourses of measurement and calculation, and ordered sets of abstract, technical terms – the registers of mathematics and science (cf. Dijksterhuis 1950/86, Part 3). This grammar was carried over through classical and medieval Latin, and also, with a significant detour via Syriac and Arabic, into the national languages of modern Europe.

A further reconstrual then took place in the 'modern' period, with the evolution of the discourses of experimental science from Galileo and Newton onwards; and it is this secondary reconstrual that I have been describing in the present chapter. This new semiotic potential provided the foundation for our discipline-based organization of technical knowledge. It could perhaps be summed up under five headings:

1) **expanding** the noun as a taxonomic resource (Section 5) (this was the goal of language planning in the 1600s, especially in England and France (cf. Salmon 1979));

94

2) **transcategorizing** processes and qualities into nouns, relators into verbs etc., with resulting semantic junction (Section 6);

3) **compacting** pieces of the argument to function (e.g. as Theme of the clause) in an "information flow" of logical reasoning (Section 7);

4) **distilling** the outcomes of 2) and 3) to create technical taxonomies of abstract, virtual entities (Section 11);

5) **theorizing**: constructing a scientific theory through the reconstruing of experience as in 1)–4), with a "favourite clause type" in which virtual entities (instantial and/or systemic) participate in virtual processes based on logical–semantic relations ("relational processes" (cf. Halliday 1985/94, Chapter 5)).

A scientific theory is a specialized, semi-designed subsystem of a natural language; constructing such a theory is an exercise in lexicogrammar. Science and technology are (like other human endeavours) at one and the same time both *material* and *semiotic* practices; knowledge advances through the combination of new techniques with new meanings. Thus 'reconstruing experience' is not merely rewording (regrammaticizing); it is also resemanticizing. The languages of science are not saying the same things in different ways – although they may be appropriated for this purpose by others wishing to exploit their prestige and power.

On the contrary; what is brought into being in this reconstrual is a new construction of knowledge; and hence, a new ideology. The connection between metaphor and ideology – metaphor in its traditional sense – is well enough documented (cf. Lakoff 1992); we shall not be surprised that grammatical metaphor has ideological import. There are two aspects to this: in metafunctional terms, the ideational and the interpersonal. Ideationally, the nominalizing grammar creates a universe of things, bounded, stable and determinate; and (in place of processes) of relations between the things. Interpersonally, it sets itself apart as a discourse of the expert, readily becoming a language of power and technocratic control. In both aspects, it creates maximum distance between technical scientific knowledge and the experience of daily life. These are familiar enough motifs (cf. Lemke 1995; Thibault 1991; Fairclough 1992; Halliday and Martin 1993, especially Chapters 2, 6, 9–11); my concern here is to emphasize how the ideology is constructed in the grammar, by the same reconstrual of experience that was central to the development of modern science in the first place. With this in mind we can hope to exploit "grammatics" to keep track of what is happening today, and perhaps predict what may happen in the next phase of semiotic reconstruction (cf. Martin's comment (1992, pp. 409–10) on the verbs in current use in computer discourse).

Every human language is stratified in the same way, and the grammar of every language has the same potential for reconstruing experience. It happened that, in the case of the particular reconstrual that accompanied the development of modern science, this potential was taken up in the first instance by a few languages that became the standard or literary languages of the European nation states; and many more languages around the world have taken it up in the present century. It is worth remarking, perhaps, that it was not taken up in the non-standard varieties of these languages: the rural dialects of Italy, England or Germany did not evolve these elaborated grammatical metaphors – they were not, after all, expected to serve in the contexts of advanced education and science. To ask whether modern science could have developed without such semiotic reconstrual is of course one of the unanswerable questions of history. Any major restructuring of knowledge is likely to demand some remodelling of grammar. But the particular form this took was the product of specific historical (including semohistorical) circumstances; and if these had been different – for example, if modern science had developed first in China or India – the grammar of scientific discourse might have taken a rather different route. But then again, it might not.

APPENDIX
Text 1

From *General Microbiology*, Fifth edition⋆

EFFECTS OF SOLUTES
ON GROWTH AND METABOLISM

Transport mechanisms play two essential roles in cellular function. First, they maintain the intracellular concentrations of all metabolites at levels sufficiently high to ensure operation or both catabolic and biosynthetic pathways at near-maximal rates, even when nutrient concentrations in the external medium are low. This is evidenced by the fact that the exponential growth rates of microbial populations remain constant until one essential nutrient in the medium falls to a very low value, approaching exhaustion. At this limiting nutrient concentration, the growth rate of the population rapidly falls to zero (Chapter 7). Second, transport mechanisms function in *osmoregulation*, maintaining the solutes (principally small molecules and ions) at levels optimal for metabolic activity, even when the osmolarity of the environment varies over a relatively wide range.⋆

Most bacteria do not need to regulate their internal osmolarity with precision because they are enclosed by a cell wall capable of withstanding a considerable internal osmotic pressure. Bacteria always maintain their osmolarity well above that of the medium. If the internal osmotic pressure of the cell falls below the external osmotic pressure, water leaves the cell and the volume of the cytoplasm decreases with accompanying damage to the membrane. In Gram-positive bacteria, this causes the cell membrane to pull away from the wall: the cell is said to be *plasmolyzed*. In Gram-negative bacteria the wall retracts with the membrane; this also damages the membrane.

Bacteria vary widely in their osmotic requirements. Some are able to grow in very dilute solutions, and some in

solutions saturated with sodium chloride. Microorganisms that can grow in solutions of high osmolarity are called *osmophiles*. Most natural environments of high osmolarity contain high concentrations of salts, particularly sodium chloride. Microorganisms that grow in this type of environment are called *halophiles*. Bacteria can be divided into four broad categories in terms of their salt tolerance: *nonhalophiles, marine organisms, moderate halophiles,* and *extreme halophiles* (Table 8.3). Some halophiles, for example *Pediococcus halophilus*, can tolerate high concentrations of salt in the growth medium, but they can also grow in media without added NaC1. Other bacteria, including marine bacteria and certain moderate halophiles, as well as all extreme halophiles, require NaC1 for growth. The tolerance of high osmolarity and the specific requirement for NaC1 are distinct phenomena, each of which has a specific biochemical basis.

Osmotic Tolerance

Osmotic tolerance—the ability of an organism to grow in media with widely varying osmolarities is accomplished in bacteria by an adjustement of the internal osmolarity so that it always exceeds that of the medium. Intracellular accumulation of potassium ions (K^+) seems to play a major role in this adjustment. Many bacteria have been shown to concentrate K^+ to a much greater extent than Na^+ (Table 8.4). Moreover, there is an excellent correlation between the osmotic tolerance of bacteria and their K^+ content. For bacteria as metabolically diverse as Gram-positive cocci, bacilli, and Gram-negative rods, relative osmotic tolerance can be deduced from their relative K^+ contents after growth in a medium of fixed ionic strength and composition. Studies on *E. coli* have shown that the intracellular K^+ concentration increases progressively with increasing osmolarity of the growth medium. Consequently, both the osmolarity and the internal ionic strength of the cell increase.⋆

The maintenance of a relatively constant ionic strength within the cell is of critical physiological importance, because the stability and behavior of enzymes and other biological macromolecules are strongly dependent on this factor. In bacteria, the diamine putrescine (Chapter 5) probably always plays an important role in assuring the approximate constancy of internal ionic strength. This has been shown through studies on *E. coli*. The concentration of intracellular putrescine varies inversely with the osmolarity of the medium; increases of osmolarity cause rapid excretion of

---

⋆ When a *solution* of any substance (*solute*) is separated from a *solute-free solvent* by a membrane that is freely permeable to solvent molecules, but not to molecules of the solute, the solvent tends to be drawn through the membrane into the solution, thus diluting it. Movement of the solvent across the membrane can be prevented by applying a certain hydrostatic pressure to the solution. This pressure is defined as *osmotic pressure*. A difference in osmotic pressure also exists between two solutions containing different concentrations of any solute.

The osmotic pressure exerted by any solution can be defined in terms of *osmolarity*. An osmolar solution is one that contains one *osmole* per liter of solutes, i.e., a 1.0 molal solution of an ideal nonelectrolyte. An osmolar solution exerts an osmotic pressure of 22.4 atmospheres at 0°C, and depresses the freezing point of the solvent (water) by 1.86°C. If the solute is an electrolyte, its osmolarity is dependent on the degree of its dissociation, since both ions and undissociated molecules contribute to osmolarity. Consequently, the osmolarity and the molarity of a solution of an electrolyte may be grossly different. If both the molarity and the dissociation constant of a solution of an electrolyte are known, its osmolarity can be calculated with some degree of approximation, as the sum of the moles of undissociated solute and the mole equivalents of ions. Such a calculation is accurate only if the solution is an ideal one, and if it is extremely dilute. Therefore, it is preferable to determine the osmolarity of a solution experimentally, e.g., by freezing-point depression.

⋆ The ionic strength of a solution is defined by the equation $I - \Sigma Mi\ Z^2$, where Mi is the molarity of a given ion and Z is the charge, regardless of sign. Since the Z term is squared, the ionic strength of an ion increases exponentially with the magnitude of its charge either positive or negative. The magnitude of ionic charge, however, does not affect osmolarity.

(from Roger Y. Stanier, John L. Ingraham, Mark L. Wheelis and Page R. Painter, *General Microbiology*, 5th edn. Basingstoke and London: Macmillan Education, 1987, pp. 204–5.) (first published Englewood Cliffs, New Jersey: Prentice Hall, 1957)

[Appendix Text 1, continued]

TABLE 8.3
Osmotic Tolerance of Certain Bacteria

Physiological Class	Representative Organisms	Approximate Range of NaCl Concentration Tolerated for Growth (%, g/100 ml)
Nonhalophiles	*Aquaspirillum serpens*	0.0-1
	Escherichia coli	0.0-4
Marine forms	*Alteromonas haloplanktis*	0.2-5
	Pseudomonas marina	0.1-5
Moderate halophiles	*Paracoccus halodenitrificans*	2.3-20.5
	Vibrio costicolus	2.3-20.5
	Pediococcus halophilus	0.0-20
Extreme halophiles	*Halobacterium salinarium*	12-36 (saturated)
	Halococcus morrhuae	5-36 (saturated)

Note: Ranges of tolerated salt concentrations are only approximate; they vary with the strain and with the presence of other ions in the medium.

putrescine. An increase in the osmolarity of the medium causes an increase in the internal osmolarity of the cell as a result of uptake of K^+; ionic strength is maintained approximately constant as a result of the excretion of putrescine. This is a consequence of the differing contributions that a multiply charged ion makes to ionic strength and osmotic strength of a solution; a change of putrescine^{2+} concentration that alters ionic strength by 58 percent alters osmotic strength by only 14 percent.

Changes in osmotic strength or ionic strength of the growth medium also trigger a cellular response that changes the proportions in the outer membrane of *E. coli* of the two major protein constituents, OmpC and OmpF. These changes are thought to be adaptive, but the mechanism by which they alter the cell's ionic or osmotic tolerance remains unclear.

The presence in the medium of the amino acid proline dramatically increases a bacterium's ability to grow in a medium of high osmotic strength.

TABLE 8.4
Intracellular Concentrations of Solutes in Various Bacteria

Organism	Concentration (%, w/v) in Growth Medium of:		Ratio of Intracellular to Extracellular Concentration of:	
	NaCl	KCl	Na$^+$	K$^+$
Nonhalophiles				
Staphylococcus aureus	0.9	0.19	0.7	27
Salmonella oranienburg	0.9	0.19	0.9	10
Moderate halophiles				
Micrococcus halodenitrificans	5.9	0.02	0.3	120
Vibrio costicolus	5.9	0.02	0.7	55
Extreme halophiles				
Sarcina morrhuae	23.4	0.24	0.8	64
Halobacterium salinarium	23.4	0.24	0.3	140

Source: Data from J.H.B. Christian and J.A. Waltho, "Solute Concentrations within Cells of Halophilic and Nonhalophilic Bacteria," *Biochem. Biophys. Acta* 65, 506 (1962).

EFFECTS OF SOLUTES ON GROWTH AND METABOLISM 205

Text 2

From David Layzer, *Cosmogenesis: the growth of order in the universe* New York and Oxford: Oxford University Press, 1990: pp. 61–2

The classical world is populated by individuals; the quantum world is populated by clones. Two classical objects – a pair of ball bearings, for example – can't be precisely alike in every respect. But according to quantum physics, all electrons are exact replicas of one another.

They are indistinguishable not only in practice but also in principle, as are all hydrogen atoms, all water molecules, and all salt crystals (apart from size). This is not simply a dogma, but a testable and strongly corroborated hypothesis. For example, if electrons weren't absolutely indistinguishable, two hydrogen atoms would form a much more weakly bound molecule than they actually do. The absolute indistinguishability of the electrons in the two atoms gives rise to an 'extra' attractive force between them. The indistinguishability of electrons is also responsible for the structure of the periodic table – that is, for the fact that elements in the same column of the table (inert gases, halogens, alkali metals, alkali earths, and so on) have similar chemical properties.

Text 3

From William Stigliani & Wim Salomons, 'Our fathers' toxic sins', *New Scientist*, 1903, 11 December 1993

Redox potential: the chemical switch

One of the fundamental requirements of life is the need to generate biochemical energy by the oxidation of organic carbon to carbon dioxide. The most efficient energy-producing mechanism is respiration, in which molecular oxygen (O_2) is the oxidising agent. In soils, waters and sediments, however, the supply of O_2 is often limited. Nonetheless, the Earth's aquatic and terrestrial ecosystems contain microorganisms which can extract oxygen from other oxygen-containing compounds. These include nitrate, manganese and iron oxides, sulphate and organic carbon.

The type of molecule used first depends on how good an oxidising agent it is in relation to others – in chemical terms, its 'redox' potential. Oxidation by molecular oxygen has the highest redox potential, so molecular oxygen is the first compound to be consumed. Nitrate has the next highest redox potential, so it is consumed next. The sequence continues with manganese oxide, ferric hydroxide, sulphate, and finally to organic carbon. The redox potential is a kind of 'chemical switch' which determines the order in which oxygen-containing chemicals are used by microorganisms to extract oxygen.

Notes

1. Note the important difference here between transcategorization and metaphor (cf. Section 6 above). There is nothing metaphorical about *poiētēs* 'maker'; it is simply an actor noun derived from a verb 'make' ('one who makes'). In the same way one can derive an adjective from a noun; e.g., in English, *venom*: *venomous*. In such cases there is no semantic junction: *venomous* is not the name of an entity, just as *poiētēs* is not the name of a process. In metaphor, on the other hand, there is semantic junction between the 'vehicle' and the 'tenor': thus *venomousness* contains not only the feature 'entity' but that of 'quality' as well.
2. From Terry A. Michalske & Bruce C. Bunker, 'The fracturing of glass', *Scientific American*, December 1987.
3. Note the difference between *behaviour* as metaphorized process 'behave' (which is accented; cf. *mechanical behaviour* = how (they) behave in terms of mechanics) and *behaviour* as dummy noun introduced in the nominalizing of another process (unaccented; cf. *feeding behaviour* = how (they) feed).
4. It is interesting to compare this with children's own theories of conservation, illustrated in these two examples:

   Nigel [4;11]:   Why does as plasticine gets longer it gets thinner?
   Father: That's a very good question. Why does it?
   Nigel: Because more of it is getting used up.
   Father: Well ... [looking doubtful]
   Nigel: [patiently] Because more of it is getting used up to make it longer, that's why; and so it goes thinner.
   (See CD 'The Complete Nigel Transcripts' accompanying Volume 4, *The Language of Early Childhood*.)

   Nick [8;]:   [in car, explaining *high beam* to his brother] On low beam the light is all spread out but on high beam it is thick, it has texture. It's like plasticine – on low beam it's like plasticine all spread out but on high beam it's like when you roll out the plasticine into a long shape like a snake so it all goes forwards instead of to the sides.
   (Beverly Derewianka, 1995, p. 108)

5. Compare Nigel's observation on the same topic at age 3:

   Nigel [3;5]:   Cats have no else to stop you from trossing them ... cats have no other way to stop children from hitting them; so they bite.
   (Halliday 1993b, p. 110)

6. Perhaps the most striking example is the class of verbs such as *correlate with*, *be associated with*, *mean*, *reflect*, which neutralize the decoding/

encoding distinction in intensive relational processes (i.e. the opposition of Token identified as Value vs. Value identified as Token (cf. Halliday 1967–8, 1985/94; Davidse 1991)); for example

the inheritance of specific genes is correlated with the inheritance of a specific chromosome

But this could also be interpreted positively: neutralizing a semantic distinction is, from another point of view, creating a new semantic category (a 'new meaning').

Chapter Four

THE GRAMMATICAL CONSTRUCTION OF SCIENTIFIC KNOWLEDGE: THE FRAMING OF THE ENGLISH CLAUSE (1999)

1 Doric and Attic styles: commonsense discourse and scientific discourse

I recently noticed a care label, of the type that is attached to clothing. It said: "Prolonged exposure will result in rapid deterioration of the item."

While I was working out what action this might call for, I asked myself: why didn't they say: "If the item is exposed for long it will rapidly deteriorate"? This would have taken no more room; in fact it is slightly shorter. But it might have seemed – what? old-fashioned? childish? colloquial? Somehow the version they used carries greater value. It is more weighty: what it is telling us is not just a fact, but a solemn, proven fact, pregnant with authority and wisdom. In other words it is more scientific.

Why does it seem like this? I have not changed the words; the lexical items are the same, varying only in their morphological shape: *deteriorate – deterioration, rapidly – rapid.* What differs between the two versions is the grammar. The differences in grammatical structure are summarized in Figure 4.1.[1]

The differences are of two kinds: differences in rank and differences in status. I want to be able to refer to pairs such as these from time to time; so let me give them names which I hope will be

'The grammatical construction of scientific knowledge: the framing of the English clause', from *Incommensurability and Translation: Kuhnian Perspectives on Scientific Communication and Theory Change*, edited by Rema Rossini Favretti, Giorgio Sandri and Roberto Scazzieri, Cheltenham: Edward Elgar, 1999.

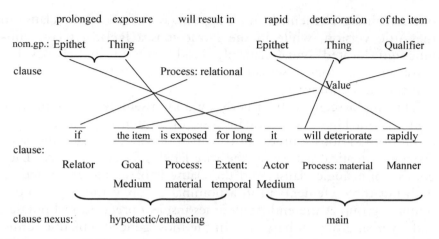

Figure 4.1 Differences in grammatical structure between 'Attic' and 'Doric' variants

transparent: I shall call the sophisticated, 'scientific' variant the Attic, and the naive, everyday variant the Doric, according to our received perception of these two cultures of ancient Greece. In rank, then, the Attic version is one clause, while the Doric version is a nexus of two clauses, forming a clause complex. In status, there are a number of differences, which could be summarized as in Figure 4.2, where to give a clearer account the status is expressed both in terms of grammatical classes and in terms of grammatical functions.

	Attic			Doric		
lexical item	*class*	*function [in]*		*class*	*function [in]*	
'long time'	verb	Epithet	[nom.gp.]	prep.phr.	Extent	[clause]
'expose'	noun	Thing	"	verbal gp.	Process	"
'rapid'	adjective	Epithet	"	advbl.gp.	Manner	"
'deteriorate'	noun	Thing	"	verbal.gp.	Process	"
'item'	noun	Qualifier	"	nomnl.gp.	Medium	"
'cause'	verbal gp.	Process	[clause]	conjunctn.	Relator	[cl. nexus]

Figure 4.2 Attic/Doric variants showing classes and functions

If we put together rank and functional status, we find that in the Attic version, almost all the lexical matter is configured in the form of nominal groups, structured as (Epithet +) Thing (+ Qualifier), with one Thing, namely *item*, located inside the Qualifier of another, *deterioration*; while in the Doric the same lexical matter is configured so as to form clauses, structured as Process plus one kind of participant, the Medium, plus two different kinds of circumstance. The one remaining element, 'cause', appears as Process in the clause in the Attic version, while in the Doric it is a Relator (class: conjunction) located syntagmatically inside one of the clauses but construing a logical-semantic relationship between the two (enhancing: conditional).

This might seem to be a fairly random assembly of grammatical features. But Figure 4.3 contains a set of written English sentences, taken from various sources, all of which display essentially the same lexicogrammatical pattern as the care label referred to above. Each consists of a single clause; and the clause is of simple construction, with just three elements in it: a nominal group at the beginning, a nominal group at the end (sometimes inside a prepositional phrase), and a verbal group in between. In the most general semantic terms, there is a participating entity, a process, and then a second entity participating either directly or circumstantially.[2]

When we investigate these further, they turn out to form a recognizable syndrome, one that is diagnostic of a certain type of highly valued, authority-laden discourse.

What we find is that all such instances of a clause of the Attic type stand in a systemic relationship to (technically, are "agnate" to) a Doric variant. Each of the Attic variants can be taken apart – unpacked, as it were – in such a way that each of the nominal groups is reworded as a clause, while the verbal group is reworded as a conjunction expressing a logical-semantic relation obtaining between this pair of clauses. The right-hand column in Figure 4.3 gives possible Doric 'translations'.

How would we interpret the relationship between the Doric and the Attic variants? Clearly it is in some sense a metaphorical relationship; but distinct from metaphor as usually understood. In metaphor in its canonical sense, the metaphoric process takes place in the vocabulary; whereas here it takes place in the grammar. The words (the lexical items) do not vary; what varies is their grammatical status – verb or adjective varying with noun, conjunction varying with verb and so on. And it is metaphor of this kind – grammatical metaphor – that is the hallmark, the characteristic motif, of scientific discourse in English. Or rather, that was once the hallmark of science, until it started to pervade most other forms of adult writing.

If we interpret something as metaphor, we are setting up a semantic relationship between two linguistic variants. Usually this relationship has been explored 'from below' – that is, by focusing on the form: here is a word, we say, and it has two meanings, one literal and another metaphorical. Thus, the English word *fruit* means, literally, 'the product of the earth, which supplies the wants of men and animals; an edible part of a plant' (*Chambers Twentieth-Century Dictionary*), and then has a second "metaphorical meaning" as product or outcome of an action. Strictly speaking, of course, each of these meanings is metaphorical by reference to the other; if one is being said to be "literal", its precedence must be established on other grounds. But first I need to shift the perspective and look at the relationship 'from above':

Fire intensity has a profound effect on smoke injection.	If a fire is intense it will give off a lot of smoke.
Sydney's latitudinal position of 33° south ensures warm summer temperatures.	Sydney is at latitude 33° south, so it is warm in summer.
Investment in a rail facility implies a long-term commitment.	If you invest in a facility for the railways you will be committing [funds] for a long term.
[The atomic nucleus absorbs energy in quanta, or discrete units.] Each absorption marks its transition to a state of higher energy.	[...] Each time it absorbs energy it (moves to a state of higher energy =) becomes more energetic.
The goal of evolution is to optimize the mutual adaption of species.	[Species] evolve in order to adapt to each other as well as possible.
[Evolutionary biologists have always assumed that] rapid changes in the rate of evolution are caused by external events [which is why ...] they have sought an explanation for the demise of the dinosaurs in a meteorite impact.	[...] when [species] suddenly [start to] evolve more quickly this is because something has happened outside [...] they want to explain that the dinosaurs died out because a meteorite impacted.
[It will be seen ... that] a successful blending of asset replacement with remanufacture is possible. Careful studies are to be undertaken to ensure that viability exists.	[...] it is possible both to replace assets and to remanufacture [current equipment] successfully. We must study [the matter] carefully to ensure that ([the plan] is viable =) we will be able to do what we plan.
The theoretical programme of devising models of atomic nuclei	As well as working theoretically by devising models of atomic nuclei

has been complemented by experimental investigations.	we have also investigated [the topic] by experimenting.
Increased responsiveness may be reflected in feeding behaviour.	[The child] is becoming more responsive, so s/he may feed better.
Equation (3) provided a satisfactory explanation of the observed variation in seepage rates.	When we used equation (3) we could explain satisfactorily (the different rates at which we have observed that seepage occurs =) why, as we have observed, [water] seeps out more quickly or more slowly.
The growth of attachment between infant and mother signals the first step in the child's capacity to discriminate among people.	Because/if/when the mother and her infant grow more attached to one another/ the infant grows/is growing/ more attached to its mother we know that/she knows that/ [what is happening is that] the child has begun/is beginning/ is going to begin to be able to tell one person from another/prefer one person over another

Figure 4.3 Examples illustrating typical metaphoric structures, with rewordings in more congruent form. The alternative rewordings shown in the last example illustrate how ambiguous such metaphor can become.

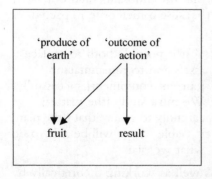

Figure 4.4 Lexical metaphor

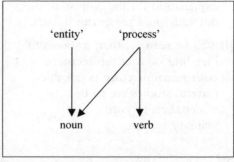

Figure 4.5 Grammatical metaphor

In grammatical metaphor, the variants realize not word meanings but category meanings. An entity is construed in the grammar as a noun, like *item*. A process is construed either as a verb (for example, *expose*) or as a noun (for example, *exposure*); it has a metaphorical as well as a congruent realization.

The reason for calling the nominalized form metaphorical is not that it is morphologically more complex. More or less any grammatical class, in English, can be derived from any other; and often there is no morphological marking at all. The reason we can interpret one form of construal as congruent (the term "literal" is not appropriate when we are looking at this from the semantic perspective) is that it is **historically** prior: in the grammar's construction of reality, the mapping of process into verb and of entity into noun **precedes** the mapping of process into noun. Indeed, the semantic categories of 'process' and 'entity' come into being only by being construed in this way by the grammar; they have no independent existence on their own. I will come back shortly to what is meant by "historical" in this context. But, since one variant is later, and therefore parasitic, on the earlier (that is, its meaning is understood by reference to a meaning already established), the two are not simply alternative wordings. As with lexical metaphors (such as *their efforts bore fruit*), so also in grammatical metaphor there is a junction of two meanings: the category meaning of the congruent form *expose* ('process') clashes with the category meaning of a noun ('entity'), and the impact generates a new meaning, 'process as (virtual) entity'. It is this semantic junction, arising from metaphoric processes in the grammar, that provides the resource for the two fundamental requirements of scientific discourse: technical concepts and reasoned argument. Either of these can, of course, occur in congruent form; but the combination of the two, in a scientific theory, seems always to rest on a foundation of grammatical metaphor.

2 Grammatical metaphor: reconstruing the relations between the grammar and the semantics

I began, as a way into the languages of science, with metaphors of nominalization: those in which a process, congruently construed as a verb, is reconstrued metaphorically as a noun. Nominalization is a familiar term, and one that is usually at the forefront when we talk about the grammar of scientific discourse; reasonably so because it is, in a sense, the driving force within the metaphoric process. At the same time, grammatical metaphor, as we find it in the theoretical discourses of science, involves much more than just turning things into nouns. Here is a representative passage from *Scientific American*, in which I have italicized all the words that I would interpret as instances of grammatical metaphor:

> Even though *the fracture of glass* can be a dramatic *event*, many *failures are preceded* by *the slow extension of preexisting cracks*. A good example of a slowly *spreading* crack is often *found* in the windshield of an automobile. *The extension of a small crack*, which may have started from *the impact of a stone*, can be followed day by day as the crack gradually propagates across the entire windshield. In other cases small, *unnoticed surface* cracks can grow during an *incubation* period and *cause a catastrophic failure* when they *reach* a critical *size*. Cracks in glass can grow at *speeds* of less than one trillionth of an inch per hour, and under *these conditions* the *incubation* period *can span* several years before *the catastrophic failure is observed*. On an atomic scale *the slow growth of cracks corresponds* to *the sequential rupturing of interatomic bonds* at *rates* as low as one bond rupture per hour. *The wide range of rates* over which glass can fracture – varying by 12 orders of *magnitude* (factors of 10) from *the fastest shatter* to *the slowest creep* – *makes the investigation of crack growth a particularly engaging enterprise.*[3]

We can distinguish three types of metaphoric process. First, there are those where the metaphorized variant is a noun functioning in the prototypical context of a noun, namely as the main element (we call this the "Thing") in a nominal group; for example, *fracture*, *failure*, *extension*, *size*. Secondly, there are those where the metaphorized word is not a noun, or, if it is, is not functioning as a Thing – but is inside the structure of a nominal group; for example, *glass*, *slow*, *preexisting*, *stone*, *surface*.[4] (The term "nominalization" is sometimes – but not always – understood as including instances of this second type.) Thirdly, there are those where the metaphorized variant is not a noun, and is not functioning inside a nominal group: for example, *are preceded*, *cause*, *reach*, *can span*, *corresponds*. This third type shows clearly that it is misleading to characterize the entire metaphoric process as one of nominalization. On the other hand, the overall effect is that of condensing large amounts of lexical material inside nominal groups. In that sense we can reasonably talk about this as a "nominal style"; although the contrast is not between nominal and verbal (as in the title of Rulon Wells's paper in an influential volume published back in 1960) but between nominal and clausal – where the Attic is a nominal, the Doric is a clausal style.

In Figure 2.3 (pp. 41–2), I have tried to set out the principal types of grammatical metaphor as I have observed this phenomenon in studying the grammar of scientific texts. I have classified them in terms of the shift (from congruent to metaphorical) in grammatical class and in grammatical function; the class shift shows the nature of the semantic junction (for example, the verb *are preceded* construes time simultaneously as a relation between processes and as a process in its own right), while the function shows how the metaphor is incorporated into the grammatical structure. The question that arises is: can anything metaphorize into anything else, or are there discernible tendencies and constraints? Can we set up a taxonomy of orders of grammatical metaphor?

It turns out, I think, that we can, provided we start from a postulate about what I am calling the "congruent" pattern. We have had to recognize congruence in order to categorize the metaphors in the first place; but it is necessary at this point to make it clear what is being asserted by it. I am assuming that a grammar – that is, the lexicogrammatical system of any and every natural language – is a theory of human experience. It is a way of imposing order, in the form of mutually defining relationships and categories, on the flux and unboundedness of the perceptual world. Each language, in the last resort, has its own special way of doing this, its unique "characterology" as Mathesius called it; but the variation is within certain limits. Since we all live on the planet's surface, and we all have the same brain structures, all grammars are likely to share certain modes of construing that are functional for our survival. These will vary with major changes in the human condition, such as that between non-settled and settled modes of existence; but all languages of settlement clearly have much in common, and English is a typical specimen of its kind. In English, then, the grammar construes *figures*. A figure is the semantic representation of a happening; human experience consists primarily of happenings, and the grammar transforms these happenings into meaning by means of its central construct, the clause. The clause, in turn, is configured out of certain parts; these are of three kinds, construed as verbs, nouns, and the rest – more accurately, (1) verbal group, (2) nominal group, (3) adverbial group or prepositional phrase. By this means the grammar deconstrues each happening into constituent *elements*: a process, a small number of entities taking part in that process, and possibly some circumstantial elements as well. Prototypically, *the oxen were dragging the plough slowly across the field*.

The grammatical categories do not appear out of nowhere; they evolve in the semiotic transformation of experience, construing the different elements that combine to make up a figure. What I have called the "congruent" pattern is simply the one in which they evolved; any cross-coupling within this pattern is by definition metaphorical. But if we want to order the various types of metaphor, we need to bring in two further elements. One is a quality, congruently construed as an adjective; from a functional perspective this is a type of noun (compare the traditional categories of "noun substantive, noun adjective"), functioning as Epithet in the nominal group (for example, *weary* in *the weary oxen*) but also on its own as Attribute in the clause (*the oxen were weary*). The other is a relator, which functions to relate one figure to another in a sequence; this is construed congruently as a conjunction (e.g. *as* in *as the sun was setting*). The general pattern of congruence between the grammatical and the semantic categories is set out in Figure 4.6.

Congruence in rank		Congruence in status (elements)	
semantic	*grammatical*	*semantic*	*grammatical*
sequence	clause nexus	entity	noun (nominal group)
figure	clause	quality	adjective [in nom.gp.]
element	group/phrase	process	verb (verbal group)
		circumstance (1)	adverb (/adverbial gp.)
		circumstance (2)	prepositional phrase
		[minor process	preposition]
		relator	conjunction

Figure 4.6 Congruence between semantic and grammatical categories

This is the point of departure from which the metaphor takes off. If we now examine the metaphoric shifts that actually occur, we find a consistent pattern of movement as shown in Figure 2.4 (p. 42).

There is an implicational scaling present here: we can range the different categories in an order such that the metaphoric shift can go only one way – to the right, as set out here. What does this mean, in semantic terms? Like metaphors of the traditional, lexical kind, grammatical metaphor always involves shifting towards the concrete. This is the grammar's way of modelling the more complex aspects of human experience, in the course of reflecting on them and theorizing about them: by making analogies with what is familiar and perceptible. The most accessible type of phenomenon is a 'thing', in its prototypical form as an entity that has extension in time and space; and the category which construes such entities is the noun. The noun is thus the ultimate target of the analogy, which as it were seeks out semantic junctions with the feature 'entity' as a way of bringing it down to earth. (This is why nominalization stands out as the salient aspect of grammatical metaphor.) Next to entities come qualities, then processes, then circumstances, the circumstance typically embodying a 'minor process' congruently construed as a preposition. The least stable element of all is the relator, because it is the most abstract: it is not even an element in a figure, but a logical-semantic relation between two figures. In the last resort, however, every corner of experience can be mapped into a 'thing'; Figure 4.7 shows the metaphoric progression of the relator 'so' from its congruent origin as a conjunction to its final resting place as a noun.

a happened; *so x* happened
x happened *because a* happened

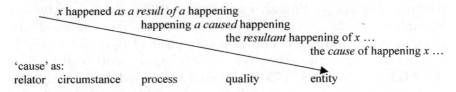

        x happened *as a result of a* happening
              happening *a caused* happening
                    the *resultant* happening of *x* ...
                          the *cause* of happening *x* ...

'cause' as:
relator   circumstance   process   quality   entity

Figure 4.7 The progression of 'cause' from relator to thing

As this progression shows, instances of grammatical metaphor seldom occur alone; rather, they tend to come in favourite clusters, or syndromes. Figure 4.8 shows one sentence from the glass-cracking text with the instances of metaphor annotated according to the taxonomy set out in Figure 2.3 above. (I have given two versions of the congruent rewording, one in which *crack* and *bond* are left in place as congruent, a second in which they are further 'unpacked' into processes; it is interesting to note the difference between the two.) As we examine more and more instances we can recognize typical patterns emerging; there are, obviously, very many of these, but the dominant motif turns out to be a complex syndrome which could be characterized in very general terms as in Figure 4.9.

Such a pattern could, of course, be identified at many different levels of generality. The description given here is a more explicit – and less inclusive – version of the informal account I gave at the beginning. But all the examples in Figure 4.3 are instances of it (and

1.   The slow growth of cracks corresponds to the sequential rupturing of
         [6   2 13]   9   [6   2   13
    interatomic bonds at rates as low as one bond rupture per hour
        6]   1   [13   2]

    Cracks grow slowly – as slowly as when the bonds between the atoms rupture one after another only once an hour.

2.   The slow growth of cracks corresponds to the sequential rupturing of
         [6   2 13 2]   9   [6   2   13
    interatomic bonds at rates as low as one bond rupture per hour
        6   2]   1   [2/13 2]

    Glass cracks slowly – as slowly as when one atom stops being bonded to another atom only once every hour

Figure 4.8 Metaphoric analysis of a sentence, showing syndromes (two versions, the second further 'unpacked')

so is the care label on my jacket). It was identified already by Huddleston et al. (1968; see also Huddleston 1971) in their investigation of scientific English back in the 1960s; their prototypical example was "*The conversion of hydrogen to helium in the interiors of stars is the source of energy for their immense output of light and heat*". It represents a "favourite clause type" for scientific writing in English (see Halliday 1988, pp. 173–4). What I have tried to do here is to suggest how this clause type relates to the grammar of English as a whole, through a number of distinct metaphorical processes combining to form a syndrome; and how it embodies, in this way, a number of semantic junctions which together account for its ability to occupy such a central role in the discourses of science.

semantic: A sequence of two figures, linked by a logical–semantic relation

grammatical:

  [congruent]   A nexus of two clauses, with relator/conjunction in secondary clause (optionally also in primary clause)

  [metaphorical]   One clause, 'relational:identifying', of three elements:

  1/2 + 9 + 1/2   Identified   +   Process   +   Identifier
                      nominal group   verbal group   nominal group

                  The nominal element may be either process [2] or quality [1]: There is a variant form with 'relational:existential' process and only one nominal, [1/2 + 12], e.g. *viability exists, bonding occurs*.

Figure 4.9 The 'favourite clause type' as metaphoric syndrome

If now we put together the syntagmatic principle of metaphors occurring in syndromes and the paradigmatic principle of an ordered series of metaphorical steps, we can see that the two axes together define a **semantic space**, within which metaphoric variation in the grammar creates its meaning. It is a highly elastic space, with enormous semogenic potential. For any given instance, there are not simply two alternative wordings, one congruent, the other metaphorical (the Doric and the Attic that I started with), but rather a range over different degrees of metaphoricness, which moreover may be spread quite unevenly across the syndrome. Every instance will of course have its own particular range of possibilities; Figure 4.10 gives a brief example, in which I have taken a clause from the glass-cracking text and moved the whole syndrome across the metaphor scale (I leave you to guess which was the original wording).

1. glass cracks more quickly the harder you press it
    'thing a undergoes process b in manner c to the extent that in manner x person w does action y to thing a'
2. cracks in glass grow faster the more pressure is put on
    '[complex] thing b-in-a acquires property d in manner c to the extent that [abstract] thing xy has process z done to it'
3. glass crack growth is faster if greater stress is applied
    '[complex abstract] thing abd has attribute c under condition that [abstract] thing xy has process z done to it'
4. the rate of glass crack growth depends on the magnitude of the applied stress
    '[complex abstract] thing c-of-abd is caused by [complex abstract] thing x-of-zy'
5. glass crack growth rate is associated with applied stress magnitude
    '[complex abstract] thing $abdc$ causes/is caused by [complex abstract] thing zyx'

Figure 4.10 Agnate series of metaphoric variants

There is also an informal semantic commentary, to which I shall return later. Note that the clause is an instance of the favoured type.

3 Dimensions of semiotic time: history of the system, of the performer, of the text

The notion of 'languages of science' implies a history: there was a time when these languages did not exist. The notion of grammatical metaphor also implies a history: there must be a (congruent) construal of meaning first, before any further meaning can be construed by departing metaphorically from it. How far do these histories coincide? About ten years ago I started looking into the history of scientific English from a grammatical point of view in order to investigate links with the history of science itself. There is a brief summary of that work in Chapter 5 below and I shall not try to replicate it here. But I will try to give a short sketch of the picture that emerged.

As we move back through the past 300 years, the favourite clause type stays with us; but it becomes less and less predominant. There are more instances of intermediate types (such as Figure 4.10 above), in which, for example, a process may remain construed as a clause but the clause as a whole is nominalized; for example, the non-finite clause in this instance from Darwin (*The Origin of Species*, p. 255): 'the security of the hive is known mainly to depend on a large number of bees being supported'. And the more extreme Attic variants become sparser. When we come to Newton's *Opticks*, written between 1685 and 1704, we find an interesting mix. The text is three discourses in one: when he describes how he experimented and what he observed, Newton writes largely in Doric style; his theoretical conclusions are of much more Attic construction; while his mathematical generalizations display a related but distinct type of nominal group structure based on multiple rankshifting of phrases and clauses inside the post-Head Qualifier. Thus while there has been steady evolution of the Attic style in the centuries since Newton wrote, his own writing already shows examples of all the different degrees of grammatical metaphor: such as 'the cause of Reflexion is not the impinging of Light on the solid impervious parts of Bodies' (*Opticks*, p. 283).

When we go back beyond Newton, however, the picture changes. Professor Altieri Biagi has studied the language of Galileo, where she finds many of the same features that I observed in Newton; and it is likely that there was some influence from Italian into English, since scientists in that century usually spent time in Italy and scientific treatises were increasingly written in Italian. I have not examined the earlier English texts from the seventeenth and sixteenth centuries, nor those of late medieval Latin. But I did study the grammar of Chaucer's *Treatise on the Astrolabe* (c. 1390), which he wrote when he gave his ten-year-old son Lowis an astrolabe as a present; Lowis didn't yet know much Latin, so Chaucer wrote the treatise in English. And here there is hardly any trace of the Attic style. The discourse is highly technical, giving instructions on how to use the instrument (unfortunately the promised chapter on theory is lost, or perhaps never got written); but, while technical terms are metaphorical in origin, once they become technicalized they cease to be metaphors, and there is almost no grammatical metaphor in Chaucer's treatise.

Thus there is one dimension of history – phylogenetic history, the history of the system – in which it is clear that the Attic style is not original but begins to emerge with the founders of experimental science, and continues to evolve throughout the "modern" period. Now let us consider another historical dimension – the ontogenetic, the history of the human child from infant to adult.

A number of intensive, diary-type studies have been carried out tracing the development of discourse in English-speaking children with particular reference to language in the construal of experience (Halliday 1975; Painter 1984, 1993; Derewianka 1995). It seems clear that in developing grammar in its ideational function, as the semiotic modelling of experience, children go through certain phases of construing. They begin with generalizing, which is a necessary condition of the move from infant protolanguage to (post-infancy) mother tongue; this enables them to progress from "proper" to "common" term (class names) and to construe the latter into taxonomies (classes of classes). Secondly, they learn to cope with abstractness: to construe terms whose meanings have no counterpart in perceptual experience. This comes typically around age 4–5 and is recognized (unconsciously) by the culture because this is when we put them into school and teach them to write – writing depends on the ability to handle abstract terms and symbols. Thirdly, they move into grammatical metaphor; this happens considerably later, around the age of puberty – they cope with particular instances of metaphor, especially interpersonal metaphors like indirect speech acts, much earlier than this, but cannot yet use metaphorical constructs to think with. So on this ontogenic dimension as well, there is a progression from the language of common-sense knowledge, which is very largely congruent in its grammar, to the metaphorical construction of knowledge in the languages of science.[5]

I have found an interesting way of taking students down the ontogenetic trail, so that they gain a sense of how children grow up to become scientifically literate – and at the same time, of how the language of science relates to that of daily life. If we consider a series of agnate clauses like those in Figure 4.10, we can think of them as variants being addressed to receivers of different ages. The last could be addressed to an educated adult of, say, 20 years of age; then the others might be addressed to young people of, say, 16, 12, 9 and 6 years old respectively. One can then take any typically Attic example from a science text and ask: how would you get this across to a child of this or that particular age? You will notice how, as you go down the age range, you are progressively unpacking the metaphor. Of course, you cannot do it if the text depends on a high level of technical knowledge. But not all clauses in scientific texts are of that kind; here are some others I have used for exploring in this way (cf. Chapter 2 above):

- fire intensity has a profound effect on smoke injection
- the patient's subsequent inability to recall the incident was attributed to the severity of the head injuries incurred
- the truest confirmation of the accuracy of our knowledge is the effectiveness of our actions.

Of course, you may have to change some of the vocabulary at the same time; for example, *subsequently/afterwards the patient was unable to/couldn't recall/remember what had happened*. But the driving force is located within the grammar.

Thus we have two histories, and they coincide: the development of the individual human being matches epigenetically the evolution of the semiotic system – in this case, the language of science, which is a subsystem, or rather a family of subsystems, of the language as a whole. Both change, over time, in the same direction: from the congruent to the metaphorical, building up new meanings through repeated instances of semantic junction. But there is still a third dimension of time to be considered: namely, the history of the text. Whereas the system of a language **evolves**, and the meaning potential of a human being **develops** (grows, matures, ages and dies), the instantiated text **unfolds** – whatever the medium, the text has a beginning, a middle and an end.

Every text creates meaning instantially as it goes along. But whereas in most registers, like casual conversation, this process is uneven and sporadic, in a scientific text, prototypically at least, the meaning progressively accumulates – this is in fact the main impetus behind grammatical metaphor, as I shall suggest in the final section: it is a way of enabling meaning to accrue. It is hard to illustrate this "logogenetic" dimension of history without working in detail through an entire text; but let me try to give a flavour of it by picking out, once again from the cracking of glass, instances of the wording of the main theoretical motif in the order in which they occurred: Figure 4.11.

THE FRACTURING OF GLASS: ... the mechanism by which *glass cracks* ... the stress needed to *crack glass* ... as a *crack grows* ... *the crack has advanced* ... make *slow cracks grow* ... *the rate* at which *cracks grow* ... *the slow growth of cracks* ... *the rate of crack growth* ... we can *decrease the crack growth rate* ... *glass fracture growth rate*

Figure 4.11 Logogenetic construal of a technical term

At the beginning of the text, there is an entity 'glass' and a process 'crack' (*crack* as verb). Step by step, the text builds up more complex meanings: the 'crack' becomes an entity, which can 'grow', more or less 'slowly'; *grow slowly* becomes *slow growth*, then *growth rate*, and at the end there is an entirely new entity called *glass fracture growth rate*. This did not exist at the beginning of the text; it has come into being instantially – and again, the grammar has moved from the congruent towards the metaphorical.

Of course, such a movement within any given text is not smoothly linear; it is tortuous and bumpy – even more so when we come to think of the entire macrotext formed by the body of texts that interleave in the course of the evolution of any one scientific subdiscipline. Some instantial creations will remain just that; others will get absorbed into the system. But the evolution of the scientific theory is a discursive process; even the short extracts I have provided here reveal how from Newton onwards the concepts and the arguments have been constructed on the hoof. We can recognize the familiar dialectic between system and instance that is a feature of all semiosis; and the movement from congruent to metaphorical within the text – the logogenetic progression – is a critical link in this process. It is the technical concepts and rational arguments built up metaphorically in the text which are available for being transported into the system: the metaphor releases the semiotic energy which enables the meaning potential to expand.

In saying that a text tends to move from the more congruent to the more metaphorical, I am not implying of course that it will stay within the same paradigm, 'saying the same thing in different words'. Paradigms are not syntagms. But we do sometimes meet with a limiting case, such as the following: *solid particles are held together by the strong attraction between them*. Such apparent tautologies are valuable precisely because they are not tautological; they illustrate the important point that metaphorical variants ("rewordings") do not in fact mean the same thing. Even if we unpack *a strong attraction [exists] between solid particles* as *solid particles are held together* the two belong in different constructions of knowledge. We may define knowledge as experience that has been transformed into meaning; but not in isolation – the meaning is within some system, and the systemic environment of two such different grammatical construals is likely to be somewhat different. The one comes from commonsense, dialogic, evolved, everyday knowledge; the other has moved towards knowledge that is scientific, monologic, designed and technical. As the grammar reconstrues in this way, it departs from the congruent beginnings with which children embark upon their mother tongue, towards a world of virtual entities which relate to one another in rather different ways, based on mathematical logic rather than on the cryptotypic logic of grammar. This world rests on two semiotic foundations: technicality, and rationality. We have to show how the grammar provides for these.

4 Why a special grammar of science?

In this final section I shall seek to problematize the issue of a special grammar for the languages of science. Why does it evolve, and what are its effects (including side-effects)?

4.1 Meaning as knowing and doing

I shall take it that human history is the interplay of two phenomenal domains, the material and the semiotic; and that it is powered by the impact between the two – an impact that becomes very visible when we observe the language development of small children. By semiotic phenomena I mean processes of meaning, with language as prototypical and also as leading edge; thus human communities are eco-social systems, with strong coupling between the semiotic and the material (Lemke 1993). I assume an account of the evolution of human consciousness along the lines worked out by Gerald Edelman (1992); but interpreting his "higher order consciousness" as consciousness based on grammar – on a stratified semiotic system. (Stratification is the decoupling of grammar from semantics.)

We are concerned with the languages of science, which means with how scientific knowledge is construed. Knowledge is semiotic transformation: to 'know' something is to have transformed it into meaning, and 'understanding' is the process of that transformation. The transformation of experience into meaning is carried out by lexicogrammar: the words and grammatical structures of a natural language. Thus the lexicogrammatical system of a language is a **theory** of human experience.

The categories and relations of our commonsense world are not given to us readymade; we construe them grammatically, using grammatical energy to theorize – to select among the indefinitely many ways in which experience could be 'parsed' and made to make sense. But meaning is a complex activity; it involves doing as well as thinking. The grammar is able to construe only because at the same time as construing it is also enacting: acting out the interpersonal encounter and the social values that make up daily life. We see this in the grammar of the clause: a clause is a mapping of transitivity and mood.

In these respects, the language of science is no different from the language of common sense. Its figures are largely statements, to be sure – in much scientific writing the declarative is simply put on cruise control; but such clauses are no less declarative in function: they are addressed to other people, as moves in an exchange of information. And there are also unwritten languages of science, like this excerpt from a discussion among three students doing their homework on the train to school (Figure 4.12). The dialogic nature of knowing is very clear! Even the most abstract kind of semiosis, like that of mathematics, is still parasitic on natural language. 'Doing science' is a form of social semiotic praxis (Lemke 1990a; Thibault 1986).

// 2 ∧ does it / matter / which one is / **added** //
// 1 what d'you / **mean** // 1 **oh** // 1 **yeah** // 1 that's why / that one doesn't / **work** /13 ∧ you see / ∧ / that one is / going / **that** way and // 1+ that one is / going / **that** way //
// 1 ∧ you /got it the / wrong way / **round** mate / ∧ // 2 **wait** a / **mo** // 1 which way has / he / **got** it //
// 1 ∧ it's a re/**duction** e/lectrode // 2 ∧ isn't / that the / way. the re/duction is / **going** //
// 1 **yeah** you// 1 got your re/actions the / wrong way / **round** mate //

119

// 2 ⌃ the el/ectrons / can't go / **that** way // 1 ⌃ the e/lectrons are /
   going / **that** way //
// 2 **no** they're / **not** //
// 1 **yeah** / ⌃ // 3 ⌃ see the e/lectrons go / **that** way …
// 3 ⌃ you see I / looked up / one of the / **tables** and they […]
// 4 ⌃ 'cause you / can't have / **positive** / ions going / there //
// 4 ⌃ no there's / nothing / wrong with / **that** // 3 all you've got
   to / do is / look up the / **tables** and // 1 see which / ones give a
   / positive / **value** //
// 1 **yeah** I // 13 **realize** / that //

Figure 4.12   Spoken science: homework on the train

4.2 Speaking and writing

If the grammar can construe, it can also reconstrue: having made the
world, it can turn it upside down, or sideways. What helps it to do
this is the move into a new medium, that of writing. Our commonsense world is construed in spoken language; it is here that congruent
patterns are laid down, setting up a rapport between the semantics
and the grammar which, once it is there, can then be challenged and
broken down. Spoken language will always have priority, because
that is where meaning is created and the categories and relations of
experience are defined. Written language can then create new
meanings by departing from this congruence, by the processes that I
have referred to as grammatical metaphor.

So when, in the literate cultures of our Eurasian culture band, a
new form of discourse evolves – educational discourse – this begins
the process whereby our experience will be reconstrued. It is a long
process, stretching phylogenetically from the iron age to the present
age of information science, and ontogenetically from initial literacy
to adulthood; and in the course of this process, knowledge becomes
designed, systemic and technical. If we now look back and compare
the world pictures that are construed in speech and in writing, we
find that each of these two modes makes the world look like itself.
The world of common sense is construed in clauses, and a clause
expresses process – doing and happening, sensing, saying and being.
In other words, the grammar of spoken language construes a world
that is fluid, transitory and without very clear boundaries, just as
speaking itself is fluid, transitory and without very clear boundaries.
By contrast, the world of educational knowledge is construed in

nominal groups, and a noun expresses entity – objects, beings, institutions and abstractions. The grammar of written language construes a world that is solid, lasting and clearly bounded, just as writing itself is solid, lasting and clearly bounded. The nominalized world looks like a written text.

4.3 Doric and Attic modes of meaning

Writing itself first arose out of the impact between grammar and pictorial, non-linguistic semiotic practices; it evolved in contexts which required text to be made permanent – inventories, calendars, inscriptions, divinations and the like. Thus it never was 'speech written down'; from the start writing construed different domains of experience, and hence was naturally at hand to serve as the medium for a different construction of knowledge – an "Attic" alongside the "Doric" mode, in the terms I have been using here.

But, as we have seen, it is only in the "modern" period, with the appearance of experimental science, that the nominalized, Attic construal of knowledge has come into being; this has been a slow and gradual process – the semiotic counterpart of the gradual evolution of material technology. Changes in the human condition are always at one and the same time both material and semiotic; alongside the technological progression from settlement and agriculture, through the iron age, to the industrial and informational revolutions we might recognize other semiotic modes along the way – perhaps an "Arcadian" preceding the Doric; an "Ionic" between the Doric and the Attic; and now something post-Attic, say Alexandrian, or better "Byzantine". Whether or not we can trace the grammar's reconstrual of human experience as something which takes place gradually through this period of technological history (it is difficult, because the grammatical processes are largely cryptotypic), it is clear that when experience is ongoingly reconstrued, we do not jettison the accumulated knowledge and wisdom of earlier ages. We build on what was there before; and what was there before is lodged in the grammar, even though typically below the level of our conscious awareness.

Thus, in each of the three histories, the present always encapsulates the past. Every scientific text, however specialized and technical, contains a mixture of levels of wording, from most congruent to most metaphorical, right up to the end. All scientific registers, likewise however specialized and technical, construe the full meta-

121

phoric range of semantic space opened up by their own histories, right up to the present. And as children grow up and go through school, they learn the Attic mode of the grammar; but they still retain the meaning potential they have built up on the way. The Attic may predominate in the workplace, especially if they become bureaucrats; but they are likely to put on the Ionic or Doric at home, and even the Arcadian might come to the surface when they are telling stories to their children.

4.4 Scientific languages and standard languages

Not all the typical features of the languages of science are specially scientific. Scientific languages evolved in the context of, and as an aspect of, the evolution of nation states, and some of their features are simply those of a "standard" (or "literary") language. In this historical context, new demands were being made on people's semiotic potential: in particular, much of the discourse of those having authority and status was now being addressed to strangers, or printed in books which would be read by persons unknown, so there were no longer the shared experiences and shared expectations which shaped the discourse of medieval societies. Parts of the grammar were topologically realigned, new meanings being created by the intersecting of features from different corners of the system. Such changes were not taken up in the tongues that survived only as rural dialects.

Since words show up on the surface of lexicogrammar, one tends to think of such changes in terms of expanding vocabulary; but they reside in the grammar as a whole. Many of the changes observable in English had to do with restructuring the flow of information – what the Prague linguists, following Mathesius (1928) who first described the phenomenon, called "functional sentence perspective"; for example, the replacement of the Subject/Actor bond by the bonding of Subject with Theme; the increased use of the passive, and the development of a recursive tense system common to passive and active; the fuzzifying of the clear distinction between participants and circumstances; the spread of thematic equative clause types, and so on (see Halliday 1990, 2003). As these examples show, these changes are taking place in the spoken as well as in the written language; and they are quantitative rather than qualitative: the grammar does not suddenly invent new devices – rather, it realigns the probabilities, often foregrounding features that up to then have had only marginal status.

Such developments in a standard language are then picked up and further extended in specialized registers such as those of science. The nominal group in English provides a typical example. Its potential for expanding was always there, and can be seen already in Chaucer's *Treatise* in a few instances such as *the arch-meridian that is contained or intercepted between the zenith and the equinoctial*; it is further exploited in standard English, in commerce and administration, but taken to considerably greater lengths in the language of physical science. The main contributory factor in this further expansion is grammatical metaphor. Let me return now to the question why grammatical metaphor was critical to the development of scientific discourse – and ultimately, therefore, to the development of science itself.

4.5 Why grammatical metaphor?

The grammar has always had the power of metaphor; it is a con-comitant of a higher-order, stratified semiotic – once the brain splits content into semantics and grammar, it can match them up in more than one way. But why is metaphor particularly favoured by the grammar of experimental science?

In the construction of a scientific theory, two semiotic conditions need to be met. One is technicality: the grammar has to create technical meanings, purely virtual phenomena that exist only on the semiotic plane, as terms of a theory; and not as isolates, but organized into elaborate taxonomies. The other is rationality: the grammar has to create a form of discourse for reasoning from observation and experiment, drawing general conclusions and progressing from one step to another in sequences of logical argument.

The grammar's most powerful resource for creating taxonomies is the nominal group. This has evolved in categorizing entities: relatively stable elements that participate in processes (either centrally, as the medium through which the process is actualized, or in some more tangential role, as agency, beneficiary, location and so on). Such entities become complex, both in their own make-up and in their relations with other entities; the grammar manages this complexity (1) paradigmatically, by organizing them in taxonomies (*fruit* is a kind of *food*, *berry* is a kind of *fruit*, *raspberry* is a kind of *berry*), and (2) syn-tagmatically, by accommodating large amounts of lexical material in the structure (like the *red-and-silver diesel-engined London Transport double-decker ninety-seven horsepower omnibus* celebrated in popular song). The latter both extend the taxonomizing power and also allow for cross-classifying and the accrual of more temporary, instantial features – temporary qualities, quantities and deictic elements.

Let us contrast this with the verbal group. It is not that processes cannot be construed as taxonomies; in a limited way they can, at least paradigmatically (*walk, run* ... are kinds of *move*; *stroll, sidle* ... are kinds of *walk*). But the verbal group typically contains only one lexical element; it expands, instead, in grammatical systems, such as tense and phase – 'moments' of unfolding in time. In other words, what the grammar construes (congruently) as processes are precisely those phenomena that are not stable enough to accrue subclassifying features; whereas what the grammar construes (congruently) as entities are phenomena that are relatively stable, and hence accrue features which group them into classes. Thus the semogenic power of the nominal groups is at once both grammatical (its structural potential) and semantic (the nature of entities – as long as the grammar remains congruent, these are different sides of the same coin). And this characteristic of entities/nominal groups has already been greatly extended by the earlier development of technology. Thus there is a payoff, both grammatically and semantically, for construing phenomena as nouns.

4.6 Construing rationality

Rationality is not, of course, a prerogative of scientific discourse; Hasan (1992) has beautifully demonstrated the importance of reasoning in the conversation of three-year-old children. What is special about scientific discourse (apart from scientists' strong convictions about what constitutes proper grounds!) is (1) that it constructs an argument out of a long sequence of connected steps, and (2) that at any one juncture a large number of previous steps may be marshalled together as grounds for the next. The steps in an argument may involve any of a variety of logical–semantic relations; that of 'cause' is only one among many, though it can perhaps be seen as prototypical.

The natural unit for construing one such step is a clause. The grammar defines the clause not only as figure (a unit of experience) but also as message (a unit of information): a flow of meaning that measures out, and also mimics, the flux of experience (compare Matthiessen 1992; Martin 1992, Chapter 6; Halliday 1985/94, Chapter 3). Structurally, this takes the form of a movement from Theme to Rheme (following the analysis of the Prague school; this seems to have been the earliest view of the clause among the sophists in ancient Athens). The Theme is the stable part, the anchor, if I may vary the metaphor; and so it is typically construed as a noun (this sense of "Theme" was in fact the first meaning of Greek *onoma*, 'name', when used as a grammatical term). The typical thematic movement in the clause is that which becomes familiar to us in our nursery rhymes: *Little Polly Flinders sat among the cinders*, *The Man in the Moon came down quite soon* – typically, a person, of course, or some personified object (the virtual entities that constitute a child's first theory of reality). Now, this entity is stable not only in the experiential context but also textually, in the discursive context: once the discourse is in motion, the Theme will typically pick up something that has gone before. So, following *The Man in the Moon* we have *He went by the south*; following *Little Polly Flinders* we have *Her mother came and caught her*, and so on; with *he*, *her mother* as the Themes.

When we come to the discourse of science, where the text is progressing as a chain of reasoning, the Theme typically becomes a résumé of the argument that has gone before; and the only way to package a piece of argument so that it becomes a natural Theme of a clause is to turn it into a nominal group:

> If electrons were not absolutely indistinguishable, two hydrogen atoms would form a much more weakly bound molecule than they actually do. The absolute indistinguishability of the electrons in the two atoms gives rise to an 'extra' attractive force between them. (Layzer 1990, pp. 61–2)

> The surface of the earth is not strong enough to support a huge mass of mountains without deforming in some way. The deformation leads to a mass deficit under the mountains that compensates the excess mass on the surface. Compensation of this type is familiar ... (Hamilton and Maruhn 1986, p. 67)

Compare the example from Newton: "the Light will not be refracted enough, and for want of a sufficient Refraction will not converge" (*Opticks*, pp. 15–16). What have been presented clausally, as process or attributes (*electrons are indistinguishable*, *the surface of the earth deforms*, *light is not refracted enough*), are nominalized when they come to function as thematic support for developing the further argument.

These were brief examples, where the reasoning was very local; but the same pattern can be observed over any longer passage of scientific text. Scientific discourse is typically constructed out of sequences of connected steps, such that at any juncture a whole battery of previous steps may be marshalled as grounds for the next.

Now, a metaphorical construct of this kind can remain purely instantial – that is, functioning solely for the immediate requirements of the text:

> American vines in French vineyards remained healthy while the European stock died. The researchers concluded that the American species were resistant to the [phylloxera] louse. ... This breeding effort was anchored in the American species' resistance to phylloxera. ... Within a few years, however, the phylloxera resistance collapsed. (*New Scientist*, 17 April 1993)

– where *phylloxera resistance* becomes a virtual entity just for the discursive occasion: it does not stabilize. But some such constructs do stabilize; and this leads us to consider technicality.

4.7 Construing technicality

We saw in the glass–cracking example how a technical concept like *glass fracture growth rate* is built up logogenetically, along as the text unfolds. We have seen that this is dependent on grammatical metaphor: the semogenic power of the nominal group is brought into play through progressive nominalizing of the processes and qualities involved: from *glass can crack* (verb) to *a glass crack* (noun); from *glass cracks can grow* to *glass crack growth*; from *glass crack growth is faster* or *slower* to *glass crack growth rate*. At each step there is a semantic junction between the meaning 'process' (as in *crack*, *grow*) or quality (as in *fast/slow*) and the category meaning of the word class "noun", that is, 'entity, thing'. Thus the new noun is not simply a rewording; it is a remeaning, the creation of a new theoretical object in which are condensed both the historical value derived from observation and reasoning and the systemic value derived from functioning within a conceptual scheme. Martin (1990) refers to this aptly by the term "distillation"; as he puts it, "technical language both *compacts* and *changes the nature of* everyday words" (Halliday and Martin 1993, p. 172). We see this distillation process at work perhaps most explicitly in definition texts, such as the text on the definition of 'redox potential' (Chapter 3, Appendix text 3).

In that text the meaning of 'redox potential' is steadily distilled from wordings such as *the need to generate biochemical energy ... the most efficient energy-producing mechanism ... molecular oxygen is the*

*oxidizing agent . . . microorganisms can extract oxygen from other compounds
. . . how good an oxidizing agent it [the type of molecule] is in relation to
others.* All of this depends on grammatical metaphor, from less
technical (*requirements of life, the sequence continues*) to more technical
(*oxidation, respiration,* and of course *redox potential* itself). It is not
possible to construe technical knowledge, and therefore not possible
to develop a scientific theory, without exploiting the metaphorical
resources of the grammar (there is no unnecessary grammatical
metaphor in the "redox potential" text).

4.8 Can scientific metaphor be 'unpacked'?

Scientific discourse rests on combining theoretical technicality with
reasoned argument; and each of these relies on the same metaphorical resource within the grammar. Semantically, each relies on the
grammar's power of condensing extended meanings in a highly
structured, nominalized form. In the latter, it is a **textual** condensation, in which stretches of preceding matter are condensed
instantly, to serve as elements – typically thematic elements – in
the ongoing construal of information. This is a syntagmatic process,
in which a metaphoric entity is created for discourse purposes; and it
can always be unpacked. Instead of *the deformation leads to a mass deficit*
we could say *because it [the surface of the earth] is deformed there is not
enough mass*; the information flow would be less clear, but the
conceptual framework would not be affected. In the case of technicality, however, the condensation is **ideational**: it is a paradigmatic
process, in which the metaphoric entity is distilled from numerous
sources of related semantic input.

This is still the product of discursive processes, whereby what is
construed instantly becomes, step-by-step, systemic. This may
happen in the course of a single text; more often it takes place
cumulatively, as the body of literature from a particular subdiscipline accrues to form a (more or less coherent) macro-text. This
is how technical meanings are created; and these metaphors can no
longer be unpacked. The "technical term" of a scientific theory is
the congruent construal of a new entity that has been created by
distillation. The metaphorical power of the grammar makes it possible to bring new semiotic 'things' into being through the unfolding
of text. In the process, the metaphor ceases to be a metaphor; if we
borrow the analogy from lexical metaphor, it is "dead".

The grammar has always had this metaphorical power; it is an essential element in theorizing human experience, in the Doric, commonsense mode as well as in the Attic mode of technology and science. We have to be able to construe phenomena from different angles, not only to categorize them but also to cross-categorize them, and to create abstract 'things' with which we can make analogies to capture the different ways in which phenomena resemble and relate one to another.[6] So metaphor is part of everyday language; and it is not really surprising that, once the languages of science have elaborated it and developed modes of discourse that are entirely dependent on it, this elaborated form should find its way back into the language of everyday life. I started with the care label in my jacket, as an example of the favourite clause type of a science text; here is an example from a popular television magazine: *he also credits his former big size with much of his career success* − which, being unpacked, might read as *he also believes it is mainly because he used to be big that he has been successful in his career.* The only difference is that here the metaphor contributed neither to the rationality of the discourse nor to the technicality of the field.

4.9 Scientific metaphor as world view

It could be argued that a technical term, far from being a dead metaphor, is one that is very much alive. It may construe some concept, say in theoretical physics, which is so far from anything accessible to our perception that only a specialist is aware of any possible renewal of connection; but it is part of the activity of 'doing science', and highly functional in at least some people's lives. The fact that 'things' like entropy or quantum gravity exist only on the semiotic plane, created by the grammar, does not make them ultimately different from the categories of our daily language, which also had to be construed in the transformation of experience into meaning − they were not 'given' to us as readymade classes of objective phenomena. Science has no beginning; it is simply the continuation of the grammar's theorizing of ourselves and our relations with our environment.

Nevertheless, there is a difference. What I have called the "scientific metaphor" is not just the construal of experience − it is a **re**construal, by which the categories of common sense are challenged and realigned. I do not mean by that simply that science is not just common sense, and often runs directly counter to it; I mean that the grammar of science constructs a very different world view from that of everyday speech. As I tried to show earlier, grammatical metaphor is a steady drift towards **things**; and the prototype of a thing is a concrete object. Not just those phenomena which are congruently construed as qualities and processes, but even the logical relations between processes like time and cause, are construed as virtual things. And in the world of classical physics, this kind of semiotic transformation is ideologically very supportive: it is holding the world still, giving it stability and permanence, while you observe it, measure it and experiment with it. Whereas the grammar of daily life tolerates – or rather, celebrates – being indeterminate, varying and flowing, the elaborated, nominalizing grammar of science imposes determinacy, constancy and stasis. It construes a world that is made ultimately of things.

4.10 Questioning the nominalizing mode

And this is precisely why it has now come into disfavour. There has always been some resistance to it – eighteenth-century humanists already felt threatened by the "objectivity" of science, and the new scientific forms of language were at least partly to blame. For one thing, the ontological status of the 'things' that scientists construed by their metaphors was far from clear: what does it mean when anything is 'reified' in this way? (This had also worried William of Occam five centuries earlier. He is often quoted as warning about the **number** of such terms; but from the passage in question it seems to me he is concerned about their **status** – how to constrain them by reference to the requirements of theory.) But more importantly, I think, there is a sense in which they **are** felt to be 'dead' metaphors; when processes or qualities are reconstructed as nouns, not only do they become fixed and determinate – they also become timeless, taken outside of history as it were. It is very much easier to think of a process as reversible if you construe it as a noun, rather than as a verb. (In this connection it is interesting that Darwin, constructing a theory in which processes were anything but reversible, used relatively fewer nominalizing grammatical metaphors.)

But in the present century it is the scientists themselves who have come to question the universal authority of the noun. A number of leading physicists, prominently Niels Bohr and Werner Heisenberg, engaged seriously with the language of their discipline. More recently, one who paid special attention to language was David Bohm, who wrote in – and about – English. Bohm (1980) recognized that "every language form carries a kind of dominant or prevailing world view", and that "one of the major defects of the ordinary mode of using language is just its general implication that it is not restricting the world view in any way at all" (p. 46). He realized that it was not possible "suddenly to invent a whole new language", and suggested instead introducing "a *new mode* of language" which he called the "rheomode" (p. 30). As the name implies, this would foreground reality as continuous flow ("the world view implied in the rheomode is ... that *all* is an unbroken and individual whole movement" (p. 47)) rather than constructing it as discrete and fragmented ("the dominant form of subject-verb-object tends continually to lead to fragmentation" (p. 31)). In our language "nouns are taken as basic" (p. 34), whereas we need forms in which primary concepts can "be expressed in terms of *events* and *processes*" (p. 124).

Unfortunately for his argument, Bohm's view of language is naive and, one has to say, fragmented. He is preoccupied with morphology ("building up language forms so that any verb may be taken as the root form" (p. 36)), and with the "literal" (that is, etymological) meanings of words (for example, "the word de-scribe literally means to 'write down'" (p. 126)). Despite his claim of "a new grammatical construction, in which verbs are used in a new way" (p. 40), his proposals largely consist in inventing new vocabulary. But what is of interest here is that Bohm's observations about "ordinary" language are not really directed at ordinary language at all; they are directed towards the language of science. It is true, of course, that our ordinary language embodies an intrinsic world view, as I myself have been stressing all along; but it is a world view that is in many respects "rheomodal", whereas it is the language of science which makes things look fixtured and discrete, with its nominalizing metaphors and its favourite clause type of "this 'thing' is the cause of that 'thing'". The grammar of our mother tongue is clausal: it maintains a compromise between stability and flux, between things and processes. One way in which Bohm might have explored the issue would have been by asking whether scientists could try moving away from the Attic mode towards more Doric ways of theorizing about the world.

4.11 A discourse of knowledge and power

We can never be sure how much the Attic forms of discourse that evolved in modern science affect the ways we think and how we behave. It is just possible that a semiotic which foregrounds things at the expense of processes and relations – precisely because we are not aware that it is doing so – may be dysfunctional for the relations between ourselves as a species and our environment, and even for our interactions one with another (see Halliday 1990, 2003). But we can surely point to another problematic feature: namely, its exclusiveness and ritualistic power. We saw above how, as you move through an agnate series from the most congruent to the most metaphorical, while you gain on the textual front (higher organization of information), you lose on the ideational (Figure 4.12). Practically nothing remains, in the nominal group, of the explicit signalling of semantic relations that is present in the structure of the clause. The result is a multiple ambiguity: a clause such as *the high price of endothermy in terms of energy use is justified by enhanced muscle performance* has very many possible interpretations. (Like everything else, this feature varies with different languages. But in the one other language of science that I have investigated, Chinese, the effect is even more striking than it is in English (see Halliday 1993a).) Informed readers, of course, discard all readings except the one intended, without even noticing that they are possible. But not all readers may be informed.

So the language of science is difficult; and this has two related consequences. On the one hand, you have to be an expert in order to understand it; it is not enough merely to be educated and inquiring. So technical discourse soon becomes technocratic discourse, written by experts with the message 'this is too hard for you to understand; better leave the decisions to us' (see Lemke 1995, Chapter 4). On the other hand, it is stamped with authority, derived from the familiar equation of 'knowledge equals power'. So technical discourse is parodied by bureaucratic discourse, in which the Attic mode has no function at all in terms of reasoning and technicality but a great deal of function in the maintenance and exercise of power: we all recognize the semiotic flavouring of a wording such as *Failure to display permits as prescribed is considered a violation of the rules and will result in the imposition of a fine.* From this point of view, the metaphoric mode imported from science does affect human behaviour, if only in widening and perpetuating the divide between those who have access to it and those who have not.

131

4.12 Conclusion

It may be questioned how far science led the way; the languages of administration and the law were probably not far behind. But it was in science that the specific features of the Attic grammar were functional in relation to the discourse, as I have tried to demonstrate here: there are reasons for choosing the metaphoric variant 'this event is the consequence of that event' rather than the congruent 'that happened, so this happened'. Taken out of time, each is metaphoric for the other; but when we take account of their histories, phylogenetic, ontogenetic and logogenetic, then in each case the Doric variant is the congruent one – the one which evolves earlier, develops earlier and unfolds earlier. The congruent is how the grammar **construes** our experience, the metaphoric is how it **re**construes, with various intermediate forms of wording along the route.

When the meaning is reworded in this way, it ceases to be the same meaning; there is a semantic junction between the category meanings of the congruent wording and the (congruent) category meanings of the classes being deployed metaphorically. The most prominent effect is that of nominalization: in *engine failure*, 'fail' is construed as a junction of 'process' and 'thing', while the congruent 'thing', the 'engine', becomes a classifier, one of a taxonomy of failures along with *crop failure*, *heart failure* and so on. But there are other junctions besides: thus, when the relator 'so' becomes a verb, *caused*, there is a hybrid of 'logical-semantic relation construed as process'. One or two such instances in isolation would carry little weight; but when new registers evolve in which the metaphorized grammar takes over, this amounts to reconstructing the model of human experience. I tried to suggest this by referring to the "Doric" and the "Attic" mode. At the same time, however, the past is always present: the linguistic system, the human speaker and the instantiated scientific text, however locked into the Attic style, draw their potential for meaning from the grammar's total range of semiotic resources.

We are all now expected to look "beyond 2000"; so I must end by asking: 'Where next?' I do not know. There are pressures for change. There are democratic pressures to make science more accessible: both in the work of some outstanding popular science writers and science journalists (and Oxford has a distinguished scholar as Professor of Public Understanding of Science, Richard

Dawkins), and in approaches to science education which take cognizance of the way science is construed in language (especially in Australia; see the extensive bibliography contained in Martin 1993). There are changes in how knowledge is structured and how knowledge is disseminated: boundaries are being redrawn along transdisciplinary, thematic lines, and people are exchanging meanings in forms of discourse which, although typically written, are dialogic and interactive in ways that were formerly restricted to speech. We can discover the ongoing effects of all these changes by analysing what happens in the grammar: noting the alternatives that emerge and exploring their semogenic potential. We can observe how semiotic junction takes place at a higher level, where different genres meet and their grammars clash. We saw something of this in earlier science fiction; I am not sure how much of this momentum has been maintained. But there is another domain where science intersects with literature, namely poetry. I believe it is just about 2100 years since Lucretius was born. Perhaps we could have a new *De rerum natura*, with those atoms now deconstrued into up, down, strange (and still stranger) quarks.

Notes

1. See Halliday 1985/94.
2. For the semantic analysis see Halliday and Matthiessen (1999).
3. From Michalske and Bunker, 'The fracturing of glass', *Scientific American*, December 1987. The analysis is fairly cautious; it could be argued that every instance of *crack* as a noun involves grammatical metaphor, the only congruent construal of *crack* being as a verb (but the evidence from child language would not support this; compare on the three 'histories', below). An analysis of this passage in terms of the different types of grammatical metaphor was given in Chapter 2.
4. More accurately: not functioning as Thing in the 'Outer' (ranking) nominal group. The instances of *glass*, in line 1, and *stone*, in line 5, are functioning as Thing, but in a non-ranking, or "rankshifted", nominal group which as a whole is functioning as Qualifier in the ranking group (*the fracture [of glass]*, *the impact [of a stone]*).
5. See Halliday and Martin (1993) for a comparison of the sciences and the humanities, especially Chapters 8–11.
6. The resources for metaphor are inherent in the nature of grammar, or rather in the higher order, stratified semiotic of which grammar is the distinctive part: since grammars can categorize, they can also cross-categorize. We can illustrate this from ancient Greek, since that is

where our western scientific discourses originated. Consider how Greek construed systematic patterns of relationship between processes and things: from ποιέω 'make', πράσσω 'do', were derived ποιητής 'one who makes', πρακτήρ (later πράκτωρ), 'one who does'; and also ποίημα 'thing made' and πρᾶγμα 'thing done'. These last, especially πρᾶγμα which came to mean 'work' and then, more abstractly, 'affair', have moved a little distance away from the concrete (the prototypical meaning of the category of noun), but they are transcategorizing derivations rather than metaphors. There is then a third type of derived noun, represented by ποίησις, πρᾶξις: these, by contrast, are metaphoric – they are the **names** of processes ('a making', 'a doing'). It was this last type that provided the resource for key terms in Greek science, like κίνησις 'motion' (later also κίνημα), φυσις, 'nature', βλέψις 'sight', αλλοίωσς 'change', παραλλαξις 'alternating motion' and so on. These metaphorical 'things' appear at the very 'beginning' of science – except that they show that science has no beginning: it is simply a continuation of the grammar's theorizing of human experience.

7. *New Scientist* 1979, 27 May 1995, p. 43, slightly adapted.

PART TWO

SCIENTIFIC ENGLISH

EDITOR'S INTRODUCTION

In Chapter 5, *On the language of physical science*, Professor Halliday explores how the 'prototypical syndrome of features that characterizes scientific English' evolved over the past four to six centuries, and how this combination of related features has come to provide the semiotic base for the emergence of physical science.

Since the focus is on scientific English, Professor Halliday begins by looking at Chaucer's *Treatise on the Astrolabe* (c. 1390), which represents a kind of technical, perhaps proto-scientific discourse which is received into English from classical Greek via classical and medieval Latin. In Chaucer's *Treatise*, Professor Halliday identifies two first steps towards nominalized discourse: (i) technical nouns, and (ii) nominal groups with iterated phrase-&-group Qualifier. A change in direction is apparent in Newton's *Treatise on Opticks* (published 1704; written 1675–87), which contains nouns which are not part of a technical taxonomy (e.g. *emergence, whiteness, inequality, propagation*), but which are instead names of processes or attributes. Nominalizing in this way – 'packaging a complex phenomenon into a single semiotic entity, by making it one element of clause structure' – served the rhetorical purposes of scientific writers, like Newton, who were engaged in the discourse of experimentation and needed 'to create a discourse that moves forward by logical and coherent steps, each building on what has gone before'. Professor Halliday notes similar developments in Priestley's *The History and Present State of Electricity, with Original Experiments*, published in three volumes in the 1760s.

A point raised in Chapter 5, and more fully developed in Chapter 6, *Some grammatical problems in scientific English*, is that learners often find scientific discourse difficult to read, causing them to feel excluded and alienated from the subject matter. Apart from it being a developmental matter – 'children find it hard to deal with grammatical metaphor until they reach about secondary school age', Professor Halliday identifies several characteristics of scientific discourse which make it problematic for learners. He illustrates and discusses these features under the following headings:

(1) interlocking definitions
(2) technical taxonomies
(3) special expressions
(4) lexical density
(5) syntactic ambiguity
(6) grammatical metaphor
(7) semantic discontinuity

The features of scientific discourse are not arbitrary. Rather, argues Professor Halliday,

> they evolved to meet the needs of scientific method, and of scientific argument and theory. They suit the expert; and by the same token they cause difficulty to the novice. In that respect, learning science is the same thing as learning the language of science. Students have to master these difficulties; but in doing so they are also mastering scientific concepts and principles.

Professor Halliday's interest in the language of science is 'as a linguist and more specifically as a grammarian' (Chapter 7, *On the grammar of scientific English*). As he explains,

> I have been interested in the evolution of scientific forms of discourse, and their relation to everyday language – especially spoken language, and especially the spoken language of small children; as well as their relation to other forms of written adult language, especially to the standard language of the modern nation state (of which in some sense scientific language is simply a particular case).

He describes his approach as being focused on the 'micro' aspects of scientific language, 'specifically on the grammar of the scientific clause; because that, to my mind, is where the essential work is done – where the meaning is made'. Although complex, dense and full of jargon, scientific language has to its credit the fact that it 'has construed for us the vast theoretical edifice of modern knowledge, constantly expanding its meaning potential without, up to the present at least, showing any signs that its capacity for expansion is limited, though presumably it must be limited in some way or other'.

As a language educator, Professor Halliday considers how children 'find their way into scientific language', expressing concern for those who never do find their way in, and 'remain always shut out from the adult modes of scientific discourse, never able to break the code'. Professor Halliday points to experience in Australia which suggests that

> children can be helped quite considerably if they are explicitly taught about the nature of technical and scientific language, including both its generic structures and its grammatical structures, at the same time as they are engaging with the scientific disciplines themselves. This as it were lets them into the secret, and helps them understand why they are faced with all these new and exotic ways of meaning.

The origins of scientific language are to be found in the language of the physical sciences; 'the semantic styles that evolved were those of physical systems and of the mathematics that is constructed to explain them', writes Professor Halliday in Chapter 8, *Writing science: literacy and discursive power*. This same discourse was later extended to other, 'more complex kinds of system: first biological, then social systems'. What began as the language of the physical sciences has since taken over as model and as norm; it is the language of literacy. What began as 'forward-looking' has since become 'increasingly anti-democratic: its arcane grammatical metaphor sets apart those who understand it and shields them from those who do not'.

What does the future hold for science and language? 'There are signs that people are looking for new ways of meaning,' writes Halliday, 'for a grammar which, instead of reconstructing experience so that it becomes accessible only to a few, takes seriously its own beginnings in everyday language and construes a world that is recognizable to all those who live in it'.

Chapter Five

ON THE LANGUAGE OF PHYSICAL SCIENCE (1988)

1

The term "scientific English" is a useful label for a generalized functional variety, or register, of the modern English language. To label it in this way is not to imply that it is either stationary or homogeneous. The term can be taken to denote a semiotic space within which there is a great deal of variability at any one time, as well as continuing diachronic evolution. The diatypic variation can be summarized in terms of field, tenor and mode: in field, extending, transmitting or exploring knowledge in the physical, biological or social sciences; in tenor, addressed to specialists, to learners or to laymen, from within the same group (e.g. specialist to specialist) or across groups (e.g. lecturer to students); and in mode, phonic or graphic channel, most congruent (e.g. formal 'written language' with graphic channel) or less so (e.g. formal with phonic channel), and with variation in rhetorical function – expository, hortatory, polemic, imaginative and so on. So for example in the research programme in the Linguistic Properties of Scientific English carried out at University College London during the 1960s the grid used was one of field by tenor, with three subject areas (biology, chemistry and physics) by three 'brows', high, middle and low (learned journals, college textbooks, and magazines for the general public).

This space–time variation in no way distinguishes scientific

'On the language of physical science', from *Registers of Written English: Situational Factors and Linguistic Features*, edited by Mohsen Ghadessy, London: Pinter, 1988. Reprinted by permission of the Continuum International Publishing Group Ltd.

English from other registers. A register is a cluster of associated features having a greater-than-random (or rather, greater than predicted by their unconditioned probabilities) tendency to co-occur; and, like a dialect, it can be identified at any delicacy of focus (cf. Hasan 1973). Whatever the focus, of course, there will always be mixed or borderline cases; but by and large "scientific English" is a recognizable category, and any speaker of English for whom it falls within the domain of experience knows it when he sees it or hears it.

In this paper I propose to focus on the physical sciences, and to adopt a historical perspective – one which in turn will restrict me to the written mode, since we have had no access to spoken scientific English until very recently. I shall look mainly at material that was written (in its time) for specialists; but seeing the specialist not as a pre-existing persona but as someone brought into being by the discourse itself. I shall concentrate on what seems to me to be the prototypical syndrome of features that characterizes scientific English; and what I hope to suggest is that we can explain how this configuration evolved – provided, first, that we consider the features together rather than each in isolation; and secondly, that we are prepared to interpret them at every level, in lexicogrammatical, semantic, and socio-semiotic (situational and cultural) terms.

Let us begin with a short example:

> The rate of crack growth depends not only on the chemical environment but also on the magnitude of the applied stress. The development of a complete model for the kinetics of fracture requires an understanding of how stress accelerates the bond–rupture reaction.
>
> In the absence of stress, silica reacts very slowly with water...
>
> (Michalske and Bunker 1987, p. 81)

Here are instances of some of the features that form part of the syndrome referred to above:

1   the expression *rate of growth*, a nominal group having as Head/ Thing the word *rate* which is the name of an attribute of a process, in this case a variable attribute: thus *rate* agnate to *how quickly?*;

2   the expression *crack growth*, a nominal group having as Head/ Thing the word *growth* which is the name of a process, agnate to *(it) grows*; and as Classifier the word *crack* which is the name of an attribute resulting from a process, agnate to *cracked* (e.g. *the glass is cracked*), as well as of the process itself,

141

agnate to (*the glass*) *has cracked; crack growth* as a whole agnate to *cracks grow*;

3   the nominal group *the rate of crack growth*, having as Qualifier the prepositional phrase *of crack growth*; this phrase agnate to a qualifying clause (*the rate*) *at which cracks grow*;

4   the function of *the rate of crack growth* as Theme in the clause; the clause itself being initial, and hence thematic, in the paragraph;

5   the finite verbal group *depends on* expressing the relationship between two things, '*a* depends on *x*': a form of causal relationship comparable to *is determined by*;

6   the expression *the magnitude of the applied stress*: see points 1 and 3 above; its function as culminative in the clause (i.e. in the unmarked position for New information);

7   the iterated rankshift (nominal group in prepositional phrase in nominal group in ...) in *the development [of [a complete model [for [the kinetics [of [fracture]]]]]*;

8   the finite verbal group *requires* expressing the relationship between two things, *development ... requires ... understanding* (cf. point 5 above);

9   the parallelism between *(rate of) growth ... depends on ... (magnitude of) stress* and *development ... requires ... understanding*, but contrasting in that the former expresses an external relationship (third person, 'in rebus': 'if (this) is stressed, (that) will grow'), while the latter expresses an internal relationship (first-&-second person, 'in verbis': 'if (we) want to model, (we) must understand') (cf. Halliday and Hasan 1976, pp. 240 ff.);

10   the expression *an understanding of how* ..., with the noun functioning as Head / Thing being the name of a mental process: agnate to *(we) must understand*; and with the projected clause *how stress accelerates ...* functioning, by rank shift, in the Qualifier;

11   the clause *stress accelerates the bond–rupture reaction*, with finite verbal group *accelerates* as the relationship between two things which are themselves processes: one brings about a change in an attribute of the other, agnate to *makes ... happen more quickly*;

12   the simple structure of each clause (three elements only: nominal group + verbal group + nominal group / prepositional phrase) and the simple structure of each sentence (one clause only);

13   the relation of all these features to what has gone before in the discourse.

To pursue the last point more fully we should have to reproduce a lengthy passage of text; but the following will make it clear what is meant. Prior to *the rate of crack growth* we had had, in the preceding five paragraphs (citing in reverse order, i.e. beginning with the nearest): *speed up the rate at which cracks grow, will make slow cracks grow, the crack has advanced*, and *as a crack grows*. If we now go right back to the initial section of the text, in the second paragraph we find (*the mechanism by which*) *glass cracks*, (*the stress needed to*) *crack glass*, and (*the question of how*) *glass cracks*; and if we pursue the trail back to the title of the paper, *The Fracturing of Glass*. The title, in other words, is a technical nominalization involving grammatical metaphor; in the text, the metaphor is constructed step by step, (*glass*) *cracks* – *to crack* (*glass*) – *a crack* (*grows*) – *the crack* (*has advanced*) – (*make*) *cracks* (*grow*) – (*rate of*) *crack growth*. We might predict that later on in the text we would find *crack growth rate*, and indeed we do: *we can decrease the crack growth rate 1,000 times*. Thus the text itself creates its grammar, instantially, as it goes along.

Whenever we interpret a text as "scientific English", we are responding to clusters of features such as those we have been able to identify in this short paragraph. But it is the combined effect of a number of such related features, and the relations they contract throughout the text as a whole, rather than the obligatory presence of any particular ones, that tells us that what is being constructed is the discourse of science.

2

Let me now attempt to give a very brief sketch of how these features evolved. In doing so I shall refer to text examples from various periods; the passages cited are typical of the texts in question, whereas the texts themselves would have been at the frontier of their genre at the time.

In around 1390 Chaucer wrote what is now known as his *Treatise on the Astrolabe*, explaining the workings of this instrument to his son Lowis, to whom he had given it as a present on his tenth birthday. In this treatise we find the two first steps towards nominalized discourse: (i) technical nouns, which are either parts of the astrolabe or geometric and mathematical abstractions (such as *latitude, declinacioun, solsticioun*), for example (I.17):

> The plate under thy riet ['grid'] is descryved ['inscribed'] with 3
> principal cercles; of whiche the leste ['smallest'] is cleped ['called'] the

143

cercle of Cancer, by-cause that the heved ['head'], of Cancer turneth evermor consentrik up-on the same cercle. In this heved of Cancer is the grettest declinacioun northward of the sonne. And ther-for is he cleped the Solsticioun of Somer; whiche declinacioun, after Ptholome, is 23 degrees and 50 minutes, as wel in Cancer as in Capricorne.

and (ii) nominal groups with iterated phrase-&-group Qualifier, especially in the more mathematical passages; for example

the latitude [of [any place [in [the region]]]] is the distance [from [the zenith]] [to [the equinoctial]]

The favoured clause types are either relational, as in the earlier passage (attributive for assigning properties, identifying for definitions), or material and mental – these latter in giving instructions, and hence typically imperative as in (II.17):

Tak the altitude of this sterre whan he is on the est side of the lyne meridional, as ney as thou mayst gesse; and tak an assendent a-non right ['straight ahead'] by som maner sterre fix which that thou knowest; and for-get nat the altitude of the firste sterre, ne thyn assendent. And whan that this is don, espye diligently whan this same firste sterre passeth any-thing the south westward, and hath him a-non right in the same noumbre of altitude on the west side of this lyne meridional as he was caught on the est side; . . .

Temporal and causal-conditional clause complexes are formed with *when, if, because* (hypotactic), and with *for, therefore* (paratactic); the causal ones are used particularly in explaining why something is called what it is. There is also another kind of hypotactic clause complex, a form of non-defining relative that is rare in modern English; an example was *which declination, after Ptolemy* . . . above (and cf. *the names of the stars are written in the margin of the grid where they are located; of which stars the small point is called the centre*). This is used for tracking an entity from one step in the text to another.

Chaucer's *Treatise* represents a kind of technical, perhaps protoscientific discourse which is received into English from classical Greek via classical and medieval Latin. It contains technical nouns, both concrete–technological and abstract–scientific; extended nominal groups, especially mathematical; clause complexes which carry forward the argument, of the form '*a*, so / then *x*' or '. . . *b* . . .; which *b* . . .'; and clauses expressing two main fields, (i) the events under study, process type typically relational, for definitions and attributions, and (ii) the activity of doing science (using the astrolabe), process types material and mental, for doing and observing +

thinking. These are the lexicogrammatical motifs of a text in which scientific English is being conceived.

3

For registering the birth of scientific English we shall take Newton's *Treatise on Opticks* (published 1704; written 1675–87). Newton creates a discourse of experimentation; in place of Chaucer's instructions for use he has descriptions of action – not 'you do this' but 'I did that'. The clauses here are again material, for doing, and mental, for observing and reasoning (*I held / stopped / removed the Prism; I looked through the Prism upon the hole*); and the observations now frequently project, as in *I observed the length of its refracted image to be many times greater than its breadth, and that the most refracted part thereof appeared violet, ...* Sample text (Experiment 4):

In the Sun's Beam which was propagated into the Room through the hole in the Window-shut, at the distance of some Feet from the hole, I held the Prism in such a Posture, that its Axis might be perpendicular to that Beam. Then I looked through the Prism upon the hole, and turning the Prism to and fro about its Axis, to make the Image of the Hole ascend and descend, when between its two contrary Motions it seemed Stationary, I stopp'd the Prism, that the Refractions of both sides of the refracting Angle might be equal to each other, as in the former Experiment. In this situation of the Prism viewing through it the said Hole, I observed the length of its refracted Image to be many times greater than its breadth, and that the most refracted part thereof appeared violet, the least refracted red, the middle parts blue, green and yellow in order. The same thing happen'd when I removed the Prism out of the Sun's Light, and looked through it upon the hole shining by the Light of the Clouds beyond it. And yet if the Refraction were done regularly according to one certain Proportion of the Sines of Incidence and Refraction as is vulgarly supposed, the refracted Image ought to have appeared round.

So then, by these two Experiments it appears, that in Equal Incidences there is a considerable inequality of Refractions. But whence this inequality arises, whether it be that some of the incident Rays are refracted more, and others less, constantly, or by chance, or that one and the same Ray is by Reflection disturbed, shatter'd, dilated, and as it were split and spread into many diverging Rays, as *Grimaldo* supposes, does not yet appear by these Experiments, but will appear by those that follow.

Such descriptions often come in the passive, as in *the Sun's Beam which was propagated into the Room through the hole in the Window-shut, one and the same Ray is by Reflection disturbed, shatter'd, dilated, and as it were split and spread into many diverging Rays*. Note that these have nothing to do with the "suppressed person" passive favoured by modern teachers and scientific editors, which came into fashion only late in the nineteenth century. They are simply the passive in its typical function in English: that of achieving the balance of information the speaker or writer intends – often describing the result of an experimental step, where the Theme is something other than the Actor in the process (*the Ray . . . is shatter'd*). If the discourse context requires Actor as Theme Newton displays no coyness about using *I*.

When describing the results of an experiment Newton often uses intricate clause complexes involving both expansion and projection, of the form 'I observed that, when I did *a*, *x* happened'. The mathematical sections, on the other hand, display the complementary type of complexity: a single clause with only three elements, but very long and complex nominal groups, as in the final two paragraphs of the following (Experiment 8):

I found moreover, that when Light goes out of Air through several contiguous refracting Mediums as through Water and Glass, and thence goes out again into Air, whether the refracting Superficies be parallel or inclin'd to one another, that Light as often as by contrary Refractions 'tis so corrected, that it emergeth in Lines parallel to those in which it was incident, continues ever after to be white. But if the emergent Rays be inclined to the incident, the Whiteness of the emerging Light will by degrees in passing on from the Place of Emergence, become tinged in its Edges with Colours. This I try'd by refracting Light with Prisms of Glass placed within a Prismatick Vessel of Water. Now those Colours argue a diverging and separation of the heterogeneous Rays from one another by means of their unequal Refractions, as in what follows will more fully appear. And, on the contrary, the permanent whiteness argues, that in like Incidences of the Rays there is no such separation of the emerging Rays, and by consequence no inequality of their whole Refractions. Whence I seem to gather the two following Theorems.

1   The Excesses of the Sines of Refraction of several sorts of Rays above their common Sine of Incidence when the Refractions are made out of divers denser Mediums immediately into one and the same rarer Medium, suppose of Air, are to one another in a given Proportion.

2   The Proportion of the Sine of Incidence to the Sine of Refraction of
one and the same sort of Rays out of one Medium into another, is
composed of the Proportion of the Sine of Incidence to the Sine of
Refraction out of the first Medium into any third Medium, and of
the Proportion of the Sine of Incidence to the Sine of Refraction
out of that third Medium into the second Medium.

Each of the two numbered paragraphs consists of one clause; the
verbal groups are *are* and *is composed of*, each having one huge
nominal on either side of it. Contrast the first sentence beginning *I
found moreover*, ..., where the nominal groups are very simple, but
the structure of the sentence, as a clause complex, is highly intricate:

$$\alpha \; \char`\^ \; `\beta(^{\times}\beta(1 \; \char`\^ \; {}^{+}2) \; \char`\^ \; \alpha(^{\times}\beta(1 \; \char`\^ \; {}^{+}2) \; \char`\^ \; \alpha(\alpha \; \char`\^ \; {}^{\times}\beta(\alpha \; \char`\^ \; {}^{\times}\beta))))$$

What about the technical terms? These fall under five main
headings: (1) general concepts, e.g. Light, Colour, Ray, Beam,
Image, Axis; (2) field: specific (optical), e.g. Incidence, Refraction,
Medium; (3) field: general (mathematical), e.g. Proportion, Excess,
Sine; (4) apparatus and its use, e.g. Prism, Lens, Superficies, Vessel;
and (5) methodology, e.g. Experiment, Trial, Theorem. These seem
to be a simple extension of what we found in Chaucer. When we
look more closely, however, we find something rather different
happening. Some of the nouns are words like *emergence*, *whiteness*,
inequality, *propagation*, which are not within the realm of the technical but are the names of processes or of attributes (agnate to *emerge*,
white, *unequal*, *propagate*); they are often printed without a capital
letter. Let us consider one example:

> Now those Colours argue a diverging and separation of the hetero-
> geneous Rays from one another by means of their unequal
> Refractions, ...

Why does Newton use nouns to refer to processes (*diverging*,
separation) which are not part of the technical taxonomies? – instead
of writing *those Colours argue that the heterogeneous Rays diverge and
separate from one another*, or even (since we and not the colours do the
arguing) *from those colours we could argue* ['infer'] *that* ....
    To explain this grammatical metaphor we have to look at the
context, which is the paragraph from *I found moreover* ... down to ...
their whole Refractions. By nominalizing in this way, Newton is
achieving two important discoursal effects:

> (1) packaging a complex phenomenon into a single semiotic
> entity, by making it one element of clause structure, so that

(2) its rhetorical function – its place in the unfolding argument – is rendered fully explicit.

What is this rhetorical function? Or rather, what are these rhetorical functions? – since there are in fact two functions in question, related to each other but distinct. One is the function of Theme, defined in terms of a Theme + Rheme structure; the other is that of New, defined in terms of a Given + New structure.

The Theme is the element that constitutes the point of departure for the message; this is signalled, in English, by first position in the clause. Provided the thematic element is also Given (i.e. non-New), the rhetorical effect is that of **backgrounding**.

The New is the element that constitutes the point of information for the message; this is signalled, in English, by nuclear prominence in the tone group. Provided the informational element is also Rheme (i.e. non-Theme), the rhetorical effect is that of **foregrounding**.

Usually, the pattern of mapping of Theme + Rheme and Given + New on to one another is of this unmarked kind: the Theme is something that is given, and the New is something that is rhematic. This is especially true in written English, where (since there can be no tonic prominence until it is read aloud) the assumption is that the New matter will come in its unmarked position, namely at the end of a clause.

Where the Theme is also Given, and thus typically refers to something that has gone before, it performs a powerful cohesive function in a text: 'you remember what I said just now? – well we're going to move on from there'. This is obviously essential to scientific discourse. But 'what I said just now' is often likely to be the summation of a fairly complex argument, as in the result of Newton's experiment by which he showed that ... *the Light ... that ... emergeth continues ever after to be white*. Newton cannot repeat the whole of this as it stands because it could not form a component part of a new clause; so he packages it into a nominalization *the Whiteness of the emerging Light*, which he can then make thematic. The element is in this way 'backgrounded' as a point of departure.

In the next sentence he also wants to present a rather complex argument, but this time having the complementary status of New. So again he uses this kind of nominalized packaging: ... *a diverging and separation of the heterogeneous Rays ... by means of their unequal Refractions*. This is put in culminative position in the clause and hence is interpreted as having tonic prominence. The element is in this way 'foregrounded' as a point of information.

Thus the device of nominalizing, far from being an arbitrary or ritualistic feature, is an essential resource for constructing scientific discourse. We see it emerging in the language of this period, when the foundations of an effective register for codifying, transmitting and extending the "new learning" are rapidly being laid down.

If so much of the lexical content is nominalized, what is left over for the verb? In *those Colours argue . . .*, what Newton is treating as the 'process' is the act of reasoning; or rather, since it is the Colours that are doing the arguing, the relationship of proof that he is setting up between his experimental results and his conclusions. This is one of two motifs that are typically represented by a verb: proving, showing, suggesting and the like. The other motif that is treated in this way is the relationship that is being set up between the processes themselves, e.g. by the verb *arises* in Experiment 4: . . . *it appears, that in Equal Incidences there is a considerable inequality of Refractions. But whence this inequality arises,* . . . It may be easier to discuss this by reference to another example taken from elsewhere in Newton's writings.

> The explosion of gunpowder arises therefore from the violent action whereby all the Mixture . . . is converted into Fume and Vapour.

The clause again contains two nominalized processes: one backgrounded, *The explosion of gunpowder* (if Newton had written *Gunpowder explodes because . . .*, this would have had only *gunpowder*, not its exploding, as Theme); the other foregrounded, *the violent action whereby . . .* (enabling the whole of 'the mixture is violently converted into fume and vapour' to be packaged into a single element). But in this instance the verb, *arises (from)*, expresses the relationship between these two processes: one is caused by the other.

In other words, what is being set up as the 'process', by being represented as a verb, is in fact a relation **between** processes: either external '*a causes x to happen*', or internal '*b causes me to think γ*'. Of course, cause is not the only relationship that can be expressed in this way; eventually most of the major categories of expansion come to be represented as verbs (i.e. exposition, exemplification, clarification; addition, variation; time, space, manner, cause, condition, concession; cf. Halliday 1985/94). But cause may have been the one that led the way.

This pattern, of a one-clause sentence consisting of process$_1$ (nominal group) + relation (verbal group) + process$_2$ (nominal group/prepositional phrase), has not yet taken over; it is just coming into prominence. The typical motifs of the *Opticks*, together with their lexicogrammatical realizations, could perhaps be summarized as follows:

(i) descriptions of experiments: intricate clause complexes; very little grammatical metaphor; abstract nouns as technical terms of physics;

(ii) arguments and conclusions from these: less intricate clause complexes; some nominalizations with grammatical metaphor; abstract nouns as non-technical terms (typically processes or attributes);

(iii) mathematical formulations: clause simplexes ('simple sentences' of one clause only), typically of the form '$a = x$', where a, x are long lexically dense nominal groups with multiple group + phrase embedding; abstract nouns as mathematical technical terms.

But this is already a form of discourse in which the textual organization of the clause, as a movement from a backgrounded 'this is where we are' to a foregrounded 'this is where we are going', has become a powerful resource for the construction and transmission of knowledge.

4

There will be space to pause once more along the journey to the present day, to look at the language used by a scientist writing some fifty years after Isaac Newton, namely Joseph Priestley. Priestley's *The History and Present State of Electricity, with Original Experiments* was published in three volumes in the 1760s. This sense of *electricity*, meaning 'the study of electricity', is less familiar today, except perhaps in the collocation *electricity and magnetism*; in Priestley's work it is one of an already large number of derivatives of *electric* using the borrowed resources of Graeco–Latin morphology: *electricity, electrical, electrify, electrification, electrician* (a researcher, not someone who comes to mend the wiring); and there is a wealth of terms built up from these, such as *electric light, electric fire* (also not in the modern sense!), *electric fluid, electric circuits, electrical battery, electrical experiment; excited electricity, communicative electricity, medical electricity, conductor of electricity; positive and negative electricity* (cf. *let a person be electrified negatively*), *electric shock* and so on. (Electric shocks were regularly administered in the treatment of paralytic conditions such as tetanus; and also as a pastime, to be transmitted along a human chain – in one instance stretched across the river Thames!) The importance of these terms is that they now begin to form a complex lexical taxonomy, for a defined branch of physics known as 'electricity'.

Meanwhile the grammar has continued to develop along the lines we have already identified. Here is a typical passage, following the section heading *The Theory of Positive and Negative Electricity*:

> According to this theory, all the operations of electricity depend upon one fluid *sui generis*, extremely subtile and elastic, dispersed through the pores of all bodies; by which the particles of it are as strongly attracted, as they are repelled by one another.
> When the equilibrium of this fluid in any body is not disturbed; that is, when there is in any body neither more nor less of it than its natural share, or than that quantity which it is capable of retaining by its own attraction, it does not discover itself to our senses by any effect. The action of the rubber upon an electric disturbs this equilibrium, occasioning a deficiency of the fluid in one place, and a redundancy of it in another.
> The equilibrium being forcibly disturbed, the mutual repulsion of the particles of the fluid is necessarily exerted to restore it....

Let us track two motifs through this piece of discourse. (1) The first paragraph contains a description, which we could modify slightly as follows: the particles of the fluid are as strongly attracted by the pores as they are repelled by one another. In the next paragraph, this is summarized in the form of an abstract technical term *equilibrium*, which functions as Head of a nominal group *the equilibrium of this fluid in any body*, this nominal group functioning as Theme in a clause which is also thematic. Equilibrium is now established as a thing, which can be maintained, disturbed and restored; and the argument can proceed. (2) One component of this equilibrium is that the particles of the fluid are repelled by one another. This too is then picked up and backgrounded: *the mutual repulsion of the particles of the fluid*. In the earlier formulation, the Theme is *the particles of the fluid*; what is news is that they are repelled by one another. This is no longer news, but is now to be taken for granted so as to lead on to some further news, in this case the effect it has in restoring the equilibrium; so it has to be packaged as a single Theme, and this can be achieved only by nominalization, so that *repel + one another* is reworded as *mutual repulsion*, with *the particles of the fluid* as its

Qualifier. This is the name of a happening; and the verbal group, *is exerted*, simply tells us that it happens.

By this complex grammatical metaphor, the process of repelling has been reworded to look like an object: *repulsion*. Under this pressure of the discourse, the nominal elements in the clause are gradually taking over the whole of the semantic content, leaving the verb to express the relationship between these nominalized processes. After this point has been elaborated, the following paragraph uses the same device to present an alternative theory:

> Some of the patrons of the hypothesis of positive and negative electricity conceive otherwise of the immediate cause of this repulsion. They say that, as the dense electric fluid, surrounding two bodies negatively electrified, acts equally on all sides of those bodies, it cannot occasion their repulsion. Is not the repulsion, say they, owing rather to an accumulation of the electric fluid on the surfaces of the two bodies; which accumulation is produced by the attraction of the bodies, and the difficulty the fluid finds in entering them? This difficulty in entering is supposed to be owing, chiefly, to the *air* on the surface of bodies, which is probably a little condensed there; . . .

Every sentence in that extract would serve to illustrate the point; let us take just the one beginning *Is not the repulsion* . . . If we 'unpack' this grammatical metaphor we might arrive at some wording such as:

> Do not [the electric atmospheres] repel each other because electric fluid has accumulated on the surfaces of the two bodies, [which in turn is] because the bodies are attracted and the fluid cannot easily enter them?

But when the happenings are expressed congruently, as verbs (*repel, accumulate, attract*), the discourse patterning is lost; we no longer have the appropriate thematic and informational movement, the periodicity of backgrounding and foregrounding. The metaphorical variant, by using nouns, gives these processes an explicit value with respect to each other in the temporal progression of the discourse; and by a further metaphor uses verbs to construct their semantic interdependency: *occasion, is owing to, is produced by*. The whole configuration is an immensely powerful resource for the semiotic construction of reality.

5

It is not that these grammatical resources were invented by scientific writers. What the scientists did was to take resources that already existed in English and bring them out of hiding for their own rhetorical purposes: to create a discourse that moves forward by logical and coherent steps, each building on what has gone before. And the initial context for this was the kind of argumentation that was called for by the experimental method in physical science.

Here is a brief summary of the features we have taken into account:

(1) Nominal elements:
  – form technical taxonomies
    (a) technological categories
    (b) methodological categories
    (c) theoretical categories
  – summarize and package representations of processes
    (a) backgrounding (given material as Theme)
    (b) foregrounding (rhematic material as New)
(2) Verbal elements:
  – relate nominalized processes
    (a) externally (to each other)
    (b) internally (to our interpretation of them)
  – present nominalized process (as happening)

In other words: concepts are organized into taxonomies, and constructions of concepts (processes) are packaged into information and distributed by backgrounding and foregrounding; and since the grammar does this by nominalizing, the experiential content goes into nominal groups. The verbal group signals that the process takes place; or, more substantively, sets up the logical relationship of one process to another, either externally (*a* causes *x*), or internally (*b* proves *y*).

By the end of the eighteenth century this has emerged as the most highly valued model for scientific writing. Two very brief examples; one from John Dalton's *A New System of Chemical Philosophy* (1827):

> Hence increase of temperature, at the same time as on one account it increases the absolute quantity of heat in an elastic fluid, diminshes the quantity on another account by an increase of pressure.

one from James Clark Maxwell, *An Elementary Treatise on Electricity* (1881):

> The amount of heat which enters or leaves the body is measured by the product of the increase or diminution of entropy into the temperature at which it takes place. ... The consequences which flow

153

from this conjecture may be conveniently described by an extension of the term 'entropy' to electric phenomena.

By this time we find a very large number of different verbs in the functions of (external) *is measured by* and (internal) *may be described by* in this last example. In terms of transitivity, those expressing external relations are relational and either intensive ('be' type, e.g. *be, become, form, equal, represent, constitute, symbolize, signal, herald, reflect, mean, serve as, act as, embody, define, manifest*) or circumstantial ('be' + a circumstantial relation 'at, on, after, with, because of, in order to etc.', e.g. *cause, lead to, accompany, follow, produce, dictate, stimulate, demand, require, correspond to, apply to, arise from, flow from, cover, result from, be associated with, be measured by*). We might include with the latter, in the sense of 'cause' (*a* causes *x*), a number of verbs expressing the causing of a specific effect, e.g. *speed up, encourage, obscure, improve, diminish* ('make faster, more likely, less clear, better, less/fewer'); these can be interpreted, in a grammar of English, either as relational or as material processes, but it is usually the relational feature that predominates when they are used in scientific contexts. There are also the verbs which merely assert that there **is** a process, as in Priestley's *repulsion . . . is . . . exerted*; cf. *rapid bonding occurs, considerable momentum develops*.

The verbs expressing internal relations are those such as *prove, show, predict, illustrate, suggest, attest, be explained by, indicate, confirm*. These may also be interpreted as relational intensive, and this interpretation is appropriate when the nominal elements are both abstractions, as in Michalske and Bunker 1987, p. 80:

> Griffith's energy balance approach to strength and fracture also suggested the importance of surface chemistry in the mechanical behaviour of brittle materials.

But many of these same verbs also function as sources of projection, as in p. 85:

> Our discovery of the importance of molecular diffusion near the crack tip indicates that surface coatings might be designed to block the opening of the crack. . . .

Here *indicate* could be interpreted as a mental process 'makes us think that' (compare expressions where the projecting process is itself nominalized, e.g. *leads us to the conclusion that . . .*); while the ones that are most clearly functioning as mental or verbal processes are those where the projection is personalized, e.g. (p. 80):

Griffith also determined that the smaller the initial crack in a piece of glass is, the greater the applied stress must be to extend it.

But as scientific discourse has come to be depersonalized, during the past hundred years or so, personal projections have tended to be increasingly hedged around: *Smith suggested that ...* was replaced by *Smith's suggestion was that ...*, and then by *Smith's suggestion that ...* followed by some other verb as process (e.g. *is confirmed by, conflicts with*); while *I suggested that ...* has disappeared almost entirely. However, in their more relational functions (including impersonal projections as in *our results show that ...*) these verbs play a central part in the syndrome of scientific English, constructing the internal steps in the argument whereby a process is paired with one that is evidence for it rather than with one that is its cause.

6

The thirteen features that we identified in the *Scientific American* text used as illustration at the beginning can all be seen as different manifestations of this underlying pattern which has been developing over the past four to six centuries. During this period, the grammar of scientific English has been continuously evolving; and we have traced this evolution by showing what is the preferred format for representing and explaining physical phenomena. This has changed, through time,

(1)   externally:
   from   *a* happens; so *x* happens
            because *a* happens, *x* happens
               that *a* happens causes *x* to happen
                  happening *a* causes happening *x*
         to   happening *a* is the cause of happening *x*

(2)   internally:
   from   *a* happens; so we know *x* happens
            because *a* happens, we know *x* happens
               that *a* happens proves *x* to happen
                  happening *a* proves happening *x*
         to   happening *a* is the proof of happening *x*

This is, of course, a highly schematic interpretation; but it shows the direction of change. The latest step to date, taken in the twentieth century, is the one **whereby the causal (or other) relation itself comes to be nominalized, as in** *the cause, the proof* above. Let us take a different example and track it backwards up the 'external' arrow of time. The following is from *Scientific American* (July 1986, p. 77):

> The resolution of the experimental difficulties associated with producing and probing exotic atomic nuclei came in the form of an online isotope-separation system (or ISOL).

To make it manageable we will leave out the embedded clause (which would have to be tracked as well in its own right). Here is the original together with a possible four regressive rewordings:

the resolution of the experimental difficulties came in the form of an ISOL

the experimental difficulties were resolved by the use of an ISOL

our using an ISOL resolved the difficulties of the experiment

by using an ISOL we solved the difficult parts of the experiment

we used an ISOL and thus could experiment even where it was difficult

Note that these do not vary much in length; despite a common belief, the more nominalized constructions are not, in fact, noticeably shorter.

All these grammatical formats may of course coexist in one paper. Instances of the latest type can be found quite early on – but they are rare. Likewise, a modern scientific article does not remain locked into the most metaphorical wordings from beginning to end; the discourse shifts within the space that grammatical metaphor defines. But there has been a steady drift towards the nominalizing region; and there will be few sentences that do not contain some of the features that we have recognized as its characteristic.

7

I have tried not just to describe how scientific English has evolved but also to suggest how to explain it. Physical scientists led the way in expanding the grammar of the language, as they found it, so as to construct a new form of knowledge; based on components that were already present in the medieval semiotic – technology on the one hand, and theory on the other – but that had not previously been combined (except perhaps in the long-forgotten practice of Roger Bacon). Up to that point, doing and thinking remain as separate moments in the cultural dynamic; in "science", the two are brought together. This process leaves room for different models of how the two are to be interrelated, which gives rise to currents of thought in humanist philosophy; but it is the practice, the activity of 'doing science', that is enacted in the forms of the language, and there has been a broad consensus about what constitutes scientific practice. It is this reality that is construed in scientific discourse.

Is this form of language more complex? Not necessarily; it depends how we define complexity. If we take lexical density (the number of lexical words per clause), and the structure of the nominal elements (nominal groups and nominalizations), it undoubtedly is more complex. On the other hand, if we consider the intricacy of the sentence structure (the number of clauses in the sentence, and their interdependencies), then it will appear as simpler: mainly one-clause sentences; and likewise with the clause structure – usually only two or three elements in the clause. We are unlikely to find anything as complex as the first sentence of Newton's Experiment 8 in scientific writing today. (Where we will find it is in casual, spontaneous speech.)

It is, however, a language for the expert; one which makes explicit the textual and logical interconnections but leaves many local ambiguities. The ambiguities arise especially in two places: (1) in strings of nouns, leaving inexplicit the semantic relations (mainly transitivity relations) among them; and (2) in the relational verbs, which are often indeterminate and may face both ways (e.g. *higher productivity means more supporting services*: does *means* mean 'brings about', 'is brought about by' or 'requires'?). Here is an example of both, from a Year 6 science textbook:

Lung cancer death rates are clearly associated with increased smoking.

What is *lung cancer death rates*: how quickly lungs die from cancer, how many people die from cancer of the lung, or how quickly people die if they have it? What is *increased smoking*: more people smoke, or people smoke more? What is *are associated with*: caused by (you die because you smoke), or cause (you smoke because you are – perhaps afraid of – dying)? We may have rejected all but the 'right' interpretation without thinking – but only because we know what it is on about already.

Because it is a language for the expert, it can often be problematic for a learner. This is partly a developmental matter: as we have seen, scientific English is highly metaphorical, in the sense of grammatical metaphor, and children find it hard to deal with grammatical metaphor until they reach about secondary school age. So for children learning science the patterns we have been investigating present a problem in their own right. Apart from this, however, they are faced with a form of language which, while they must use it to construe a whole new realm of experience, tends to leave implicit precisely the experiential meanings that they most depend on for its construction.

To see the language from the point of view of a learner, and especially if one hopes to intervene in the learning process, it is important to understand how it works. For this one needs a *grammatics* (a model of grammar); I have used systemic grammar, this being the sort of task to which its paradigmatic-functional design is particularly appropriate. (For the framework of analysis, see Halliday 1985, 1985/94; for a detailed systemic treatment of the grammar of modern scientific English, Huddleston et al. 1968; for scientific English in school, Wignell, Martin and Eggins 1987/93.) But 'how it works' is only part of the story. A newly evolving register is always functional in its context (whether the context itself is one of consensus or of conflict); the language may **become** ritualized, but it cannot start that way, because to become ritualized a feature must first acquire value, and it can acquire value only by being functional. Thus despite the extent to which scientific English comes to be ritualized, and carried over as a language of prestige and power into other contexts where its special features make no sense **except** as ritual (for example in bureaucratic discourse), all the characteristics that we observed, as contributing to the syndrome that was illustrated at the beginning of the paper, are in origin functional in the effective construction of reality, whatever we may feel about the way they are deployed today. And it is this that our "grammatics" has to be able to account for. Systemic grammar enables us to ask why scientific English evolved the way it did, and how it was able to provide the semiotic base for the emergence of physical science.

Chapter Six

SOME GRAMMATICAL PROBLEMS IN SCIENTIFIC ENGLISH (1989)

In any typical group of science students there will be some who find themselves in difficulty – who find the disciplines of physics, or biology, or mathematics forbidding and obscure. To such students, these subjects appear decidedly unfriendly. When their teacher tries to diagnose the problems the students are having, it is usually not long before the discussion begins to focus on language. Scientific texts are found to be difficult to read; and this is said to be because they are written in "scientific language", a "jargon" which has the effect of making the learner feel excluded and alienated from the subject-matter.

This experience is not confined to those who are studying their science in English. It often happens in other languages also that scientific forms are difficult to understand. But here I shall be concentrating on English; and it is important to stress that it is not only ESL students who find problems with scientific English – so also do many for whom English is the mother tongue. My impression is that, while these two groups – those for whom English is mother tongue and those for whom it is second language – may respond to scientific English in different ways, it is largely the same features that cause difficulties to both. For example, a pile-up of nouns as in *form recognition laterality patterns*, or *glass crack growth rate*, is hard to understand both for ESL and for EL1 students of science. The two groups may use different strategies for decoding these

'Some grammatical problems in scientific English', from *Symposium in Education*, Society of Pakistani English Language Teachers, Karachi: SPELT, 1989.

structures; but decoding strategies vary according to other factors also, for example the age of the learner. In so far as "scientific English" presents special problems of its own, distinct from those of other varieties of English, the problems seem to be much the same for everybody.

In any case, in today's multilingual cities such as Birmingham, Toronto or Sydney, there is no clear line between first and second language groups of learners. A typical secondary level science class may include monolingual English speakers at one end, students who have had almost no experience of English at the other end, with the remainder spread out all the way along the continuum in between. In this situation the teacher is forced to think of the problem in terms which apply to all. But this perspective is also relevant to countries such as those of South and Southeast Asia, where the students will have been taught using a variety of different languages as their medium of instruction.

Once their attention has been directed on to the language, science teachers usually think of the difficulties first in lexical terms: that is, as difficulties of vocabulary. This is what is implied by the term "jargon", which means a battery of difficult technical terms. The word "jargon" often carries a further implication, namely that such terms are unnecessary and the same meaning could have been conveyed without them, in the everyday language of ordinary common sense. And this is, in fact, one view of scientific language: some people think that it is an unnecessary, more or less ritualistic way of writing, and that science – scientific concepts and scientific reasoning – could just as well be expressed in everyday, non-technical terms. They refer to this other kind of language as "plain English", "simple words" and the like.

We could contrast this view with the opposite opinion, which is that science is totally dependent on scientific language: that you cannot separate science from how it is written, or rewrite scientific discourse in any other way. According to this view, "learning science" is the same thing as learning the language of science. If the language is difficult to understand, this is not some additional factor caused by the words that are chosen, but a difficulty that is inherent in the nature of science itself. It is the subject-matter that is the source of the problem.

Usually when sensible people can hold such opposite points of view, the reality lies somewhere in between; and this is certainly the case in this instance. It would not be possible to represent scientific knowledge entirely in commonsense wordings; technical terms are not simply fancy equivalents for ordinary words, and the conceptual structures and reasoning processes of physics and biology are highly complex and often far removed, by many levels of abstraction, from everyday experience. Hence the language in which they are constructed is bound to be difficult to follow. At the same time, it is often made more difficult than it need be; the forms of scientific discourse can take over, imposing their own martial law, so that writers get locked in to patterns of writing that are unnecessarily complicated and express themselves in highly technical wording even in contexts where there is no motive for it. This is the point where we can justifiably talk about "scientific jargon": where the writer is following a fashion by which he seeks (unconsciously, in all likelihood) to give extra value to his discourse by marking it off as the discourse of an intellectual elite.

It is important to arrive at a balanced view on this question, because we not only need to identify what the problematic features of scientific English are; we also need to try and explain them – to show what functions these things have in the discourse as a whole, and why they have evolved as part of the language of science. This will help us to know whether, in any particular passage, the features that made it difficult to understand were motivated or not – in other words, whether there is some good reason why the text has been written the way it is. Might it be precisely where the complexity is not motivated – where there was no reason for the writer to have adopted that particular wording at that stage in the argument – that the students are finding difficulties? It will take careful, well-informed classroom research to enable us to answer this last question; but we can suggest some explanations, of a general kind, for why these problematic features are found in scientific writing. The language of science, however much it may become a matter of convention, or a way of establishing the writer's own prestige and authority, is not, in origin, an arbitrary code.

But in order to understand why scientific writing became difficult in certain ways, we shall need to get rid of our obsession with words. The difficulty lies more with the grammar than with the vocabulary. In the last resort, of course, we cannot separate these from each other; it is the total effect of the wording – words and structures – that the reader is responding to, and technical terms are part of this overall effect. Nevertheless technical terms are not, in themselves, difficult to master; and students are not particularly dismayed by them. It is usually the teacher who puts technical terms in the centre of the picture, because vocabulary is much more obvious, and easier to talk about, than grammar. But the generalizations we have to make, in order to help students cope with scientific writing, are mainly generalizations about its grammar. The problems with technical terminology usually arise not from the technical terms themselves but from the complex relationships they have with one another. Technical terms cannot be defined in isolation; each one has to be understood as part of a larger framework, and each one is defined by reference to all the others.

I shall suggest seven headings which can be used for illustrating and discussing the difficulties that are characteristic of scientific English:

(1) interlocking definitions
(2) technical taxonomies
(3) special expressions
(4) lexical density
(5) syntactic ambiguity
(6) grammatical metaphor
(7) semantic discontinuity

This should not be taken as a definitive listing of categories; all these features could be organized in different ways, or subdivided further, and more could certainly be added. These are simply the headings that I have found useful as a framework for working on the problem. In what follows, I have drawn on various sources, but particularly on the work of my colleagues in Sydney: Charles Taylor's study of the language of high school textbooks, with special reference to the problems of second language learners; Martin and Rothery's discussion of writing in primary schools; Wignell, Martin and Eggins' analysis of geography textbooks at junior secondary level; and Louise Ravelli's treatment of grammatical metaphor. My own analysis of scientific texts, reported on in a lecture series at the National University of Singapore, included material from four different points of origin: (i) secondary and upper primary science and mathematics textbooks from Australia, (ii) science lectures recorded at the University of Birmingham in England, (iii) writings from the *Scientific American*, and (iv) for a historical survey, works by Chaucer, Newton, Priestley, Dalton, Darwin and Clerk Maxwell. I found it necessary to undertake this kind of historical study in order to investigate how, and especially why, the features that were causing such problems of understanding today had themselves originally evolved.[1]

(1) Interlocking definitions. Here is an example of how a series of definitions is presented to children in upper primary school:[2]

> A circle is a plane curve with the special property that every point on it is at the same distance from a particular point called the *centre*. This distance is called the *radius* of the circle. The *diameter* of the circle is twice the radius. The length of the circle is called its *circumference*.

Here *circle, centre, radius, diameter* and *circumference* all figure in a series of interlocking definitions. Within this set, *circle, centre* and *radius* are mutually defining: they are all used to define each other, through the intermediary of two other terms which are assumed to be already known, namely *distance* and *plane curve*. The remaining terms, *diameter* and *circumference*, are then defined each by reference to one of the first three; and here two other terms are assumed to be known and mastered, namely *length* and *twice*. The pattern of definitions is as in Figure 6.1:

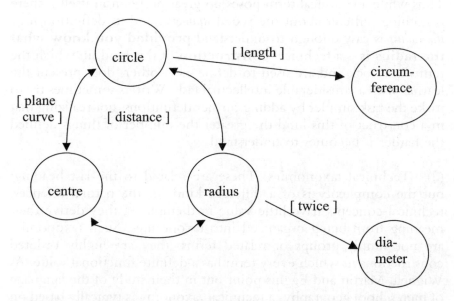

Figure 6.1   Interlocking definitions of five technical terms

Now, there are certain difficulties here which are specific to this example: the notions of 'plane curve', of 'every point on a curve', and of 'the length of a circle'. Likewise, any example chosen would probably present special problems of its own. But at the same time the overall semantic structure is strikingly complex; and this is something that may be found anywhere in maths and science textbooks. The learner has first to reach an understanding of a cluster of related concepts, all at the same time, and then immediately use this understanding in order to derive more concepts from the first ones. Note that these relationships are set up by means of a grammatical construction which faces both ways: '*a* is defined as *x*', '*x* is called *a*' – both of which may occur in the same clause, as happens in the first sentence of the extract:

'*a* is defined as an *x* which has feature *y* which is called *b*'

Furthermore the 'hinge' element *y* is itself fairly complex grammatically:

with the special property that every point on it is at the same distance from a particular point

Thus while a technical term poses no great problem in itself – there is nothing difficult about the **word** *diameter*, and its definition *twice the radius* is easy enough to understand **provided you know what the radius is** – a technical **construction** of this kind, in which the terms interlock and are used to define each other, does present the learner with a considerable intellectual task. Writers sometimes try to make the task simpler by adding further definitions, not realizing that in a construct of this kind the greater the number of things defined the harder it becomes to understand.

(2)   Technical taxonomies. These are related to the last heading; but the complexity is of a different kind. In the natural sciences, technical concepts have little value in themselves; they derive their meaning from being organized into taxonomies. Such taxonomies are not simply groups of related terms; they are highly ordered constructions in which every term has a definite functional value. As Wignell, Martin and Eggins point out in their study of the language of high school geography, a technical taxonomy is typically based on two fundamental semantic relationships: '*a* is a kind of of *x*' (superordination) and '*b* is a part of *y*' (composition). Thus in their example of *climate*, climate is divided into certain **kinds** (Figure 6.2) and is composed of certain **parts** (Figure 6.3):

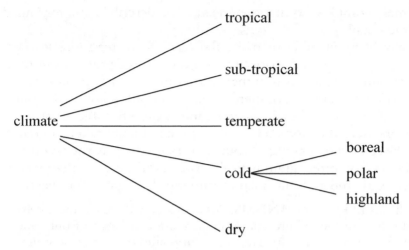

Figure 6.2 Kinds of climate (superordination)

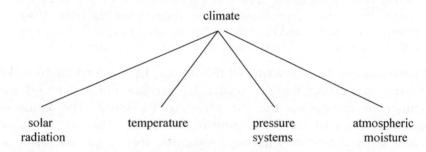

Figure 6.3 Parts of climate (composition)

It will be seen that the first is an 'either/or' relationship: 'every climate is **either** tropical **or** subtropical **or** ...'; the second is a 'both + and' relationship: 'every climate is **both** temperature **and** solar radiation **and** ...'. (We have to stretch the meaning of *either* and *both* here so that they are no longer limited to just two.)

Three problems can arise with such constructions. The first is that these taxonomies can become very complicated, with many layers of organization built into them. The second is that they are usually not made explicit; there are often neither lists nor diagrams (the figures above do not appear in the textbook), so the student is left to work them out for himself from reading the text. The third problem is that the criteria on which these taxonomies are set up can also be extremely complex, so that they need to be described and explained in some detail.

It would be possible to make the reading matter more learner-friendly by dealing systematically with these three problems in turn: first introducing the terms in their taxonomic order (e.g. *there are five kinds of climate, namely . . .*), then setting them out in lists or diagrams, and finally describing each category and, where possible, explaining it. In practice, the first and third steps are usually taken together, with the second one being left out; as a result, the way the taxonomy is presented is often grammatically very confusing, with no clear pattern of theme and information running through it. For example,

> ONE-CELLED ORGANISMS. Some organisms, such as the ameba and others in the culture you examined, are composed of only one cell. These organisms are said to be **unicellular**. Living in water, these animals are in close contact with the food, water, and oxygen they need. A one-celled animal takes in its own food. Along with this food, the animal also takes in some water. Additional water enters the animal cell by diffusion. The normal movement of the cytoplasm carries the food, water, and oxygen throughout the cell. Waste materials are eliminated directly to the outside of the cell. Most one-celled organisms can survive only in a watery environment.

It is very likely that the writer of this passage has been trying to make it more interesting for the reader by varying the order and the manner of presenting the categories to be learnt: the kinds of organism, the parts of the organism and so on. Thus every clause begins with a new theme: *some organisms, these organisms, living in water, a one-celled animal, additional water, the normal movement of the cytoplasm, waste materials, most one-celled organisms.* Unfortunately, while this kind of variation may be an admirable goal for a literary text, if scientific texts are written in this way they are much harder to read and to learn from. It is very difficult to construct the relevant taxonomies on the basis of this kind of writing.

(3) Special expressions. Some expressions used in mathematical language have a special grammar of their own, for example *solving the open sentence over D*. Here it is the expression as a whole that gets to be defined, rather than any particular word in it:

> If D is the domain of a variable in an open sentence, the process of finding the truth set is called *solving the open sentence over D*.

This is 'technical grammar', rather than technical terminology; it is not particularly problematic once it has been explained (provided the learner does not ask what happens if *D* is **not** the domain of a variable in an open sentence).

This kind of special grammar is more common in mathematics than in science; mathematicians have often had to stretch the grammar a little in order to say what they want. Already in Isaac Newton's writings we find some very long nominal constructions, like the following from the *Treatise on Opticks*:

> The Excesses of the Sines of Refraction of several sorts of Rays above their common Sine of Incidence when the Refractions are made out of divers denser Mediums immediately into one and the same rarer Medium, suppose of Air, . . .

– all of which is merely the Subject of the clause. This kind of stretching of the grammar is less usual in scientific discourse. However, the language of science has brought its own innovations, stretching the grammar in ways which are at first sight less obvious but which, partly because they are less obvious, tend to cause greater difficulties of comprehension. Here is an example from an upper primary school textbook:

> Your completed table should tell you what happens to the risk of getting lung cancer as smoking increases.

The *table* is, of course, a table of figures; that is understood. But how does a table *tell you* something? – tables do not talk, even tables of figures. And what kind of an object is a *risk*, such that we can ask what *happens to* it? And what does *smoking increases* mean: that more smoke is put out by some combustion process? What kind of relationship is being expressed by the *as*: does it mean 'while' (time), 'because' (cause), or 'in the same way that' (manner)?

What is being illustrated here is not, in fact, a single phenomenon. It is a set of interrelated phenomena: features which tend to go together in modern scientific writing, forming a kind of syndrome by which we recognize that something is written in the language of science. But although these features commonly go together, in order to understand the problems they pose to a student we will need to separate them out; and this will occupy the next three headings. The present section will serve as a bridge leading into them, because when we see them in their historical perspective they do constitute a special mode of expression that evolved in scientific discourse, although we are now so used to them that we no longer think of them as special. It is only when they occur in a fairly extreme form that they stand out, as in the following (taken from an abstract):[3]

> [These results] are consistent with the selective perceptual orientation hypothesis if it is assumed that both word recognition and concurrent verbal memory produce more left than right hemisphere activation and that in the case of mixed lists in the present study this activation had not dissipated on form recognition trials.

(4)   Lexical density. This is a measure of the density of information in any passage of text, according to how tightly the lexical items (content words) have been packed into the grammatical structure. It can be measured, in English, as the number of lexical words per clause.

In the following examples, each of which is one clause, the lexical words are underlined; the lexical density count is given at the right:

(a)   But we never did anything very much in <u>science</u>   2
      at our <u>school</u>.
(b)   My <u>father</u> used to <u>tell</u> me about a <u>singer</u> in his   4
      <u>village</u>.
(c)   A <u>parallelogram</u> is a <u>four-sided</u> <u>figure</u> with its   6
      <u>opposite</u> <u>sides</u> <u>parallel</u>.
(d)   The <u>atomic</u> <u>nucleus</u> <u>absorbs</u> and <u>emits</u> <u>energy</u> in   8
      <u>quanta</u>, or <u>discrete</u> <u>units</u>.

In any piece of discourse there is obviously a great deal of variation in the lexical density from one clause to the next. But there are also some general tendencies. In informal spoken language the lexical density tends to be low: about two lexical words per clause is quite typical. When the language is more planned and more formal, the lexical density is higher; and since writing is usually more planned than speech, written language tends to be somewhat denser than spoken language, often having around four to six lexical words per clause. But in scientific writing the lexical density may go considerably higher. Here are three clauses with a lexical density of 10–13, all from *Scientific American*:[4]

(e)   Griffith's <u>energy</u> <u>balance</u> <u>approach</u> to <u>strength</u> and   13
      <u>fracture</u> also <u>suggested</u> the <u>importance</u> of <u>surface</u>
      <u>chemistry</u> in the <u>mechanical</u> <u>behaviour</u> of <u>brittle</u>
      <u>materials</u>.
(f)   The <u>conical</u> <u>space</u> <u>rendering</u> of <u>conical</u> <u>strings</u>'   10
      <u>gravitational</u> <u>properties</u> <u>applies</u> only to <u>straight</u>
      <u>strings</u>.

(g) The <u>model</u> <u>rests</u> on the <u>localized</u> <u>gravitational</u>   13
<u>attraction</u> <u>exerted</u> by <u>rapidly</u> <u>oscillating</u> and
extremely <u>massive</u> <u>closed</u> <u>loops</u> of <u>cosmic</u> <u>string</u>.

When the lexical density goes up to this extent, the passage becomes difficult to read. Of course, the difficulty will also depend on the particular lexical items that are used and on how they are distributed in the grammatical structure; but the lexical density is a problematic factor in itself. In much scientific writing, almost all the lexical items in any clause occur inside just one or two nominal groups (noun phrases); compare examples (e) – (g) above, where this applies to all except one in each case (*suggested, applies, rests*). Perhaps the hardest examples to process are those which consist of strings of lexical words without any grammatical words in between, such as Griffith's *energy balance approach, conical strings' gravitational properties*; likewise those cited at the beginning of the paper, *form recognition laterality patterns* and *glass crack growth rate*. Even where the words themselves are perfectly simple and well known, as in the last of these four examples, the expressions are not easy to understand. Another example was *the increasing lung cancer death rate*, which appeared in the same passage as the example quoted in the last section. Here, however, another factor contributes to the difficulty, that of grammatical ambiguity; and this leads us in to our next heading.

(5)   Syntactic ambiguity. Consider examples such as the following:

(h) Increased responsiveness may be reflected in feeding behaviour.
(i) Lung cancer death rates are clearly associated with increased smoking.
(j) Higher productivity means more supporting services.

All have a very simple structure: a nominal group, functioning as Subject, followed by a verbal group, followed by another nominal group with (in two instances) a preposition introducing it. If we focus attention on the verbal expressions, *may be reflected (in), are . . . associated (with), means*, we find that they are ambiguous; and they are ambiguous in two respects. In the first place, we cannot tell whether they indicate a relationship of cause or of evidence. Is one thing being said to be the **effect of** another, or is it merely the **outward sign of** it? For example: in (h), does the feeding behaviour **demonstrate that** responsiveness has increased, or does it **change**

as a result of the increase? In the second place, supposing that we can identify a relationship of cause, we still cannot tell which causes which. In (j), for example, is higher productivity **brought about by** more supporting services, or does it **cause** more supporting services to be provided? It may seem obvious to the writer, and also to a teacher, which meaning is intended; but it is far from obvious to a learner, and teacher and learner may interpret the passage differently without either of them being aware that another interpretation was possible.

The expression *are associated with*, in (i), can also face in either direction: either 'cause' or 'are caused by'. **We** may know that smoking causes cancer, and hence that the more you smoke, the more likely you are to die from cancer of the lung. But this sentence **could** mean that lung cancer death rates **lead to** increased smoking: perhaps people are so upset by fear of lung cancer that they need to smoke more in order to calm their nerves. It is even possible that the writer wanted not to commit himself to a choice between these two interpretations of the statistics. But when we start to explore the meaning of this example more carefully, we find that it contains a great deal more ambiguity in addition to that which we have already seen in the verb.

For example, what does *lung cancer death rates* mean? Is it 'how many people die from lung cancer', or 'how quickly people die when they get lung cancer'? Or is it perhaps 'how quickly people's lungs die from cancer'? And does *increased smoking* mean 'people smoke more', or 'more people smoke' – or is it a combination of the two, 'more people smoke more'? Having reached some understanding up to this point, such as 'more people smoke ... more people die of cancer', we still do not know whether they are the same people or not – is it just the smokers who die more, or everyone else as well? Nor do we know whether the situation is real or hypothetical: is it 'because more people are smoking, so more are dying', or 'if more people smoked, more would die'? If we combine all these possibilities we have already reached some fifty possible interpretations, most of which were quite plausible; they are genuine alternatives faced by a human reader, not fanciful simulations of some computerized parsing program.

Where does this ambiguity come from? It arises from various sources. We have already referred to polysemous verbs like *mean, be associated with*; there are probably between one and two thousand verbs of this class in use in scientific English. But the main cause of ambiguity is that clauses are turned into nouns. That is to say, something that would in spoken English be typically expressed as a clause is expressed instead as a group of words centring on a noun. If I say *Mary announced that she had accepted*, I am making it clear who did what; but if I say *the announcement of Mary's acceptance*, you cannot tell (i) whether Mary made the announcement herself or someone else did, (ii) whether Mary was accepting (something) or being accepted, (iii) whether she had accepted/been accepted already or would accept/be accepted in the future. Thus the single nominal group *the announcement of Mary's acceptance* corresponds to many different wordings in the form of a clause: *Mary announced that she would accept, they announced that Mary had been accepted*, and so on. A great deal of semantic information is lost when clausal expressions are replaced by nominal ones.

Scientific writing uses very many nominal constructions of this kind, typically in combination with verbs of the type illustrated in (h) − (j) above. Both these features are, as we have seen, highly ambiguous, although we usually do not recognize the ambiguity until we try to reword the passage in some other form. Here is a further example:

(k) The growth of attachment between infant and mother signals the first step in the development of the child's capacity to discriminate amongst people.

Possible rewordings of this might be:

$$\left\{ \begin{array}{l} \text{When} \\ \text{If} \end{array} \right\} \text{an infant and} \left\{ \begin{array}{l} \text{its} \\ \text{a} \end{array} \right\} \text{mother} \left\{ \begin{array}{l} \text{start to grow} \\ \text{grow more} \end{array} \right\} \text{attached to one}$$

$$\text{another,} \left\{ \begin{array}{l} \text{this shows that} \\ \text{this is because} \end{array} \right\} \text{the child} \left\{ \begin{array}{l} \text{is taking} \\ \text{has taken} \end{array} \right\} \text{the first steps}$$

$$\text{towards} \left\{ \begin{array}{l} \text{becoming} \\ \text{becoming more} \end{array} \right\} \text{capable of} \left\{ \begin{array}{l} \text{distinguishing} \\ \text{preferring} \end{array} \right\} \text{one person}$$

from / to another.

Combining these we get $2^7 = 128$ possible interpretations. But in this instance I find it difficult to opt for any one of them; none of the rewordings seems to be particularly convincing.

(6) Grammatical metaphor. The high lexical density and the ambiguity discussed in the last two sections are both by-products of a process I shall refer to as "grammatical metaphor". This is like metaphor in the usual sense except that, instead of being a substitution of one **word** for another, as when we say *you're talking tripe* instead of *you're talking nonsense*, it is a substitution of one grammatical class, or one grammatical structure, by another; for example, *his departure* instead of *he departed*. Here the words (lexical items) are the same; what has changed is their place in the grammar. Instead of pronoun *he* + verb *departed*, functioning as Actor plus Process in a clause, we have determiner *his* + noun *departure*, functioning as Deictic plus Thing in a nominal group.[5] Other examples are *her recent speech concerned poverty* instead of *she spoke recently concerning poverty*; *glass crack growth rate* instead of *how quickly cracks in glass grow*. Often the words may change as well as the grammar, as in the last example where *how quickly* is replaced by *rate* – we do not usually say *glass crack growth quickness*; but the underlying metaphor is in the grammar, and the lexical changes follow more or less automatically.

I am not suggesting that there will always be some absolute, non-metaphorical form to which these grammatical metaphors can be related; metaphor is a natural historical process in language and modes of expression involving different degrees of metaphor will always exist side by side. We can often take two or three or even more steps in rewording a grammatical metaphor in a less metaphorical, more congruent form; for example, we might say that 'cracking' is really a process – something happening – rather than a thing, so that *cracks in glass*, with *cracks* as a noun, is a metaphor for *glass cracks* with *cracks* as verb. As another example,

> (1) [The 36 class only appeared on this train] in times of reduced loading, or engine failure.

could be reworded as *when loadings were reduced, or the engine failed*; but we might then reword the first part over again as *when the load was smaller* or even *when fewer goods were being carried*.

What is the nature of this rewording? One way of thinking of it is by imagining the age of the reader, or listener. In talking to a nine-year-old, we would never say *in times of engine failure*; we would say *whenever the engine failed*. Notice that we have not had to simplify the vocabulary; there are no difficult words in the first version – it is the grammar that is difficult for a child. Similarly we would change *slow down the glass crack growth rate* to *make the cracks in glass grow more slowly*, or *stop the cracks in glass from growing so quickly*. What we are doing, when we reword in this way, is changing the grammar (with some consequential changes in vocabulary) by making it **younger**. Children learn first to talk in clauses; it is only later – and only when they can already read and write with facility – that they are able to replace these clauses with nominal groups.

As far as we can tell, this also reflects what happened in the history of the language. In English, and other languages of Europe, the older pattern is the clausal one; and it is based on certain principles of wording which we might summarize as follows:

(1) processes (actions, events, mental processes, relations) are expressed by verbs;
(2) participants (people, animals, concrete and abstract objects that take part in processes) are expressed by nouns;
(3) circumstances (time, place, manner, cause, condition) are expressed by adverbs and by prepositional phrases;
(4) relations between one process and another are expressed by conjunctions.

For example:

participant	process	circumstance	relation between processes	participant	process	circum-stance
the cast	acted	brilliantly	so	the audience	applauded	for a long time
[noun]	[verb]	[adverb]	[conjunction]	[noun]	[verb]	[preposi-tional phrase]

If this is now reworded metaphorically as:

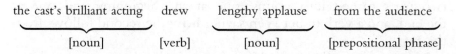

the cast's brilliant acting	drew	lengthy applause	from the audience
[noun]	[verb]	[noun]	[prepositional phrase]

a number of changes have taken place. The processes *acted* and *applauded* have been turned into nouns, *acting* and *applause*; the participant *the cast* has become a possessive, while *the audience* has become part of a prepositional phrase. The circumstances *brilliantly* and *for a long time* have both become adjectives inside nominal

173

groups; and the relation between the two processes, showing that one of them caused the other, has become a verb, *drew*. This makes it sound as though acting and clapping were things, and as if the only event that took place was the causal relation between them (... *acting drew* ... *applause*). All these changes illustrate what is meant by grammatical metaphor.

This kind of metaphor is found particularly in scientific discourse, and may have evolved first of all in that context. It is already beginning to appear in the writings of the ancient Greek scientists; from them it is carried over into classical Latin and then into medieval Latin; and it has continued to develop – but to a far greater extent – in Italian, English, French, German, Russian and the other languages of Europe from the Renaissance onwards. And although it has spread across many different registers, or functional varieties, of language, in English at least the main impetus for it seems to have continued to come from the languages of science.

Why did scientific writers, from Isaac Newton onwards, increasingly favour such a mode of expression? – one in which, instead of writing 'this happened, so that happened', they write 'this event caused that event'? These were not arbitrary or random changes. The reason lies in the nature of scientific discourse. Newton and his successors were creating a new variety of English for a new kind of knowledge; a kind of knowledge in which experiments were carried out; general principles derived by reasoning from these experiments, with the aid of mathematics; and these principles in turn tested by further experiments. The discourse had to proceed step by step, with a constant movement from 'this is what we have established so far' to 'this is what follows from it next'; and each of these two parts, both the 'taken for granted' part and the new information, had to be presented in a way that would make its status in the argument clear. The most effective way to do this, in English grammar, is to construct the whole step as a single clause, with the two parts turned into nouns, one at the beginning and one at the end, and a verb in between saying **how** the second follows from the first.

I have written about the history of this development elsewhere, with illustrations from some of the earlier texts.[6] What I am presenting here is a very simplified account; there are, obviously, countless variations on the pattern described above. Nevertheless these variants all derive from the basic principle of organizing information into a coherent form that suited the kind of argumentation that came to be accepted as 'scientific'. Here is a contemporary example, taken from the *Scientific American*:

> The atomic nucleus absorbs and emits energy only in quanta, or discrete units. Each absorption marks its transition to a state of higher energy, and each emission marks its transition to a state of lower energy.

Notice how, in the second sentence, each clause consists of (i) a 'taken for granted' part, nominalizing what has been said before (*the atomic nucleus absorbs energy* → *each absorption*; *the atomic nucleus emits energy* → *each emission*) (ii) a 'new information' part, pointing forward to what is to come, and also nominalized (*its transition to a state of higher/lower energy*) and (iii) the relation between them, in the form of a verb (*marks*). Frequently the 'taken for granted' part summarizes the whole of a long previous discussion; for example, the same article contains the sentence:

> The theoretical program of devising models of atomic nuclei has of course been complemented by experimental investigations.

This has exactly the same pattern; but here the 'taken for granted' part (*the theoretical program . . . atomic nuclei*) is referring back to many paragraphs of preceding text.

If we reword these so as to take the metaphor out, the entire balance of the information is lost. For the last example we might write:

> We devised models of atomic nuclei, in a program of theoretical [research], and in addition of course we investigated [the matter] by doing experiments.

But this would give us no indication that the first part was a summary of what had gone before, or that the last part was going to be taken up and developed in what followed. What is equally important, it would fail to make it clear that each step – devising theoretical models and investigating experimentally – is to be understood as a unity, a single phenomenon rather than an assembly of component parts.

It would be wrong to give the impression that in developing this favourite type of clause structure, and the grammatical metaphor that made it possible, the scientists were guided by any conscious planning. They were not. Newton and his contemporaries did discuss the best ways of constructing a scientific paper, and they tried to

175

regulate the use of vocabulary for building elaborate taxonomies, especially in biology (and taken up later on in chemistry); but they were not aware of their own use of grammar, and these forms evolved naturally in response to pressure from the discourse.[7] It is only when we analyse this discourse grammatically, using a functional grammar, that we can appreciate how the patterns relate to what the scientists were trying to achieve.

I have not presented the detailed grammatical analysis here; it would need too much space. But it is helpful, I think, to bring out the nature of grammatical metaphor, and the sense in which these forms can be said to be metaphorical, because almost every sentence in scientific writing will contain some example of it, and it does present problems to the learner. This is partly a question of maturity: students well into secondary school may still find it difficult to comprehend, even if they have been educated throughout in English medium.[8] For those who are taking up English just as a language for science and technology, the problem may be greater or less depending on the degree and kind of grammatical metaphor found in the language(s) they have used as medium of education before.

It seems likely that part of the difficulty arises, however, because these metaphorical expressions are not just another way of saying the same thing. In a certain sense, they present a different view of the world. As we grew up, using our language to learn with and to think with, we have come to expect (unconsciously, until our teachers started to give us lessons in grammar) that nouns were for people and things, verbs for actions and events. Now we find that almost everything has been turned into a noun. We have to reconstruct our mental image of the world so that it becomes a world made out of things, rather than the world of happening – events with things taking part in them – that we were accustomed to. Some of the problem may even be ideological: the student may want to resist this view of reality that he feels is being imposed on him by the language of science. It is worth noting, in this connection, that the scientists themselves are now becoming dissatisfied with the language they use in their writings. They too feel that it has gone too far in this direction, and that if they are to continue to develop new ideas in science they will need to return to less nominalized forms of expression.[9]

(7) Semantic discontinuity. This is my final heading; I am using it to point out that writers sometimes make semantic leaps, across

which the reader is expected to follow them in order to reach a required conclusion. Let me discuss just one example:

> In the years since 1850, more and more factories were built in northern England. The soot from the factory smokestacks gradually blackened the light-coloured stones and tree trunks.
>
> Scientists continued to study the pepper moth during this time. They noticed the dark-coloured moth was becoming more common. By 1950, the dark moths were much more common than the light-coloured ones.
>
> However, strong anti-pollution laws over the last twenty years have resulted in cleaner factories, cleaner countryside and an increase in the number of light-coloured pepper moths.

The first two paragraphs are rather straightforward; but in the third paragraph, problems arise. Taken as a whole, it is a typical example of the structure described in the last section: two processes, with a logical connection between them. The sense is '*a* happened, so *x* happened', expressed metaphorically in the form of 'happening *a* caused happening *x*' (*strong anti-pollution laws ... have resulted in cleaner factories ...*). We might reword this part as:

> Over the last twenty years, [the government have passed] strong laws to stop [people] polluting; so the factories [have become] cleaner...

We saw above that the main reason for choosing the metaphorical form was that 'happening *a*' was something that had been presented before, and so here was being referred to as a whole, as a kind of package or summary of what was to be taken for granted and used as a point of departure for the next step in the argument. However, in this instance happening *a* has not been presented before; this is the first time we have heard of any "anti-pollution laws". So the reader has to (i) discover that it is new information, (ii) decode it and (iii) use it as a stepping-off point for understanding something else.

But let us suppose that the reader has coped with this difficult assignment. He now comes to 'happening *x*' and finds that this is a co-ordination of three processes, all of them presented metaphorically: *cleaner factories, cleaner countryside and an increase in the number of light-coloured pepper moths*. Rewording this, he begins to understand:

> ...the factories have become cleaner, the countryside has become cleaner, and there are more light-coloured pepper moths than before.

– that is, the moths have also become cleaner: only a few of them are now affected by dirt in the air. But that is not at all the intended message. What the reader is supposed to do is to insert another logical relationship between each pair of these resulting processes, and then draw a highly complex conclusion from them:

> . . . the factories have become cleaner, [so] the countryside has become cleaner, and [so] there are getting to be more of the light coloured pepper moths [because they don't show up against clean trees, and therefore do not get eaten by the birds as much as they did when the trees were dirty].

In other words, the learner is expected to work out for himself the principle of natural selection.

This is a particularly problematic example. The language is highly metaphorical, in the sense of grammatical metaphor; the first part of the sentence is misleading because it suggests that we know about the "strong anti-pollution laws" already, and in the second part the reader is required to perfom two complicated semantic leaps − inserting the two causal connectives, and working out the implications of the second one. It is not uncommon to find semantic discontinuities of one kind or another in scientific writing; the specialist has no trouble with them − but for learners they are an additional hazard. Of all the kinds of difficulty discussed in these few pages, this is the one a teacher can do least towards helping students to solve. The teacher can give a few illustrations, and warn the students to be on their guard; but every instance seems to be unique, and it is hard to find any general principles behind them all.

★ ★ ★ ★ ★ ★ ★

Most of the features described under these seven headings could in principle occur independently of each other. But they are all closely related, and, excepting perhaps those mentioned under (3), 'special expressions' (in mathematics), they tend to cluster together as characteristics of scientific discourse. I have tried to show that they are not arbitrary − that they evolved to meet the needs of scientific method, and of scientific argument and theory. They suit the expert; and by the same token they cause difficulty to the novice. In that respect, learning science is the same thing as learning the language of science. Students have to master these difficulties; but in doing so they are also mastering scientific concepts and principles.

At the same time, it must be said that many of those who write in the language of science write it very badly. They leave implicit things that need to be made explicit, create multiple ambiguities that cannot readily be resolved, and use grammatical metaphor both inappropriately and to excess. The language thus becomes a form of ritual, a way of claiming status and turning science into the prerogative of an elite. Learners who complain that their science texts are unnecessarily difficult to read may sometimes be entirely justified. And we are all familiar with those who, not being scientists, have borrowed the trappings of scientific language and are using it purely as a language of prestige and power – the bureaucracies and technocracies of governments and multinational corporations.[10] In bureaucratic discourse these features have no reason to be there at all, because there is no complex conceptual structure or thread of logical argument. But they serve to create distance between writer and reader, to depersonalize the discourse and give it a spurious air of being rational and objective.

In my view the best tool we have for facing up to this kind of language, criticizing it where necessary but above all helping students to understand it, is a functional model of grammar. This enables us to analyse any passage and relate it to its context in the discourse, and also to the general background of the text: who it is written for, what is its angle on the subject matter, and so on. Grammatical analysis is a fairly technical exercise, and not something that students can be expected to undertake for themselves unless they are specializing in language. But science teachers (provided they can be persuaded to discard traditional prejudices about grammar!) may find it interesting and rewarding to explore the language of their own disciplines; and also, where this applies, to compare scientific English with scientific registers that have evolved, or are now evolving, in the major languages of the region in which they work.

Notes

1. See entries in the Bibliography for Taylor (1979), Martin and Rothery (1986), Wignell, Martin and Eggins (1987), Ravelli (1985). Primary texts for the historical survey were Geoffrey Chaucer, *A Treatise on the Astrolabe* (1391); Isaac Newton, *Optiks* (1704); Joseph Priestley, *The History and Present State of Electricity* (1767); John Dalton, *A New System of Chemical Philosophy* (1827); Charles Darwin, *The Origin of Species* (1859); James Clerk Maxwell, *An Elementary Treatise on Electricity* (1881). Texts from the *Scientific American* were Hamilton and Maruhn, 'Exotic atomic nuclei' (July 1986); Michalske and Bunker, 'The frac-

turing of glass' (1987); Vilenkin, 'Cosmic strings' (Dec 1987). For the University of Birmingham studies see King (in press). A sketch of some features of the grammar of scientific English is contained in Halliday (1988); the work from which the present paper is mainly derived was presented in lecture form in Halliday (1986).

2. Sources for the upper primary/lower secondary science and mathematics texts quoted in this paper are A. McMullen and J. L. Williams, *On Course Mathematics* (Macmillan Australia, 1971); Intermediate Science Curriculum Study, *Well-being: probing the natural world* (Martin Educational, 1976); A. A. Parkes, K. E. Couchman and S. B. Jones, *Betty and Jim: year six mathematics* (Shakespeare Head Press, 1978); R. L. Vickery, J. H. Lake, L. N. McKenna and A. S. Ryan, *The Process Way to Science* (Jacaranda Press, 1978). The taxonomies of climate are from C. Sale, G. Wilson and B. Friedman, *Our Changing World* (Longman Cheshire, 1980), quoted in Martin, Wignell, Eggins and Rothery (1988).

3. From the Abstract to J. B. Hellige, 'Visual laterality patterns for pure- versus mixed-list presentation' (*Journal of Experimental Psychology* 4.1, 1978).

4. December 1987, pp. 80, 58, 58.

5. For the analysis of the grammar see Halliday (1985/94), Chapters 5 and 6.

6. See Halliday (1988).

7. For the evolution of the scientific article see Bazerman (1988). For an account of the work of the scientific language planners at the time of Newton, see Salmon (1966, 1979).

8. See Lemke (1982, 1983) for the results of a detailed investigation of the teaching of science in American high schools. For discussion of science education in Britain, with reference to the language of science, see White (1986).

9. This point is discussed briefly in Halliday (1987b).

10. For a study of the language of written communication within a government department see Hardaker (1982). For an analysis of the nature and function of technocratic discourse see Lemke (1990b).

Chapter Seven

ON THE GRAMMAR OF SCIENTIFIC
ENGLISH (1997)

The discourse of science has been a popular topic in recent years, no doubt because it is important to so many different groups of people: to language educators, concerned with problems of teaching and learning science in school; to historians of ideas, concerned with the construction and dissemination of scientific knowledge; to specialists in cultural studies, concerned with scientific language in its relations to structures of power and control in society; to translators, concerned with the special problems of scientific translation in international projects and debates; to computational linguists engaged in natural language processing, where scientific texts are among the main candidates for text generation and parsing; and to linguists interested in the evolution of scientific forms of discourse, their relation to standard languages, to everyday speech and the like. And scientific researchers themselves have become increasingly aware of how fundamental language is to the success of their own enterprise. See Martin and Veel (1998) for a recent overview of the field.

Much of the research has concentrated on structural and rhetorical aspects of scientific genres: the evolution of the various generic forms, such as published articles, reports presented to scientific academies; the forms themselves, and the more or less explicit conventions that have grown up around them; and the rhetorical criteria that have been used to evaluate scientific texts – criteria such as being clear, being objective, being impersonal, being persuasive

'On the grammar of scientific English', from *Grammatica: studi interlinguistici*, edited by Carol Taylor Torsello, Padova: Unipress, 1997.

and so on. Major studies such as Bazerman's (1988) *Shaping Written Knowledge*, on the one hand, and Lemke's (1990a) *Talking Science: Language, Learning, and Values* on the other, have shown, with reference to English, the extent to which science **is** scientific discourse; instead of the old notion that science is a set of ideas, a body of theory that has to be communicated in language but somehow exists independently of language, it is recognized that a scientific theory is itself a linguistic (or at least a semiotic) object – a 'system of related meanings', in Lemke's words.

My own interest, as a linguist and more specifically as a grammarian, has been closely related to these questions – but in a sense also complementary to them. I have been interested in the evolution of scientific forms of discourse, and their relation to everyday language – especially spoken language, and especially the spoken language of small children; as well as their relation to other forms of written adult language, especially to the standard language of the modern nation state (of which in some sense scientific language is simply a particular case). But I have concentrated more on the 'micro' aspects, and specifically on the grammar of the scientific clause; because that, to my mind, is where the essential work is done – where the meaning is made. All discourse is powered by grammatical energy, so to speak; and scientific discourse is a very high-energy form. However much we may complain about it – it is complex, it is dense, it is full of jargon etc. – the fact is that it has been amazingly successful. Scientific language has construed for us the vast theoretical edifice of modern knowledge, constantly expanding its meaning potential without, up to the present at least, showing any signs that its capacity for expansion is limited, though presumably it must be limited in some way or other. And I have always wanted to know why.

I have also been very much concerned, as a language educator, with how children find their way into scientific language. Some of them, of course, never do find their way in; they remain always shut out from the adult modes of scientific discourse, never able to break the code. Yet all children are budding scientists: they pose problems, they reason about them, and they look for solutions. But they use a very different grammar: the grammar of daily life. And that, I think, is the best place to begin thinking about scientific English, or the scientific registers of any particular language (cf. Halliday and Martin 1993).

I shall assume that the grammar of every natural language is (among other things) a **theory** of human experience (see Halliday and Matthiessen 1999). I mean by this the ordinary, everyday spoken language that we learn as our mother tongue; and by the grammar I mean, as always, the grammatical systems and structures – the clause complexes, clauses, phrases, groups and words, as well as the lexical items themselves, the vocabulary. So 'grammar' here is short for lexicogrammar. The essential point is that lexicogrammar (the syntax, morphology and vocabulary of a language all taken together) is one stratum within the overall organization of language; and underlying all of it is a network of *systems*. When we look at the grammar in this way, systemically, we are able to see it all as a single resource, a unified force for transforming our experience into meaning.

Let me try to make this point a little clearer. The categories and relations we use to talk about things – the names we use, their systematic relationships to each other, the configurations in which they occur – define for us what we think of as 'reality'. Reality is what our language says it is. But these categories and relations were not given to us ready-made. The world as we **perceive** it is not clearly bounded and classified. We have to **impose** the categories ourselves, grouping together sets of different and often quite disparate phenomena that for purposes of human survival can be treated as alike. So, when I look outside my study window I see various objects sticking up out of the ground. Some are *trees*, some are *shrubs*, some are *bushes*, some are *flowers*, some are *herbs*, and some are *weeds*. They are all different kinds of *plants*; but they are distinguished from each other by a range of different and quite mixed criteria (a *weed*, for example, is a plant that ought not to be growing where it is), and all of them are indeterminate and overlapping categories – they are fuzzy sets. And I can say *plants grow*, but I can also say *I grow plants*, as well as *I plant* (*trees, flowers* etc.), and even *I plant plants* (as in *I planted a lot of native Australian plants in my garden this year*). All this everyday talk embodies a great deal of theory, about what things are, and how they relate to each other and to us. But it is theory that we subscribe to quite unconsciously. Of course, we had to learn it all, when we were children; but we have long forgotten how and where we learnt it. We know so much; but we do not know that we know it. And if later on, in school or university, any of our teachers refers to this kind of everyday, commonsense knowledge, it will usually be in order to disparage it – to dismiss it as worthless because it does not correspond to the new reality we are being required to master. The teacher says, 'Of course, grass trees aren't really trees at all' – just as spiders aren't insects, dolphins aren't fishes, and so on. When we go to school, we have to learn a new kind of knowledge: educational knowledge, which has its own categories, its own ways of reasoning about them – and its own language. Of course, many of these scientific categories and ways of reasoning do correspond to the unconscious categories and unconscious rationality of the language of daily life; but many of them do not – and even when they do, children often don't realize that they do, because they have to learn them all over again in a different grammar.

So children learn (to take an example from a primary school textbook):

Some animals protect themselves with bites and stings.

Now every child of 8 or 9 years old knows perfectly well that lots of creatures can bite you or can sting you. But they wouldn't say it the way the book said it. They probably wouldn't call a lot of them animals (for example wasps, spiders, even snakes); and they certainly wouldn't say *with bites and stings*. They would say (once they had got over the idea that the wasp only stung them in order to protect itself) *by biting and stinging*, using verbs rather than nouns to make the point. And when they came to the next sentence:

Some animals rely on their great speed to escape from danger.

they would find it hard to make any sense of this at all.

So how does this new, elaborated, semi-designed language of scientific knowledge differ from the evolved language of common-sense with which they started?

I will not be able here to track scientific language through the school in the way that children come to experience it; instead I will move straight on to the language of science as it is written for adults, which school learners are exposed to gradually, over the years. If you ask speakers of English what is distinctive about the language of science, they typically refer to its vocabulary: they say that it is full of technical terms, or else that it is full of "jargon", which simply means technical terms that the speaker doesn't understand. So it is perhaps useful to look at a passage of scientific writing (taken from the *Scientific American*) which shows that technical terminology is not a necessary feature of all scientific discourse:

Our work on crack growth in other solids leads us to believe that the general conclusions developed for silica can explain the strength behaviour of a wide range of brittle materials. The actual crack tip reactions appear to vary from material to material and the chemistry of each solid must be considered on a case-by-case basis.

(Michalske and Bunker 1987)

Let me make it clear what I am saying. I am not saying that scientific English does not contain technical vocabulary; of course it does. What I am saying is that we do not **need** technical vocabulary to recognize that a passage of English comes from a scientific text. There are other features also at work. Take for example the clause (*that*) *the general conclusions developed for silica can explain the strength behaviour of a wide range of brittle materials*: we may note the expression *the strength behaviour of . . . materials*, and also the wording *the conclusions . . . can explain the . . . behaviour*. If we focus just on this particular clause, I would draw attention to three of its lexico-grammatical features. (i) It has a very simple structure: just three elements, which (if we represent them in terms of grammatical classes) are nominal group + verbal group + nominal group. (ii) The process construed by the clause is one of a clearly recognized type, 'a explains *x*', incorporating a verb *explain* (cf. *prove, show, demonstrate, suggest* etc.) which sets up a particular logical relationship between the two nominal expressions – it is a subtype of circumstantial relational clause, one where the verb is such that it can also function as a verbal process or projection with a human sayer, as in *Smith explained that* . . . (iii) The Head nouns in the two nominal groups are both nominalizations of processes: *conclusion* > *conclude*, *behaviour*> *behave*.

It is possible to identify here something that could be regarded as the prototypical clause of modern scientific English, a kind of 'favourite clause type' that runs throughout the discourse of science. By 'favourite clause type' I don't mean that it is the most frequent. That would be a meaningless claim, since it would make sense only if we first defined (a) the exact population of clauses that constituted 'scientific English', in terms of the variables that I talked about earlier, (b) the exact boundaries of this 'favourite clause type' itself, and (c) the degree of detail to which other clause types would need to be specified in order to distinguish them from the 'favourite' one. It certainly is very frequent. But in saying that it is the favourite clause type, I am talking in qualitative terms – in terms of the semantic load that it carries: its critical role in furthering the argument, and in constructing scientific theories.

The following is a set of examples, taken from different technical and scientific texts, illustrating this favourite clause type:

a) the net effect of electron emission *is* the conversion of a neutron to a proton

b) segregation of DNA into daughter cells *is a simple consequence of cell growth*

c) gene recombination *results from* some sort of physical exchange, or crossover, between chromatids

d) this input of energy to produce conformational change leading to strong binding *appears to be the factor behind* the frequent occurrence of normally 'buried' hydrophobic side-chains as contact residues for antibody

e) simple addition of certain 16 amino acid peptides from influenza nucleoprotein to uninfected cells *conferred* susceptibility to T-cell lysis

f) the inheritance of specific genes *is correlated with* the inheritance of a specific chromosome

g) the induction of mutations by causing base-pair transitions *is to be contrasted with* the mechanism of induction of mutations by certain acridine dyes

h) any change in the electrons' energy *arises because of* their interaction with the gas atoms

i) disc braking *can only occur* in very young stars

j) the balance between the different effects *should depend on* the strength of the magnetic field

k) fire intensity *has a profound effect on* smoke injection

l) the theoretical program of devising models of atomic nuclei *has been complemented by* experimental investigations

m) the failure to be stimulated by the pigeon peptide in association with B10.A(5R) *seems* therefore *to be due to* an inability of the antigen to complex with the I-E of B10.A(5R)

I have italicized that part of the clause which expresses the logical-semantic relation between the two processes that are nominalized (or, in example i, the 'happening' of the one single process). It will be clear that the 'favourite clause type' is a broadly defined category, with a range of what look like very different verbs – it is, in fact, a fairly indeterminate, or 'fuzzy', category, in the sense that however explicitly we define it there will always be doubtful cases. But it is possible to characterize it reasonably accurately, providing we first describe the principles on which the everyday grammar works in constructing its model of 'reality'. This is what I referred to earlier in saying that a grammar was a theory of human experience – where likewise I was referring to the grammar of daily life.

I am talking here, of course, about the daily life grammar of English. But in order to make the points that I want to make about scientific English, and the differences between the two, I shall need to refer just to one or two very general principles; and these are principles that seem to be common to all human languages. The details of how these principles work out are highly variable, from one language to another; but this variation does not affect the overall direction of the argument.

In all human languages, the grammar construes experience in terms of *figures*. A figure is a complex semantic unit of which the organizing concept is that of a process – something happens; this is the raw material of human experience, some change taking place in the environment, or else inside our own body or our own consciousness. The figure is a theoretical model of this process, in terms of the different elements that go to make it up: the process itself, the entity or entities participating in the process and circumstantial elements like where, when, how or why it happens. Let us suppose we are standing by the road on the side of a mountain; everything is peaceful, until suddenly something happens – there is a rapid downhill movement, and a large object on wheels comes rushing past. We construe this, through our grammar, as a figure: a process 'drive', two participating entities 'bus' and 'person driving', and two circumstantial elements 'down the hill' and 'very fast'. The last of these we might combine with a value judgment: not just 'very fast' but 'too fast'. So we say *the driver was driving the bus too fast down the hill*.

The grammatical configuration that construes this figure is a *clause*; and the elements of the figure are construed as *groups* and *phrases*. The groups and phrases are of different kinds:

verbal group	construing process	e.g. *was driving*
nominal group	construing participant	e.g. *the bus, the driver*

and for the circumstantial elements:

adverbial group	construing circumstance (manner)	e.g. *too fast*
prepositional phrase	construing circumstance (place)	e.g. *down the hill.*

187

A clause consists of some combination of groups and phrases; it has a nucleus consisting of the process plus one participant, the one in which the process comes to be actualized (here 'drive' and 'bus': *was driving the bus*).

One further step. There can of course be any number of figures; but sometimes the grammar construes two figures into a ***sequence***, with a particular logical-semantic relation set up between them. This might be, for example, a relation of 'cause': suppose the event we just construed had an unfortunate consequence, we might continue *so the brakes failed*, where the second clause *the brakes failed* is linked to the first by a conjunction *so*. The grammar construes this sequence of two figures as a ***clause nexus***. Of course, a sequence can go on for a number of figures, so we need the more general concept, in the grammar, of a ***clause complex***, a structure made up of any number of conjoined clauses. (For details of the grammatical analysis see Halliday 1985/94).

Now the point that needs to be emphasized here is this. The sequences, figures and elements are not 'given': they are constructed, or (as I prefer to say, since it is a semiotic construction) 'construed' by the grammar. The phenomenon as we perceive it is unanalysed and unbounded; it is the grammar that construes it as a configuration consisting of process, participants and circumstances. The grammar transforms human experience into meaning. The different ranks in the semantics – sequence, figure, element – and the different types of semantic element – process, participant, circumstance, relator, and also quality (of participant, which was not illustrated just now, but could have been, say *the reckless driver*) – do not exist as prior mental constructs: they are created by the grammar, as a theoretical schema or model of experience. We can set out the basic pattern, as it appears in English, as in Figure 7.1; and the illustrative example can then be analysed as in Figure 7.2.

There is thus, in our everyday language of commonsense, a regular pattern of relationship between the grammatical categories (clause, verbal group etc.) and the semantic ones (figure, process etc.). I shall refer to this pattern of relationship between the grammar and the semantics as "congruent". Of course, if the grammar never departed from this pattern, we would not need to refer to it by any name at all; we would just take it for granted, without even needing to distinguish between what is "grammatical" and what is "semantic" – we could treat the whole as just one level of organization. But what the grammar has construed it can also deconstrue, and reconstrue into

	semantic		lexico grammatical
ranks	sequence [of figures]	realized by	clause nexus
	figure	"	clause
	element [in figure]	"	group/phrase
types of element	process	"	verbal group
	participating entity	"	nominal group
	quality	"	adjective (in nominal group)
	circumstance	"	adverbial group or prepositional phrase
	relator	"	conjunction

Figure 7.1 Congruence between semantic and grammatical categories

the driver	drove	the bus	too rapidly	down the hill	so	the brakes	failed
nominal group	verbal group	nominal group	adverbial group	prepositional phrase	conjunction	nominal group	verbal group
entity	process	entity	circumstance	circumstance	relator	entity	process

Figure 7.2 Example of sequence, showing figures and elements

quite a different pattern; and it is this potential that is exploited in the language of science. If our everyday, commonsense grammar is a transformation of experience into meaning, our elaborated grammar of science is a retransformation, a reconstrual along rather different lines. Figure 7.3 shows what happens to the bus when its unfortunate demise is written up in a scientific paper.

the driver's	overrapid	downhill	driving	of the bus	caused	brake	failure
Deictic (my friend's	Epithet new	Classifier sports	Thing car	Qualifier from Italy)		Classifier	Thing
nominal group						nominal group	

Figure 7.3 The same sequence reconstrued as one clause

The elaborated pattern is entirely familiar; it has been recognized in grammar for a very long time, under the term **nominalization**, which means turning other things into nouns, or at least getting

189

them to behave as if they were nouns. What is significant here is the particular way it happens. The nominal group, in its origin as a congruent construction, is an expansion outwards from a noun, the noun standing at the head of the construction. This noun construes the entity itself; we say, in our functional grammar, that it functions as the Thing. This then gets expanded by the addition of various other items, in a fairly regular order (the order of course differs from one language to another, though again there can be seen to be common principles at work). In English, as you move 'to the left' (that is, preceding the noun that is functioning as Thing), you first come to the Classifier, which assigns the element to a class, like *sports* in *sports car*; then to Epithet, which gives it a descriptive quality, like *new* in *new sports car*; before that comes Numerative, which characterizes it by quantity or place in order, like *second* in *second new sports car*; and finally (that is, right at the beginning) a Deictic, which allocates this particular instance to some recognizable point of reference, like *this* or *my*, or *my friend's* in *my friend's second new sports car*. Then, coming (in English) after the Thing, functioning as Qualifier, we may have phrases or clauses which add further specification, like *from Italy* in *my friend's second new sports car from Italy*; these are either circumstantial elements or figures that enter into the identification and definition of the Thing in question.

Now, the striking feature about nominalization is that the grammar uses precisely these same structural resources for (re)construing a figure: *the driver's overrapid downhill driving of the bus* is made up of functional elements identical with those of *my friend's new sports car from Italy*. The process 'drive' has become a Thing, *driving*; the circumstance *down the hill* has become a class of this Thing called *driving*, namely *downhill driving*; the circumstance of Manner *too rapidly* has become an Epithet; and the two participants, *the bus* and *the driver*, have become (i) a phrase functioning as Qualifier, *of the bus*, and (ii) a possessive Deictic *the driver's*.

In similar fashion, the figure 'brake + fail' has become another nominal group, with the process 'fail' construed as a Thing, *failure*, and the entity 'brake' construed as a class of failures – along with *heart failure, power failure, engine failure, crop failure* and so on. So instead of two clauses, we now have two nominal groups, with head nouns *driving* and *failure*.

But two nominal groups don't make a clause; they usually need a verbal group as well, to set up some configurational relation between them. Besides reconstruing the processes as nouns, as if they were entities, the grammar at the same time reconstrues the logical-semantic relation, 'so', as a verb, *cause* – as if this, in fact, was the process in which these entities were participating. Hence *the driver's overrapid downhill driving of the bus caused brake failure.*

This of course was a contrived example; I invented it. But all the examples cited earlier followed exactly the same general pattern. We could take any one of those examples and reword it as two clauses linked by a relator; e.g. (b) *cells grow, so DNA is segregated into daughter cells.* This is where the favourite clause type that I was talking about a short while ago comes from. As I said, we can define it in various ways, either more or less inclusively; but essentially it arises where the grammar deconstrues the **congruent** version of its modelling of human experience and reconstrues it in a different way, with processes and qualities made to look like things and the logical relation between processes made to look like the process itself. So, to take another very brief example, that of (k) above, we could say, congruently, *if (a) fire is intense it injects a lot more smoke* (we might want to add *into the atmosphere*, or else change *injects* to *gives off*); but what the text actually said – and these are all examples taken from scientific or technical texts – was *fire intensity has a profound effect on smoke injection.*

I shall refer to this phenomenon – the way the grammar shifts from a predominantly **clausal** to a predominantly **nominal** mode of construal – as "grammatical metaphor", since it is closely analogous to metaphor in its canonical, lexical sense. In lexical metaphor, one **word** (lexeme) is replaced by another; in grammatical metaphor, one grammatical **class**, or a whole grammatical **structure**, is replaced by another. And the effect, in both cases, is to bring out a new confluence of meanings.

We have to ask, then, why scientific English is typically written in this fashion: what is the payoff, from this kind of metaphoric reconstruction? I think we can investigate this from two points of view. One is from the point of view of its immediate context in the discourse: how it helps the argument along, how it contributes to the ongoing reasoning in the text. The other is from the point of view of its long-term context in the theory: how it helps in constructing a framework of technical concepts which are related to each other taxonomically and which operate at a highly abstract level where each term condenses in itself a large amount of accumulated knowledge.

To illustrate these effects properly would require at the least an entire text, and preferably even a text sequence, a 'macro-text' extending over the development of some particular branch of scientific theory. But let me do what I can with just a few lines of a fairly simple text. What I will try to illustrate is the twofold significance of the nominalizing metaphor: that it is both ***instantial*** and ***systemic***, in such a way that a system of meaning potential (which is what a scientific theory is) is built up out of instances of related scientific text. That is how theories are constructed.

First, Figure 7.4 will serve as a reminder of the nature of this ***grammatical metaphor***; it shows the relation between the clausal grammar of *an electron moves in an orbit* and the nominal grammar of *the orbital motion of an electron*.

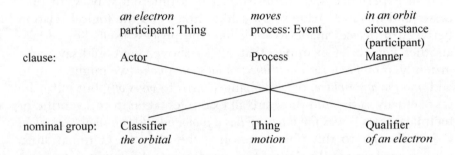

Figure 7.4 Grammatical metaphor: shifts in class and functional status

Let me use this as a point of reference for some observations on the following passage. This text is a short extract from an article in the *New Scientist*; we could characterize it as adult, semi-technical, non-specialized scientific discourse. I have italicized those portions which exemplify what I am talking about.

> Life on Earth involves a myriad species interacting with each other in ways that constantly change as *they evolve, differentiate and become extinct*. ... *This model of evolution* predicts that *life does not evolve gradually but intermittently*, interrupted by *bursts of change* which *are characterized by mass extinctions* and *the emergence of many new species*. ... In 1972, Eldredge ... and Gould ... proposed from their study of fossil records that the evolution of single species takes place in steps separated by *long periods of stability*. They named this phenomenon '*punctuated equilibrium*'. ... Evolutionary biologists have always assumed that *rapid changes in the rate of evolution* are caused by external events – which is why, for example, they have sought *an explanation for the demise of the dinosaurs* in *a meteorite impact*. On the other hand, if

life organizes into a critical state, *catastrophes* ... are *a natural part of evolution*.

(Per, Flyvberg and Sneppen, *New Scientist*, 12 March 1994)

We are told in the first sentence, in congruent, clausal form, that species evolve, differentiate and become extinct. The next sentence nominalizes *evolve* to *evolution* as part of the Theme of the clause, the point of departure for the next step in the argument where the writers refer to their own model – it would be difficult to get this into the Theme without nominalizing it. The model then *predicts*; this is one of the verbs from our favourite clause type, in its variant '*a proves x*' – but what it predicts is again first introduced in congruent form: *life does not evolve gradually but intermittently*. The next clause, beginning with *interrupted*, then nominalizes the other two processes from the first sentence: *mass extinctions*, and *the emergence of many new species* – again with a critical role in the discourse, although here not as Theme but as the culminative element or 'New-Rheme', the focus of information within the message. Again it is the nominalizing which makes this possible, because it is the only way of construing all this content as a single element in the clause. Notice that it uses both the Classifier (*mass extinction*, like *orbital motion*) and the Qualifier (*emergence of species*, like *motion of an electron*). Then likewise we find *long periods of stability* as New-Rheme, and *rapid changes in the rate of evolution* as Theme, both of them again packaging together much of what has gone before. This packaging into nominal groups is what makes it possible for large chunks of information to take on critical values in the flow of discourse, either as Theme or as culminative New-Rheme. They cannot take on these functional values if they remain in congruent, clausal form.

All these are instantial effects; they help to construct the discourse as a progression of steps in reasoning. Note the by now familiar verbs with which they are configured: *involves, are characterized by, predicts, takes place, are caused by, sought an explanation for* and finally simply *are*: *catastrophes are a natural part of evolution*.

And this leads into the complementary aspect of the payoff from grammatical metaphor – the systemic. Consider the technical terms within this passage. Some of them (*evolution, extinction, fossil records*) are long-established terms; they contain a vast store of accumulated knowledge and of argument, and a clearly defined status in a technical taxonomy, typically condensed into a single noun. The reason it is a noun rather than a verb or adjective has to do with the

193

semogenic potential of **entities**: these are construed by the grammar as being both stable in time and highly complex in the features they can accrue (recall here the very elaborate structure of the nominal group), whereas processes are typically transient and do not readily create or fit into taxonomies. But we can also see, in the same discourse, new theory in the making; and at one point this is made quite explicit: *they named this phenomenon 'punctuated equilibrium'* – using, as always, a nominal group with which to name it. Here we can see the process of condensation at work, because *this phenomenon* refers to the whole of the clause *the evolution of single species takes place in steps separated by long periods of stability* – behind which, again, lies a considerable body of related scientific text. *Punctuated equilibrium* now becomes a theoretical entity, an abstract or perhaps a virtual object that exists on the semiotic plane, and other people can now reason with it and write theses about it.

But having got this far, we can now see that the two kinds of effect that we recognized earlier, the immediate, instantial effect and the long-term, systemic effect, are ultimately all part of the same phenomenon, the creation of new meaning through the grammar's potential for metaphor. Many of the instantial effects are of course just that – they remain purely local in the discourse, like the word *emergence* in the present text. That one is not on the way to becoming a technical term. Others, like *catastrophe*, are perhaps on the borderline; here it clearly has a technical function, packaging much of the preceding matter into a Theme for a powerful sum-marizing clause. But it is already a technical term in mathematics, and there is presumably a resonance with that sense of *catastrophe* here. But in the last resort the discursive process, whereby the grammar creates these nominalizations to suit the needs of the argument, is the same process as that of generalization and abstrac-tion, which leads to the formation of theoretical terms and taxo-nomies. What we see in the discourse is scientific knowledge in the making. How it works out in detail, of course, will depend on the context, especially the tenor: a textbook writer, for example, is not developing new knowledge but leading the learner towards some-thing that is already known. But it is new, of course, to the reader; and it is noticeable that textbook writers, and writers on science for the public, often use the grammar in just this way, combining the flow of discourse with the construction of theory in a single voyage of discovery, like that leading towards *punctuated equilibrium* in the example I have just been considering.

I have been stressing the positive, meaning-creating power of scientific language because I think it is important to ask why the grammar evolved in the way it did. The grammar was not planned; it evolved in the context of pressure on the resources of the language – on the resources of all the emerging standard languages of Europe at that time – for construing new forms of knowledge, based on experimentation, observation and measurement, and reasoning therefrom. I have tried to suggest that, if we analyse the grammar, focusing on the features which distinguish it from everyday language, we will recognize how it came to have this extraordinarily powerful effect (see also Halliday 1999/2004).

But it soon got a bad reputation, in England, at least, for being artificially alien and obscure. So we need to explain also its negative effects.

It can be, unquestionably, extremely dense; and this denseness is something we can quantify, in a fairly simple fashion. We can measure the *lexical density* of scientific writing. There are various ways of doing this, and what works for one language won't necessarily work for another; but in English we can count the number of lexical words per ranking clause. By "lexical words" I mean content words, those which belong in the dictionary rather than in the grammar (the latter are the grammatical, or function, words). This distinction, between content words and function words, is a cline, or continuous scale, with no very clear boundary separating the two; but people have strong intuitions about it, and provided we draw the line consistently when we are comparing different texts it doesn't matter exactly where we draw it. By "ranking clauses" I mean those that are not embedded, and hence have their full status as clauses in the discourse (if we count embedded clauses separately, then the words which occur inside them have to be counted over again). If we look at the clauses set out as (a) to (m) above, we find they have a lexical density of anything up to nearly twenty:

a	b	c	d	e	f	g	h	i	j	k	l	m
7	8	7	19	13	7	11	7	4	7	6	9	12

But I have counted quite extensive passages of scientific text and the average lexical density that I have found is typically somewhere around six. By contrast, informal speech typically has around two lexical words per clause. If we take a sentence of moderately technical writing and 'translate' it step by step into an informal spoken

195

version, going from the most metaphorical to the most congruent, in the terms that I have been using, we might produce something like the following (original version first; lexical words italicized, clause boundaries indicated by ||):

(i)   the *use* of this *method* of *control unquestionably leads* to *safer* and *faster train running* in the most *adverse weather conditions*

(ii)   if this *method* of *control* is *used* || *trains* will *unquestionably* (be able to) *run safelier* and *faster* || (even) when the *weather conditions* are most *adverse*

(iii)   you can *control* the *trains* this way || and if you do that || you can be quite *sure* || that they'll be able to *run safelier* and *faster* || no matter how *bad* the *weather* gets

As you move from the nominal to the clausal mode, you get more clauses, naturally; but the number of lexical words does not go up – it may even go down, because empty lexical words like *conditions* tend to disappear. Here the comparative figures for the three versions were as follows:

	no. of clauses	no. of lexical words	lexical density
(i)	1	12	12
(ii)	3	11	3.67
(iii)	5	8	1.6

Where do the lexical items go, in these highly dense forms of discourse? How would ten or more content words be distributed within one clause? The answer to this has already become clear: they go inside nominal groups. Let me construct another example, again by rewording a sentence from a scientific text, this time in five different versions:

1   glass cracks more quickly the harder you press it
2   cracks in glass grow faster the more pressure is put on
3   glass crack growth is faster if greater stress is applied
4   the rate of glass crack growth depends on the magnitude of the applied stress
5   glass crack growth rate is associated with applied stress magnitude

Here is a commentary showing what semantic information is obtainable from the grammatical structure in each of the five variants:

1   'thing *a* undergoes process *b* in manner *c* to the extent that in manner *x* person *w* does action *y* to thing *a*'

2 '(complex) thing *b-in-a* acquires property *d* in manner *c* to the extent that (abstract) thing *xy* has process *z* done to it'

3 '(complex abstract) thing *abd* has attribute *c* under condition that (abstract) thing *xy* has process z done to it'

4 '(complex abstract) thing *c-of-abd* is caused by (complex abstract) thing *x-of-zy*'

5 '(complex abstract) thing *abdc* causes/is caused by (complex abstract) thing *zyx*'

It can be seen that in (1), which is the most congruent, the structural information is very explicit: if you say *glass cracks more quickly the harder you press it* you know from the grammar that some *thing* undergoes some *process* in some *manner* to the extent that in some *other manner* some *person* does some *action* upon it. As you move down towards (5), this information is gradually lost, until by the end all you know is that some *complex abstract thing* either *causes* or *is caused by* some other *complex abstract thing*. In other words, as one moves from the clausal mode of grammar to the nominal mode, one tends to gain in discursive power; but by the same token one tends to lose most of the ideational–semantic information, because all that the nominal group provides is a long string of modifying words. These can be obscure and highly ambiguous if one does not know what they mean in advance.

This is not necessarily a problem if such expressions have been steadily built up by reasoning throughout the text, in the way I have been describing in this paper. In the present text it was, so that by the time you had reached version (4), which by the way was the original wording, you knew well enough what the sentence meant – what general theoretical principle it was formulating. But this does not always happen. Writers are not always careful to lead up to such nominalized wordings in ways which reveal their internal structure.

There is a particular problem here for younger learners, because of the intrinsic nature of grammatical metaphor as a meaning-creating process. As I suggested at the start, the ordinary everyday grammar is a construal of human experience; and when children first learn their mother tongues, they are both learning the language and at the same time learning through the language – that is, using it as a means of learning in general. These two developments, learning language and learning through language, are really two facets of the same learning process: the semiotic construction of reality. The problem with grammatical metaphor is that it is in a sense sabotaging this process, deconstruing the patterns that the children have been working so hard in order to learn. It is not until the years of transition to adolescence that children really master these metaphorical structures; and this sets a critical task for language educators to take on. Experience in Australia is suggesting that children can be helped quite considerably if they are explicitly taught about the nature of technical and scientific language, including both its generic structures and its grammatical structures, at the same time as they are engaging with the scientific disciplines themselves. This as it were lets them into the secret, and helps them understand why they are faced with all these new and exotic ways of meaning. (For further information see Martin et al. 1988; Martin 1993.)

And it is here that I think the grammatical analysis can be helpful, in showing the essential continuity between the language of science and the language of daily life. Even the most abstruse scientific text is ultimately based in the grammar of the mother tongue, and depends on the primary construal of experience that that embodies. It is not the case that every clause in every paragraph is construed at this highly metaphorical level; on the contrary, every text incorporates both congruent and metaphorical forms of wording, and furthermore there is a tendency for the more metaphorical patterns to be built up gradually throughout the text from relatively congruent beginnings. In fact we can think of the language of science in terms of all three dimensions of its history: the evolution of the system, the growth and development of the human learner, and the unfolding of the individual text – these are all governed by the same general principle, that the congruent clausal world comes into existence first. This is what makes the eventual reconstruction of it in nominal terms so effective as a means of understanding. It is because you already know that *evolve* (say) is a process that you gain additional insight by reconstruing it as if it was a thing, *evolution*. It is not the nominal but the nominalized – not just being a noun, but being a noun that had first been something else – that gives us an extra dimension, the way of looking at the world in two different and contradictory ways at once which is the essence of the scientific understanding. That is something that may turn out to be common to all the different languages of science.

Chapter Eight

WRITING SCIENCE: LITERACY AND DISCURSIVE POWER (1993)

Adults may choose to deny it, but children in school know very well that there is a 'language of science'. They may not be able to say how they know it; but when they are faced with a wording such as:

> One model said that when a substance dissolves, the attraction between its particles becomes weaker,...
>
> (Junior Secondary Science Project 1968, pp. 32–3)

they have no trouble in recognizing it as the language of a chemistry book. And they tend to feel rather put off by it, especially when they find themselves challenged with a question like one that follows:

> What might happen to the forces of attraction which hold the particles of potassium nitrate together,...?
>
> (ibid.)

If children do get put off by this, we respond, as seems natural to us, by giving their feeling a name. We call it 'alienation'. We have now labelled the condition; we think that in labelling it we have diagnosed it, and that in diagnosing it we are halfway towards curing it. In reality, of course, we have only made the condition worse. Nothing could be more alienating than to learn that you are suffering from alienation. But in responding in this way we have helped to demonstrate how scientific discourse works.

It is not only schoolchildren who have felt alienated by the

'Introduction to writing science: literacy and discursive power' from *Writing Science: Literacy and Discursive Power*, M. A. K. Halliday and James Martin, London: RoutledgeFalmer, 1993. Reprinted by permission of RoutledgeFalmer.

discourse of science. Within a century of the so-called 'scientific revolution' in Europe, people were feeling disturbed by the picture that science presented, of a universe regulated by automatic physical laws and of a vast gulf between humanity and the rest of nature. Prigogine and Stengers, in their remarkable book *Order out of Chaos* (1984), show how this feeling arose; and they point to the disturbing paradox between the humanist origins of natural science and its contemporary image as something unnatural and dehumanizing:

> Science initiated a successful dialogue with nature. On the other hand, the first outcome of this dialogue was the discovery of a silent world. This is the paradox of classical science. It revealed to men a dead, passive nature, a nature that behaves as an automaton which, once programmed, continues to follow the rules inscribed in the program. In this sense the dialogue with nature isolated man from nature instead of bringing him closer to it. A triumph of human reason turned into a sad truth. It seemed that science debased everything it touched.
>
> (p. 6)

To understand this paradox, we have to take account of the kind of language in which science is construed. In his revealing account of science education, based on a study he carried out in New York secondary schools, Jay Lemke (1990a pp. 129–30) put it in this way:

> How does science teaching alienate so many students from science? How does it happen that so many students come away from their contact with science in school feeling that science is not for them, that it is too impersonal and inhuman for their tastes, or that they simply 'don't have a head for science'? One way this happens, I believe, is through the way we talk science. The language of classroom science sets up a pervasive and false opposition between a world of objective, authoritative, impersonal, humourless scientific fact and the ordinary, personal world of human uncertainties, judgments, values, and interests.

But the language of classroom science is simply the language of science adapted to the classroom. It fails to overcome the problem; but it did not create it in the first place. The issue is that of the discourse of science itself.

Where children are most likely to be put off is in the early years of secondary school, when they first come face to face with the language of their "subjects" – the disciplines. Here they meet with unfamiliar forms of discourse; and since these often contain numbers of technical terms, when we first reflect on scientific language we usually think of these as the main, perhaps the only, source of the difficulty. There are a lot of technical terms, of course, and they may be quite hard to master if they are not presented systematically. But children are not, on the whole, bothered by technical terms – they often rather enjoy them; and in any case textbook writers are aware of this difficulty and usually manage to avoid introducing too many of them at once. It is not difficult, however, to find passages of wording without many technical terms which are still very clear instances of scientific writing; for example

> ...One property at least (the colour) of the substance produced is different from the substances that were mixed, and so it is fairly certain that it is a **new substance**.
> (Junior Secondary Science Project 1968, p. 43)

Compare this example:

> Your completed table should help you to see what happens to the risk of getting lung cancer as smoking increases.
> (Intermediate Science Curriculum Study 1976, p. 59)

And this is not simply a feature of the language of science textbooks; the following extract from the *Scientific American* contains hardly any technical terms:

> Our work on crack growth in other solids leads us to believe that the general conclusions developed for silica can explain the strength behaviour of a wide range of brittle materials. The actual crack tip reactions appear to vary from material to material and the chemistry of each solid must be considered on a case-by-case basis.
> (Michalske and Bunker 1987, p. 81)

Of course, technical terms are an essential part of scientific language; it would be impossible to create a discourse of organized knowledge without them. But they are not the whole story. The distinctive quality of scientific language lies in the lexicogrammar (the "wording") as a whole, and any response it engenders in the reader is a response to the total patterns of the discourse.

Naturally it would engender no response at all unless it was a variety of the parent language. Scientific English may be distinctive, but it is still a kind of English; likewise scientific Chinese is a kind of Chinese. If you feel alienated by scientific English this is because you are reacting to it as a form of a language you already know very well, perhaps as your mother tongue. (If on the other hand you are confronting scientific English directly as a second language, you may find it extraordinarily difficult, especially if it is your first encounter with a language of science; but that is very different from being alienated by it.) It is English with special probabilities attached: a form of English in which certain words, and more significantly certain grammatical constructions, stand out as more highly favoured, while others correspondingly recede and become less highly favoured, than in other varieties of the language. This is not to imply that there is one uniform version of it, any more than when we talk of British English or Australian English we are implying that there is one uniform version of each of these dialects. Any variety of a language, whether functional or dialectal, occupies an extended space, a region whose boundaries are fuzzy and within which there can be considerable internal variation. But it can be defined, and recognized, by certain syndromes, patterns of co-occurrence among features at one or another linguistic level – typically, features of the expression in the case of a dialect, features of the content in the case of a functional variety or "register". Such syndromes are what make it plausible to talk of "the language of science".

Given the view of language that prevails in western thought, it is natural to think of the language of science as a tool, an instrument for expressing our ideas about the nature of physical and biological processes. But this is a rather impoverished view of language, which distorts the relationship between language and other phenomena. The early humanists, founders of modern science in the west, paid more serious attention to language in their endeavours. In part, this was forced upon them because they were no longer using the language that had served their predecessors, Latin, and instead faced the job of developing their various emerging 'national' languages into resources for construing knowledge. But their concern with language went deeper than that. On the one hand they were reacting against what they saw as (in our jargon of today) a logocentric tendency in medieval thought; the best-known articulation of this attitude is Bacon's 'idols of the marketplace' (*idola fori*), one of the four *idola* or false conceptions which he felt distorted scientific thinking. The *idola fori* result, in Dijksterhuis' (1961/86) words,

> ... from the thoughtless use of language, from the delusion that there must correspond to all names actually existing things, and from the confusion of the literal and the figurative meaning of a word; ...
>
> (p. 398 [IV: 184])

The "delusion" referred to here had already been flagged by William of Occam, whose often quoted stricture on unnecessary entities was in fact a warning against reifying theoretical concepts such as 'motion'; the perception that lay behind this suspicion of language was later codified in the nominalist philosophy of John Locke, summed up by David Oldroyd (1986) as follows:

> The important point, of course, is that the new philosophy claimed that new knowledge was to be obtained by experimentation, not by analysis of language or by establishing the correct definitions of things. If you wanted to know more about the properties of gold than anyone had ever known before you would need a chemical laboratory, not a dictionary!
>
> (pp. 91–2)

On the other hand, the scholars of the new learning were at the same time extremely aware of how crucial to their enterprise was the role that language had to play. Since "language" now meant 'languages', the perception of this role differed somewhat from one country to another; it was stated most explicitly in England and in France, partly perhaps because of the historical accident that these languages, which had changed catastrophically in the medieval period, were having more trouble sorting out their orthographies than Italian, German or Dutch. Whatever the reason, English and French scholars devoted much effort to designing a language of science; the work in England is described and evaluated by Vivian Salmon in her book *The Study of Language in Seventeenth Century England*, published in 1979. This work went through several phases, as those concerned progressively refined their conception of what it was that was needed to make their language effective as a resource for the new knowledge.

The earliest effort was simply to devise a form of shorthand, a writing system that would be simpler and more expeditious in codifying knowledge in writing; for example Timothy Bright's *Characterie*, published in 1588. Bright's work however already embodied a second, more substantial aim: that of providing a universal character, a system of writing that would be neutral among the various different languages, in the way that numerical symbols are. Bright appreciated the lexigraphic nature of Chinese writing (that its symbols stood for words, or their parts), which had then recently become accessible in Europe, and used that as a model for his purpose.

Within the next few decades, a more ambitious goal was being pursued, that of a universal "philosophical language": that is, a fully designed, artificial language that would serve the needs of scientific research. Among those who conceived of plans for such a philosophical language, Vivian Salmon refers to William Petty, Seth Ward, Francis Lodowick, George Dalgarno and John Wilkins; it was the last of these who actually carried out such a plan to the fullest extent, in his famous *Essay Towards a Real Character and a Philosophical Language*, published in 1668. Wilkins' impressive work was the high point in a research effort in which scholars from many countries had been deeply engaged, as they worked towards a new conception of the structure and organization of scientific knowledge.

A "philosophical language" was not simply a means of writing down, and hence transmitting, knowledge that had already been gained; more than that, it was a means of arriving at new knowledge, a resource for enquiring and for thinking with. The ultimate goal in the conception of scientific language design was subsequently articulated by Leibniz, who (in Oldroyd's words) "envisaged the construction of a general science of symbols which could be applied to experience" – a project, however, which "remained unfulfilled in Leibniz' time and remains so to this day" (Oldroyd 1986, pp. 104–5). But from the efforts and achievements of Wilkins and his contemporaries, and in particular from the extent to which the scientists themselves supported and participated in these efforts, we can gain a sense of the significance accorded to language in seventeenth- century scientific thought. Language was an essential component in enlarging the intellectual domain.

The biggest single demand that was explicitly made on a language of science was that it should be effective in constructing technical taxonomies. All natural languages embody their own folk taxonomies, of plants and animals, diseases, kinship structures and the like; but these are construed in characteristically messy ways, because of the need to compromise among conflicting criteria, and they were seen rather as an obstacle to developing the systematic technical taxonomies that were required by the new science. So when the scientists came to design their own artificial languages much of the emphasis was placed on building up regular morphological patterns for representing a classificatory system in words.

Clearly this had to be one of the central concerns. Unlike commonsense knowledge, which can tolerate – indeed, depends on – compromises, contradictions and indeterminacies of all kinds, scientific knowledge as it was then coming into being needed to be organized around systems of technical concepts arranged in strict hierarchies of kinds and parts. In the event, none of the artificial languages was ever used for the purpose; but the experience of linguistic design that went into creating them was drawn upon in subsequent work, for example in constructing systematic nomen-clatures for use in botany and in chemistry. Even where no special linguistic structures have been developed for the purpose, an essential feature of all scientific registers since that time has been their systems of technical terms.

But there is another aspect of scientific language that is just as important as its technical terminology, and that is its technical grammar. Interestingly, the C17 language planners paid no attention to this. Wilkins' philosophical language did, of course, incorporate a grammar – otherwise it would not have been a language, in any practical sense; but it was a grammar of a conventional kind, without any of the innovatory thinking that had gone into the lexical morphology. Yet if we examine how scientists such as Newton were actually using language in their own writings, we find innovations in the grammar which are no less striking than those embodied in the construction of technical terms. People are, of course, less conscious of grammar than they are of vocabulary; no doubt this is one reason for the discrepancy. The other reason would have been, perhaps, that the grammatical developments were more gradual; they were just one further move in a steady progression that had been taking place since the time of Thales and Pythagoras in ancient Greece, and they did not involve creating new grammatical forms so much as systematically deploying and extending resources that were poten-tially already there.

It is convenient to think of the new resources that came into scientific English (and other languages: for example the Italian of Galileo) at this time as falling under these two headings, the lexical and the grammatical. The lexical resources were highly visible, in the form of vast numbers of new technical terms; what was sig-nificant, however, was not so much the terms themselves as the potential that lay behind them. On the one hand, as we have seen, they could be formed into systematic taxonomic hierarchies; on the other hand, they could be added to *ad infinitum* – today a bilingual dictionary of a single branch of a scientific discipline may easily contain 50,000–100,000 entries. The grammatical resources were the constructions of nominal groups and clauses, deployed so that they could be combined to construe a particular form of reasoned argument: a rhetorical structure which soon developed as the prototypical discourse pattern for experimental science. Any passage of Newton's writings could be taken to illustrate these resources, both the lexical and the grammatical; for example the following passage taken from the *Opticks*:

> If the Humours of the Eye by old Age decay, so as by shrinking to make the *Cornea* and Coat of the *Crystalline Humour* grow flatter than before, the Light will not be refracted enough, and for want of a sufficient Refraction will not converge to the bottom of the Eye but to some place beyond it, and by consequence paint in the bottom of the Eye a confused Picture, and according to the Indistinctness of this Picture the Object will appear confused. This is the reason of the decay of sight in old Men, and shews why their Sight is mended by Spectacles. For those Convex glasses supply the defect of Plumpness in the Eye, and by increasing the Refraction make the Rays converge sooner, so as to convene distinctly at the bottom of the Eye if the Glass have a due degree of convexity. And the contrary happens in short-sighted Men whose Eyes are too plump.
>
> (Newton 1704, pp. 15–16 (Book One, II, Ax. VII))

This is not the place to discuss such language in detail; but we can illustrate the two sets of resources referred to above. Lexically, expressions such as *Crystalline Humour* (here shown to be a kind of *Humour*), *Refraction* (defined earlier in association with *Reflexion*), *Convex* and *Convexity* (contrasted a few lines further down with *the Refractions diminished by a Concave-glass of a due degree of Concavity*) are clearly functioning as technical terms. Grammatically, a pattern emerges in which an expression of one kind is followed shortly afterwards by a related expression with a different structural profile:

> will not be refracted enough ... for want of a sufficient Refraction
>
> paint (.) a confused Picture ... according to the Indistinctness of this Picture
>
> make the Cornea (.) grow flatter ... supply the defect of Plumpness in the Eye
>
> those Convex glasses ... if the Glass have a due degree of convexity ...

In each of these pairs, some verb or adjective in the first expression has been reworded in the second as a noun: *refracted – Refraction, confused – Indistinctness, (grow) flatter – (the defect of) Plumpness, Convex*

– *convexity*; and this has brought with it some other accompanying change, such as *will not be refracted enough – for want of a sufficient Refraction, a confused Picture – the Indistinctness of this Picture.* In each case a grammatical process has taken place which enables a piece of discourse that was previously presented as new information to be re-used as a 'given' in the course of the succeeding argument.

But when we observe these two features, technical vocabulary and nominalized grammar, in a passage of scientific text – even a very short extract like the one just cited – we can see that they are interdependent. Creating a technical term is itself a grammatical process; and when the argument is constructed by the grammar in this way, the words that are turned into nouns tend thereby to become technicalized. In other words, although we recognize two different phenomena taking place (as we must, in order to be able to understand them), in practice they are different aspects of a single semiotic process: that of evolving a technical form of discourse, at a particular 'moment' in socio-historical time.

There is no mystery about this being, at one and the same time, both one phenomenon and two. When we look at it from the standpoint of the wording – lexicogrammatically, or 'from below' in terms of the usual linguistic metaphor – it involves two different aspects of the language's resources, one in the word morphology, the other in the syntax. When we look at it from the standpoint of the meaning – semantically, or 'from above' – we see it as a single complex semogenic process. Lexicogrammatically, it appears as a syndrome of features of the clause; semantically, it appears as a feature of the total discourse. To get a rounded picture, we have to be able to see it both ways.

Here we can, obviously, offer no more than a while-you-wait sketch of one facet of the language of science – although an important one; but it will be enough, perhaps, to enable us to take the next step in our own argument. The language of science is, by its nature, a language in which theories are constructed; its special features are exactly those which make theoretical discourse possible. But this clearly means that the language is not passively reflecting some pre-existing conceptual structure; on the contrary, it is actively engaged in bringing such structures into being. They are, in fact, structures of language; as Lemke has expressed it, "a scientific theory is a system of related meanings". We have to abandon the naive, 'correspondence' notion of language, and adopt a more con-structivist approach to it. The language of science demonstrates

207

rather convincingly how language does not simply correspond to, reflect or describe human experience; rather, it interprets or, as we prefer to say, "construes" it. A scientific theory is a linguistic construal of experience.

But in that respect scientific language is merely foregrounding the constructive potential of language as a whole. The grammar of every natural language – its ordinary everyday vocabulary and grammatical structure – is already a theory of human experience. (It is also other things as well.) It transforms our experience into meaning. Whatever language we use, we construe with it both that which we experience as taking place 'out there', and that which we experience as taking place inside ourselves – and (the most problematic part) we construe them in a way which makes it possible to reconcile the two.

Since we all live on the same planet, and since we all have the same brain capacities, all our languages share a great deal in common in the way experience is construed. But within these limits there is also considerable variation from one language to another. Prigogine and Stengers (1984) remark, in the preface to the English translation of their book:

> We believe that to some extent every language provides a different way of describing the common reality in which we are embedded.
>
> (p. xxxi)

– and they are right. Much of this variation, however, is on a small scale and apparently random: thus, the minor differences that exist between English and French (the language in which their book was originally written), while irritating to a learner and challenging to a translator, do not amount to significantly different constructions of the human condition. Even between languages as geographically remote as English and Chinese it is hard to find truly convincing differences – perhaps the gradual shift in the construction of time from a predominantly linear, past/future model at the western end of the Eurasian continent (constructed in the grammar as tense) to a predominantly phasal, ongoing/terminate model at its eastern end (constructed in the grammar as aspect) would be one example, but even there the picture is far from clear. By and large there is a fair degree of homogeneity, in the way our grammars construe experience, all the way from Indonesia to Iceland.

This is not really surprising. After all, human language evolved along with the evolution of the human species; and not only along with it but as an essential component in the evolutionary process.

The condition of being human is defined, *inter alia*, by language. But there have been certain major changes in the human condition, changes which seem to have taken place because, in some environments at least, our populations tend inexorably to expand (see for example Johnson and Earle 1987; on p. 16 they sum up their findings by saying "The primary motor for cultural evolution is population growth"). The shift from mobility (hunting and gathering) to settlement (husbanding and cultivating) as the primary mode of subsisting was one such catastrophic change; this may have been associated with quite significant changes in the way experience is construed in language. The classic statement on this issue was made by Benjamin Lee Whorf (Carroll 1956), in his various papers collected under the title *Language, Thought and Reality*; despite having been 'refuted' many times over this remains as viable as it was when it was first written. More recently, Whorf's ideas have come to be discussed with greater understanding, e.g. by Lee (1985), Lucy (1985), and Lucy and Wertsch (1987) (see their articles listed in the Bibliography).

It would be surprising if there were not some pervasive differences in world view between two such different patterns of human culture. Since some sections of humanity have continued to pursue a non-settled way of life, it ought to be possible to compare the language of the two groups; but this has still not been satisfactorily achieved – for two main reasons. One is that the random, local variation referred to earlier gets in the way; if we focus on grammatical structure, then all types of language will be found everywhere, but it is the underlying 'cryptotypic' grammar that would vary in systematic ways, and we have hardly begun to analyse this. The other reason is that many linguists have felt discouraged by the risk of being attacked as naive historicists (at best, and at worst as racists) if they ventured to suggest any such thing. But to recognize that the changeover from mobility to settlement, where it took place, was an irreversible process is not in any way to attach value to either of these forms of existence. The point is important in our present context, because there appear to have been one, or perhaps two, comparably significant changes in the course of human history, likewise involving some populations and not others; and the "scientific revolution" was one. (The other, perhaps equally critical, was the "technological revolution" of the iron age.)

Let us be clear what we are saying here. It is not in dispute that, for whatever reason, certain human societies evolved along particular lines following a route from mobility to settlement; among those that settled, some evolved from agrarian to technological, and some of these again to scientific–industrial. The question we are asking is: what part does language play in these fundamental changes in the relationship of human beings to their environment? One answer might be: none at all. It simply tags along behind, coining new words when new things appear on the scene but otherwise remaining unaffected in its content plane (its semantics and its grammar). In this view, any changes that took place in language were merely random and reversible, like the changes from one to another of the morphological language 'types' set up in the nineteenth century (isolating, agglutinative, inflexional).

We reject this view. In our opinion the history of language is not separate from the rest of human history; on the contrary, it is an essential aspect of it. Human history is as much a history of semiotic activity as it is of socio–economic activity. Experience is ongoingly reconstrued as societies evolve; such reconstrual is not only a necessary condition for their evolution – it is also an integral part of it. We have barely started to understand the way this happens; partly because, as already stressed, our descriptions of languages are not yet penetrating enough, but also because we do not yet fully comprehend how semiotic systems work. (We shall come back to this point below.) But while we may not yet understand how meaning evolved, this is no reason for denying that it did evolve, or for assuming that all semantic systems were spontaneously created in their present form.

When we come to consider a special variety of a language, such as the language of science, we may be better able to give some account of how this evolved; not only has it a much shorter history, but also we can assume that whatever special features it has that mark it off from other varieties of the language have some particular significance in relation to their environment. Or rather, we can assume that they had some particular significance at the time they first appeared; it is a common experience for such features to become ritualized over the course of time, once the social context has changed, but it is virtually certain that they would have been functional in origin. Scientific discourse has been instrumental in constructing and maintaining extraordinarily complex ideological edifices, and the grammar has evolved to make this discourse possible. In the process, the grammar has been reconstruing the nature of experience.

It is not too fanciful to say that the language of science has reshaped our whole world view. But it has done so in ways which (as is typical of many historical processes) begin by freeing and enabling but end up by constraining and distorting. This might not matter so much if the language of science had remained the special prerogative of a priestly caste (such a thing can happen, when a form of a language becomes wholly ceremonial, and hence gets marginalized). In our recent history, however, what has been happening is just the opposite of this. A form of language that began as the semiotic underpinning for what was, in the world-wide context, a rather esoteric structure of knowledge has gradually been taking over as the dominant mode for interpreting human existence. Every text, from the discourses of technocracy and bureaucracy to the television magazine and the blurb on the back of the cereal packets, is in some way affected by the modes of meaning that evolved as the scaffolding for scientific knowledge.

In other words, the language of science has become the language of literacy. Having come into being as a particular kind of written language, it has taken over as model and as norm. Whether we are acting out the role of scientist or not, whenever we read and write we are likely to find ourselves conjured into a world picture that was painted, originally, as a backdrop to the scientific stage. This picture represents a particular construction of reality; as Prigogine and Stengers (1984) remind us,

> Whatever **reality** may mean, it always corresponds to an active intellectual construction. The descriptions presented by science can no longer be disentangled from our [i.e. the scientists'] questioning activity...
>
> (p. 55)

But it is a picture that is far removed from, and in some ways directly opposed to, the 'reality' of our ordinary everyday experience. Of course, this too is a construct; it is constructed in the grammar of the ordinary everyday language – the "mother tongue" that first showed us how the world made sense. But that simply makes it harder for us to accept a new and conflicting version. If you feel that, as a condition of becoming literate, you have to reject the wisdom you have learnt before, you may well decide to disengage. The "alienation" that we referred to at the beginning is in danger of becoming – some might say has already become – an alienation from the written word.

★ ★ ★ ★ ★ ★ ★ ★ ★ ★

211

In concentrating on the grammar, we are not excluding from the picture the generic aspects of scientific discourse; questions of genre are clearly significant. The structure of a scientific paper was explicitly debated by the founders of the Royal Society in London; and although ideas have changed about what this structure should be, editors of journals have always tended to impose their rather strict canons of acceptable written presentation, as regards both the textual format and (more recently also) the interpersonal style. But this aspect of scientific discourse has been rather extensively treated (for example in Charles Bazerman's (1988) book *Shaping Written Knowledge*); whereas almost no attention has been paid to the distinctive features of its grammar. Yet it is the grammar that does the work; this is where knowledge is constructed, and where the ideological foundations of what constitutes scientific practice are laid down.

The evolution of science was, we would maintain, the evolution of scientific grammar. We do not mean by this scientific **theories** of grammar — a scientific "grammatics"; we mean the grammatical resources of the natural languages by which science came to be construed. In case this seems far-fetched, let us make the point in two steps. The evolution of science was the evolution of scientific thought. But thought — not all thought, perhaps, but certainly all systematic thought — is construed in language; and the powerhouse of a language is its grammar. The process was a long and complex one, and it has hardly yet begun to be seriously researched; but we can try, very briefly, to identify some of the milestones along the way. We shall confine our account to western science, because it was in the west that the move from technology into science first took place; but it should be remembered that the original languages of technology evolved more or less simultaneously in the three great iron age cultures of China, India and the eastern Mediterranean.

As a first step, the early Greek scientists took up and developed a particular resource in the grammar of Greek, the potential for deriving from the lexical stem of one word another word of a different class (technically, the transcategorizing potential of the derivational morphology). Within this, they exploited the potential for transforming verbs and adjectives into nouns. In this way they generated ordered sets of technical terms, abstract entities which had begun as the names of processes or of properties, like *motion, weight, sum, revolution, distance* — or in some cases as the names of relations between processes, like *cause*. Secondly, these scholars — and more specifically the mathematicians — developed the modifying potential of the Greek nominal group; in particular, the resource of extending the nominal group with embedded clauses and prepositional phrases. In this way they generated complex specifications of bodies and of figures; these functioned especially as variables requiring to be measured, for example *the square on the hypotenuse of a right-angled triangle*. As in English (where the structure of the nominal group is very similar) this device was applicable recursively; its semogenic power can be seen in mathematical expressions such as the following from Aristarchus of Samos:

> The straight line subtending the portion intercepted within the earth's shadow of the circumference of the circle in which the extremities of the diameter of the circle dividing the dark and the bright portions in the moon move...
>
> (Heath 1913, p. 393)

These resources were then taken over by calquing (systematic translation of the parts) into Latin — without much difficulty, since the two languages were related and reasonably alike (although the second step was slightly problematic because the Latin nominal group was less inclined to accommodate prepositional phrases).

More than anything else, these two potentials of the grammar, that for turning verbs or adjectives into nouns, and that for expanding the scope of the nominal group — including, critically, the potential of combining the two together — opened up a discourse for technology and the foundations of science. In Byzantium, where Greek remained the language of learning, this discourse was eventually absorbed into Arabic, which had itself meanwhile emerged independently as a language of scholarship. In western Europe, where Latin took over, it continued to evolve into medieval times; by then, however, while the outward form was still Latin, the underlying semantic styles were those of the next generation of spoken languages, Italian, Spanish, French, English, German and so on, and further developments, even if first realized in Latin, were more an extension of these languages than of Latin itself. Probably the main extension of the grammar that took place in medieval Latin was in the area of relational processes (types of 'being'), which construed systems of definitions and taxonomies of logical relationships.

Early examples in English of the language of medieval technology and science can be found in Chaucer's *Treatise on the Astrolabe* and *Equatory of Planets*. For scientific English these serve as a useful point of departure. If one then compares the language of these texts with that of Newton, one can sense the change of direction that is being inaugurated in Newton's writing, where the grammar undergoes a kind of lateral shift that leads into 'grammatical metaphor' on a massive scale. Examples such as those given earlier, where e.g. *will not be refracted enough* is picked up by *for want of a sufficient Refraction*, are seldom found in the earlier texts. Expressions such as *a sufficient Refraction* and *the Indistinctness of this Picture*, each by itself so slight as to be almost unnoticeable, foreshadow a significant change of orientation in the discourse.

Why do we say these constitute a grammatical metaphor? Because a process, that of 'refracting', which was first construed as a verb (the prototypical realization of a process), then comes to be reconstrued in the form of a noun (the prototypical realization of a thing). The second instance is metaphorical with respect to the first, in the same way that the shift from *imagination* to *painted scenes and pageants of the brain* (from Abraham Cowley, quoted by Peter Medawar in *Pluto's Republic* (1984), p. 48) is metaphorical. Here, 'the faculty of producing mental images' is first represented "literally" as *imagination* and then re-represented as *pageants* which literally represents 'elaborate colourful parades'; this is metaphor in its regular, lexical sense. In grammatical metaphor, instead of a lexical transformation (of one word to another) the transformation is in the grammar – from one **class** to another, with the word (here the lexical item *refract-*) remaining the same. In the same way, in *a confused Picture . . . the Indistinctness of this Picture* a property, 'unclear', which was first construed as an adjective (the prototypical realization of a property), likewise comes to be reconstrued as a noun. (Here there happens to be also a lexical change, from *confused* to *indistinct*; but this does not involve any further metaphor.)

Now of course there has always been grammatical metaphor in language, just as there has always been lexical metaphor; the original derivations of nouns as technical terms in ancient Greek were already in this sense metaphorical. But there are certain significant differences between these and the later developments. The earlier process was one of transcategorization within the grammar; the meaning construed in this way is a new technical abstraction forming part of a scientific theory, and its original semantic status (as process or property) is **replaced by** that of an abstract theoretical entity – thus *motion* and *distance* are no longer synonymous with *moving* and *(being) far*. This semogenic process did not of course come to an end;

it continues with increasing vigour – it is hard to guess how many new technical terms are created in English each day, but it must amount to quite a considerable number. But in the later development the nominalized form is not in fact being construed as a technical term; rather, it is a temporary construct set up to meet the needs of the discourse, like *plumpness* or *indistinctness*, which still **retain** their semantic status as properties. We can think of instances like these, of course, as being technicalized for the nonce, and such "instantial" technicalizations may in time evolve into technical terms; but there is still a difference between the two. This difference can be seen in our first example, where *refraction* is being used not in its role as a technical term of the theory but as a metaphorical nominalization of the verb *refracted* – and so brings with it a little cluster of other grammatical metaphors, whereby the expression of the degree of the process, construed (in prototypical fashion) adverbially as *not . . . enough*, is reconstrued metaphorically as a noun *want* plus an adjective *sufficient* modifying the metaphorized process *refraction* (*for want of a sufficient Refraction*, where *Refraction* is still referring to the **process** of being refracted).

Such a small beginning may hardly seem worthy to be mentioned. But there is a steady, unbroken evolution in scientific English from this small beginning to the kinds of wording which are typical of written science today:

> A further consequence of the decreasing electronegativity down Group VII is that the relative stability of the positive oxidation states increases with increasing relative atomic mass of the halogen.
>
> (Hill and Holman 1978/83, p. 243)

> Let us imagine a hypothetical universe in which the same time-symmetric classical equations apply as those of our own universe, but for which behaviour of the familiar kind (e.g. shattering and spilling of water glasses) coexists with occurrences like the time-reverses of these.
>
> (Penrose 1989, p. 397)

> The subsequent development of aerogels, however, was most strongly promoted by their utility in detectors of Cerenkov radiation.
>
> (Jochen Fricke, 'Aerogels', *Scientific American*, May 1988, p. 93)

Here the effect of grammatical metaphor can be clearly seen, in expressions such as: the *development of x was promoted by their utility in y* (less metaphorically, *x were developed because they could be used in y*); *behaviour of the familiar kind, e.g. x-ing of y, coexists with occurrences like*

215

z-w (less metaphorically, *things behave not only in familiar ways, like y x-ing, but also in ways where the w is z-ed*); *the relative stability of x increases with increasing y of z* (less metaphorically, *x becomes more stable as z acquires more y*). These examples were not drawn from academic journals; they were taken from randomly opened pages of a senior secondary textbook, a book written for non-specialists, and an issue of the *Scientific American*. Articles written for specialists typically display a considerably denser concentration of grammatical metaphor, which reaches an extreme in the abstracts that are provided at the beginning.

The birth of science, then (if we may indulge in a well-worn lexical metaphor), from the union of technology with mathematics, is realized semiotically by the birth of grammatical metaphor, from the union of nominalization with recursive modification of the nominal group. This emerging variety of what Whorf called 'Standard Average European', instantiated for example in Galileo's Italian and in Newton's English (in reality, of course, a far more complex construction than this brief sketch can hope to suggest), provided a discourse for doing experimental science. The feature we have picked out as salient was one which enabled complex sequences of text to be 'packaged' so as to form a single element in a subsequent semantic configuration.

But by the same token, something else was also happening at the same time. When wordings are packaged in this way, having started off as (sequences of) clauses, they turn into nominal groups, like *the subsequent development of aerogels* nominalized from *aerogels (were) subsequently developed*. It is this nominalization that enables them to function as an element in another clause. But it also has another effect: it construes these phenomena as if they were **things**. The prototypical meaning of a noun is an object; when *stable, behave, occur, develop, useful* are regrammaticized as *stability, behaviour, occurrence, development, utility* they take on the semantic flavour of objects, on the model of the abstract objects of a technical taxonomy like *radiation, equation* and *mass*. Isolated instances of this would by themselves have little significance; but when it happens on a massive scale the effect is to reconstrue the nature of experience as a whole. Where the everyday 'mother tongue' of commonsense knowledge construes reality as a balanced tension between things and processes, the elaborated register of scientific knowledge reconstrues it as an edifice of things. It holds reality still, to be kept under observation and experimented with; and in so doing, interprets it not as changing with time (as the grammar of clauses interprets it) but as persisting – or rather, persistence – through time, which is the mode of being of a noun.

This is a very powerful kind of grammar, and it has tended to take over and become a norm. The English that is written by adults, in most present-day genres, is highly nominalized in just this way. Discourse of this sort is probably familiar to all of us:

> Key responsibilities will be the investment of all domestic equity portfolios for the division and contribution to the development of investment strategy.
>
> (*Sydney Morning Herald*, 1 February 1992, p. 32)

But whereas this nominalizing was functional in the language of science, since it contributed both to technical terminology and to reasoned argument, in other discourses it is largely a ritual feature, engendering only prestige and bureaucratic power. It becomes a language of hierarchy, privileging the expert and limiting access to specialized domains of cultural experience.

Lemke characterizes a language as a dynamic open system: a system that is not stable, but is metastable, able to persist through time only by constantly changing in the course of interacting with its environment. One way in which a language typically changes is that new registers or functional varieties evolve along with changing historical conditions. The evolution of a register of science is a paradigm example of this.

The "scientific revolution" took place in the context of the physical sciences; it was here that the new conception of knowledge was first worked out. Thus the leading edge of scientific language was the language of the physical sciences, and the semantic styles that evolved were those of physical systems and of the mathematics that is constructed to explain them. This discourse was then extended to encompass other, more complex kinds of system: first biological, then social systems. In calling these "more complex", we are obviously not comparing them in terms of some overall measure of complexity; we are referring specifically to their relationship to each other as classes of phenomena. A physical system, at least as construed in classical Newtonian physics, is purely physical in nature; but a biological system is both biological and physical, while a social system is at once all three. Hence it was progressively more difficult to understand the kind of abstraction that was involved in construing these various systems: a 'biological fact' is more problematic than a

217

'physical fact', and a 'social fact' is more problematic still. To put this in other terms, the relationship of an observable *instance* to the underlying *system* changes with each step; and the grammar, which developed around the semantics of a physical fact, has to come to terms with, and to naturalize, each of these new types of instantiation.

What the grammar does, as we have seen, is to construe phenomena of all kinds into a scientific theory. While there is some minor variation among the different languages in the way this is typically done – for example between English and French, where the former constructs reality more along empiricist, the latter more along rationalist lines – the grammar of scientific theory is largely in common. But what kind of a system is a scientific theory? A theory is a system of yet another kind – a *semiotic* system. A semiotic system is a system of the fourth order of complexity: that is, it is at the same time physical and biological and social.

The most general case of a semiotic system is a language (in the prototypical sense of this term: a natural language, spoken by adults, and learnt as a mother tongue). This involves a physical medium (typically sound waves), a biological organism as transmitter/receiver, and an interactive social order. Such a system constitutes, as we have expressed it, a general theory of experience: with it we construe our commonsense knowledge of the world, the 'reality' that lies about us and inside us. But construing organized knowledge, in the shape of a scientific theory, means evolving a dedicated semiotic system: a special register of a language which will be orthogonal to, and at the same time a realization of, a system (or rather a universe of systems) of one or more of these four kinds.

It seems to have taken two or three generations for people to come to terms with each new kind of system. If we use the century as a crude but convenient peg, we can say that physical systems were interpreted in C17–18, biological systems in C19 and social systems in our own C20. Of course, scholars had always been thinking about systems of the more complex kinds, and had tried to account for their special characteristics; already, among the ancient Greek scholars, the Stoics had recognized the need for a special theory of the sign to account for semiotic systems such as language. But in the main currents of thought the natural strategy was to map the more complex system on to a kind that is well understood. Thus in the modern period language was modelled first as matter, then as matter plus life, until in the early C20 Saussure imported from sociology the concept of value. Since a language is a phenomenon of all these kinds, it was possible to learn a great deal about it; but what was learnt did not yet amount to a science of language, because the special nature of semiotic systems had not yet been understood. Language has a fourth sphere of action, one that lies beyond those of matter, of life and of value; it has *meaning*. The unique property of semiotic systems is that they are systems of meaning.

Meaning arises when a dynamic open system of the social kind – one based on value – becomes stratified. Stratification is the feature that was first adumbrated in the classical theory of the sign; the technical name for the relationship that is brought about by stratifying is *realization*. We discuss below how the concept of realization may best be construed in a theory of language, given that we still understand relatively little about it. Lemke (1984) has suggested that it may be formalized through the notion of 'metaredundancy' as the analogue of the cause and effect of a classical physical system. But it is widely misinterpreted; nearly a century after Saussure there are still those who treat it as if it was a relation of cause and effect, asking about a stratal relationship such as that between semantics and lexicogrammar the naive question 'which causes which?' Realization is a relationship of a very different kind, more akin to that of token and value, where the two can only come into existence, and remain in existence, simultaneously.

Linguists often notice how, when highly sophisticated thinkers from other sciences turn their attention to language, they often ignore altogether the findings of linguistics and regress to treating language at the level at which it is presented in the early years of secondary school. We agree that this is a pity; but we are inclined rather to seek the reason why they do it. To us it seems that this happens because they consider that linguistics has not yet evolved into a science; in the formulation we used earlier, the nature of a 'semiotic fact' is still not properly understood. In our view the C20 scholar who came nearest to this understanding was Hjelmslev (1961) Whorf (Carroll ed. 1956) Trubetzkoy (1967) Lamb (1966, 1999) Chomsky (1961, 1964) Hagège (1981), with significant contributions from Whorf, from Firth and from Trubetzkoy; one of the few who have tried to build on Hjelmslev's work is Sydney Lamb. Chomsky oriented linguistics towards philosophy, where it had been located for much of its earlier history; but that did not turn it into a science. As one of the leaders of contemporary linguistics, Claude Hagège, has pointed out, it is the working practices of scientists – how they construct theories to explain the phenomena of experience – that provide the model for those (including linguists) who want to 'do science', rather than philosophers' interpretations of these, which are theories constructed to explain how scientists work.

There is no virtue in doing science for its own sake; and in any case linguistics does not become 'scientific' by slavishly following the methods of the physical or other sciences. If the semiotic sciences do develop alongside the others this will change our conception of what 'doing science' means. It will not change the principles of theory construction, or the essentially public nature of scientific activity; but it will add a new type of instantiation, and hence a new relation between the observer and the phenomenon, which will broaden our conception of possible kinds of reality. At present, because the relation between observable instance and underlying system is obscure there is a huge gulf in linguistics between the study of language and the study of text; and this is of practical significance, in that it adversely affects all forms of activity involving language, whether in language education, language pathology or language planning. In this respect, at least, there would seem to be room for a more 'scientific' approach.

Clearly whatever limitations there are to our understanding of language as a whole apply also to our understanding of the language of science. We have tried in the chapters in this book to close the gap between the system and the instance – which are, in fact, different observer positions, not different phenomena – and to interpret the language of science both as system, or potential, and as instantiated in text. We find it helpful, in this context, to locate it in its historical dimension – or rather, its historical dimensions, because a semiotic system moves along three distinct axes of time. First there is phylogenetic time: the system itself evolves, and here "system" may refer to human language as a whole, to a specific language such as English, or to a specific variety of a language, like scientific English. Secondly, there is ontogenetic time: the language of each human being grows, matures and dies. Thirdly there is what we might call "logogenetic" time, using *logos* in its original sense of 'discourse': each text unfolds, from a beginning through a middle to an end.

We confront all of these histories when we come to explain grammatical metaphor in the language of science. Given a pair of variants like (*how/that*) *aerogels subsequently developed* and *the subsequent development of aerogels*, if we view them synoptically all we can say is

220

that each one is metaphorical from the standpoint of the other. But if we view them as related in time, then there is a clear temporal priority. The clausal variant precedes the nominal one in all three dimensions of history: it evolved earlier in the English language (and probably in human language as a whole); it appears earlier in life, as children develop their mother tongue; and it tends to come at an earlier point in the unfolding of a particular text. It is these dynamic considerations that lead us to call the nominal variant metaphorical.

Can we discern any general historical trends that are relevant to the language of science? It seems to us that two things are happening that may influence the way the language of science goes on to evolve in the future. One is that semiotic processes are all the time becoming relatively more prominent in human life in general; the other is that systems of other kinds are coming to be interpreted more and more in semiotic terms. In both these developments language is at the centre, and in particular the language of systematized knowledge. However, it also seems to us that in both these contexts this language is likely to change, and to change in a particular direction. Language is, as we have tried to suggest, both a part of human history and a realization of it, the means whereby the historical process is construed. This is what we mean by language as "social semiotic": while it accommodates endless random variation of a local kind, in its global evolution it cannot be other than a participant in the social process.

It is a truism to say that we are now in the midst of a period of history when people's lifestyles are changing very fast. With our late C20 technology, many of us no longer spend our time producing and exchanging goods and services; instead, we produce and exchange information. The hub of a city of the industrial revolution was its railway station or its airport, where people and their products were moved around; that of a C21 city – a "multi function polis", as it has been ineptly named – will be (we are told) its information centre, or teleport. The citizens of Osaka, who regard their city as the technological capital of the world (what Osaka thinks today Tokyo will think tomorrow), call it an "information–oriented international urban complex of the 21st century"; its teleport will be

> an information communication base integrating satellite and overland optical fibre network communications systems; it is a port of information communication.
> (Osaka Port and Harbour Bureau, c. 1987, p. 7)

In this sort of environment, people will be interfacing more and more with semiotic systems and less and less with social, biological or physical ones – a way of life that is familiar to many human beings already.

As a concomitant of this, scientists are increasingly using semiotic models to complement their physical and biological models of the universe. This began with relativity, as David Bohm (1980) makes clear:

> A very significant change of language is involved in the expression of the new order and measure of time plied [*sic*] by relativistic theory. The speed of light is taken not as a possible speed of an **object**, but rather as the maximum speed of propagation of a **signal**. Heretofore, the notion of signal has played no role in the underlying general descriptive order of physics, but now it is playing a key role in this context.
>
> The word 'signal' contains the word 'sign', which means 'to point to something' as well as 'to have significance'. A signal is indeed a kind of **communication**. So in a certain way, significance, meaning, and communication become relevant in the expression of the general descriptive order of physics (as did also information, which is, however, only a **part** of the content or meaning of a communication). The full implications of this have perhaps not yet been realized, i.e. of how certain very subtle notions of order going far beyond those of classical mechanics have tacitly been brought into the general descriptive framework of physics.
>
> (p. 123)

Many physical, chemical and biological phenomena are coming to be interpreted as semiotic events. Prigogine and Stengers (1984) give the example of periodic chemical processes ("chemical clocks") that occur in far-from-equilibrium states of matter:

> Suppose we have two kinds of molecules, 'red' and 'blue'. Because of the chaotic motion of the molecules, we would expect that at a given moment we would have more red molecules, say, in the left part of a vessel. Then a bit later more blue molecules would appear, and so on. The vessel would appear to us as 'violet', with occasional irregular flashes of red or blue. However, this is **not** what happens with a chemical clock; here the system is all blue, then it abruptly changes its colour to red, then again to blue. Because all these changes occur at **regular** time intervals, we have a coherent process.
>
> Such a degree of order stemming from the activity of billions of molecules seems incredible, and indeed, if chemical clocks had not been observed, no one would believe that such a process is possible.

> To change colour all at once, molecules must have a way to 'communicate'. The system has to act as a whole. We will return repeatedly to this key word, communicate, which is of obvious importance in so many fields, from chemistry to neurophysiology. Dissipative structures introduce probably one of the simplest physical mechanisms for communication.
>
> (pp. 147–8)

Here "communicate" is picked out as a "key word", a word that is "of obvious importance in so many fields". But this, in fact, is where we have to demur. The **word** "communicate" in itself is of very little importance; nor is the fact that "the word 'signal' contains the word 'sign'", whatever that "contains" is taken to mean. What is important is the system of meanings that constitute a scientific theory of communication (that is, of semiotic systems and processes), and the lexicogrammatical resources (the *wordings* as a whole) by which these meanings are construed.

And here we come to a problem and a paradox. The problem is this. The language of science evolved in the construal of a special kind of knowledge – a scientific theory of experience. Such a theory, as we have said, is a semiotic system; it is based on the fundamental semiotic relation of realization, inhering in strata or cycles of token and value. But this means that scientists have all along been treating physical and biological processes as realizations – and hence as inherently communicative (Prigogine and Stengers refer to science as "man's dialogue with nature"). (We remind the reader here of our earlier note, that "system" is short for "system-&-process"; communicating is simply semiotic process.) The problem, now that semiotic systems are being explicitly invoked as explanatory models in science, is to direct the beam of scientific enquiry on to such systems and study them as phenomena in their own right. They can hardly serve an explanatory role if they are not themselves understood.

The prototype of a semiotic system is, as we have said, a natural language; and this leads us in to the paradox. In adapting natural languages to the construction of experimental science, the creators of scientific discourse developed powerful new forms of wording; and these have construed a reality of a particular kind – one that is fixed and determinate, in which objects predominate and processes serve merely to define and classify them. But the direction of physics in C20 has been exactly the opposite: from absolute to relative, from object to process, from determinate to probabilistic, from stability to flow. Many writers have been aware of the contradiction that this

223

has brought about, and have hoped somehow to escape from it by redesigning the forms of language – without realizing, however, that it is not language as such, but the particular register of scientific language, that presents this overdeterminate face. The language they learnt at their mothers' knees is much more in harmony with their deepest theoretical perceptions.

So while there is no reason to doubt that the language of science, as a variety of present-day English (and its counterpart in other languages), will continue to evolve in the twenty-first century, we may expect that it will change somewhat in its orientation. It is likely to shift further towards semiotic explanations, both at the highest level of scientific abstraction and at the technological level in line with the "information society" (the vast output of computer documentation has already constituted a special sub-register at this level). But at the same time it is likely to back off from its present extremes of nominalization and grammatical metaphor and go back to being more preoccupied with processes and more tolerant of indeterminacy and flux.

In order to do this while still functioning at the technical and abstract level of scientific discourse the grammar would need to be restructured in significant ways. This would not be a matter of inventing a few new verbs; it would mean recasting the nominal mode into a clausal one while developing the verbal group as a technical resource. Note in this connection Whorf's (1950) observation about Hopi:

> Most metaphysical words in Hopi are verbs, not nouns as in European languages ... Hopi, with its preference for verbs, as contrasted with our own liking for nouns, perpetually turns our propositions about things into propositions about events.
>
> (pp. 61, 63)

It is doubtful whether this could be done by means of design; a language is an evolved system, and when people have tried to design features of language they have almost always failed – although it has to be said that they have usually done so without knowing much about what language is or how it works. But however it came about, any change of this kind would have important social consequences, because it would help to lessen the gap between written language and spoken, and between the commonsense discourse of home and neighbourhood and the elaborated discourse of school and the institutions of adult life.

Two other factors seem to tend in the same direction. One is the way that information technology has developed. The semo-technology of the scientific revolution was print; this made the written language predominant, and greatly exaggerated the difference between writing and speech. Eventually the status of writing was undermined by speech technology – telephone and radio; this redressed the balance somewhat but did not bring the two closer together. The disjunction is being overcome, however, by tape recorders and computers: spoken language can now be preserved through time as text, while written language can be scrolled in temporal sequence up the screen. Instead of artificially forcing the two apart, the new technology tends to mix them up together, as happens for example in electronic mail, which is an interesting blend of spoken and written forms.

But there is another, deeper tendency at work, a long-term trend – however faltering and backtracking – towards more democratic forms of discourse. The language of science, though forward-looking in its origins, has become increasingly anti-democratic: its arcane grammatical metaphor sets apart those who understand it and shields them from those who do not. It is elitist also in another sense, in that its grammar constantly proclaims the uniqueness of the human species. There are signs that people are looking for new ways of meaning – for a grammar which, instead of reconstructing experience so that it becomes accessible only to a few, takes seriously its own beginnings in everyday language and construes a world that is recognizable to all those who live in it. We would then no longer be doomed, as Prigogine and Stengers put it, "to choosing between an antiscientific philosophy and an alienating science" (1984, p. 96).

BIBLIOGRAPHY

Bazerman, C. (1988) *Shaping Written Knowledge: the genre and activity of the Experimental Article in Science*. Madison, WI: The University of Wisconsin Press.

Biagi, M. L. A. (1995) 'Diacronia dei linguaggi scientifici', in R. Rossini Favretti (ed.), *Proceedings of the International Conference 'Languages of Science'*, Bologna, 25–27 October 1995.

Bohm, D. (1980) *Wholeness and the Implicate Order*. London: Routledge.

Bühler, K. (1934) *Sprachtheorie: die Darstellungsfunktion der Sprache*. Jena: Fischer.

Butt, D. G. (2000) 'The meaning of a network: linguistic networks for modelling complex behaviour', in D. G. Butt and C. M. I. M. Matthiessen (eds) *The Meaning Potential of Language: mapping meaning systemically*. Macquarie University Linguistics Department (mimeo).

Butt, D. G. (2001) 'Firth, Halliday and the development of systemic functional theory', in K. Koerner et al. (eds), *History of the Language Sciences* Vol. 2. Berlin and New York: Walter de Gruyter.

Carroll, J. B. (ed.) (1956) *Language, Thought and Reality: selected writings of Benjamin Lee Whorf*. Cambridge, MA: MIT Press.

Chaucer, G. (c.1390) *A Treatise on the Astrolabe*.

Chomsky, N. (1961) 'Generative grammar' *Word* 17.

Chomsky, N. (1964) 'Topics in the theory of generative grammar' in T. A. Sebesk (ed.) *Theoretical Foundations*. The Hague: Mouton (Current Trends in Linguistics 3).

Dalton, J. (1827) *A New System of Chemical Philosophy*. London: George Wilson.

Darwin, C. (1859) *The Origin of Species by Means of Natural Selection*. New York: Avenel Books, 1979.

Davidse, K. (1992a) 'A semiotic approach to relational clauses'. *Occassional Papers in Systematic Linguistics* 6.

Davidse, K. (1992b) 'Existential constructions: a systemic perspective'. *Leuvense Bijdragen* 81.

Davidse, K. (1999) *Categories of Experiential Grammar*. University of Nottingham: Monographs in Systemic Linguistics.

Dawkins, R. (1982) *The Extended Phenotype: the long reach of the gene*. Oxford and New York: Oxford University Press.

Derewianka, B. (1995) *Language Development in the Transition from Childhood to Adolescence: the role of grammatical metaphor*. Macquarie University, PhD thesis.

Dijksterhuis, E. J. (1961/86) *The Mechanization of the World Picture: Pythagoras to Newton*. Princeton, NJ: Princeton University Press.

Edelman, G. M. (1992) *Bright Air, Brilliant Fire: on the matter of the mind*. New York: Basic Books.

Eggins, S. (1994) *An Introduction to Systemic Functional Linguistics*. London: Pinter.

Ellis, J. M. (1993) *Language, Thought, and Logic*. Evanston, IL: Northwestern University Press.

Fairclough, N. (1992) *Discourse and Social Change*. Cambridge: Polity Press.

Firth, J. R. (1957a) 'A synopsis of linguistic theory', in J. R. Firth et al., *Studies in Linguistic Analysis*. Oxford: Blackwell (for the Philological Society). Reprinted in Palmer (ed.), 1968.

Firth, J. R. (1957b) *Papers in Linguistics 1934–1951*. London: Oxford University Press.

Fries, P. H. (1992) 'The structuring of written English text', *Language Sciences* 14.4.

Fries, P. H. (1995) 'Themes, methods of development, and texts', in Hasan and Fries (eds).

Goatly, A. (1995) 'Congruence and ideology', *Social Semiotics* 5.1.

Hagège, C. (1981) *Critical Reflections on Generative Grammar*, translated by Robert A. Hall Jr. Lake Bluff IL: Jupiter Press.

Halliday, M. A. K. (1967–8) 'Notes on transitivity and theme in English, Parts 1–3', *Journal of Linguistics* 3.1, 3.2, 4.1. In Collected Works, Vol. 7.

Halliday, M. A. K. (1975) *Learning How to Mean: explorations in the development of language*. London: Edward Arnold. Some parts in Collected Works, Vol. 4, chaps. 2–3, 2004.

Halliday, M. A. K. (1978) 'Meaning and the construction of reality in early childhood', in H. L. Pick Jr. and E. Saltzman (eds), *Modes of Perceiving and Processing of Information*. Hillsdale, NJ: Lawrence Erlbaum. In Collected Works, Vol. 4, chap. 5, 2004.

228

Halliday, M. A. K. (1979) 'One child's protolanguage', in M. Bullowa (ed.), *Before Speech: the beginnings of interpersonal communication*. Cambridge: Cambridge University Press. In Collected Works, Vol. 4, chap. 4, 2004.

Halliday, M. A. K. (1983) 'On the transition from child tongue to mother tongue', *Australian Journal of Linguistics* 3.2. In Collected Works, Vol. 4, chap. 9, 2004.

Halliday, M. A. K. (1984a) 'Language as code and language as behaviour: a systemic functional interpretation of the nature and ontogenesis of dialogue', in R. Fawcett et al. (eds), *The Semiotics of Culture and Language* Vol. 1. London: Frances Pinter. In Collected Works, Vol. 4, chap. 10, 2004.

Halliday, M. A. K. (1984b) *Listening to Nigel: conversations of a very small child*. Sydney: Linguistics Department, University of Sydney. In Collected Works, Vol. 4, CD Rom, 2004.

Halliday, M. A. K. (1985) *Spoken and Written Language*. Geelong, Australia: Deakin University Press.

Halliday, M. A. K. (1985/94) *An Introduction to Functional Grammar*. London: Edward Arnold (2nd edn, 1994).

Halliday, M. A. K. (1986) *Language and Learning: linguistic aspects of education and scientific knowledge*. Lecture series at National University of Singapore.

Halliday, M. A. K. (1987a) 'Spoken and written modes of meaning', in R. Horowitz and S. J. Samuels (eds), *Comprehending Oral and Written Language*. New York: Academic Press. In Collected Works, Vol. 1, chap. 12, 2002.

Halliday, M. A. K. (1987b) 'Language and the order of nature', in N. Fabb, D. Attridge, A. Durant and C. MacCabe (eds), *The Linguistics of Writing: arguments between language and literature*. Manchester: Manchester University Press. In Collected Works, Vol. 3, chap. 5, 2003.

Halliday, M. A. K. (1988) 'On the language of physical science'. This volume, chapter 5.

Halliday, M. A. K. (1990) 'New ways of meaning: a challenge to applied linguistics', *Journal of Applied Linguistics (Greek Applied Linguistics Association)* 6. Reprinted in Martin Pütz (ed.), *Thirty Years of Linguistic Evolution: studies in honour of René Dirven*. Philadelphia, PA and Amsterdam: John Benjamins, 1992. In Collected Works, Vol. 3, chap. 6, 2003.

Halliday, M. A. K. (1993a) 'The analysis of scientific texts in English and Chinese', in Halliday and Martin. In Collected Works, Vol. 8.

Halliday, M. A. K. (1993b) 'Towards a language-based theory of learning', *Linguistics and Education* 5.2. In Collected Works, Vol. 4, chap. 14, 2004.

Halliday, M. A. K. (1995) 'The grammatical construction of scientific knowledge: the framing of the English clause'. This volume, chapter 4.

Halliday, M. A. K. (1998) 'Language and knowledge: the "unpacking" of text'. This volume, chapter 2.

Halliday, M. A. K. (1999) 'Grammar and the construction of educational knowledge' in Roger Berry et al. (eds), *Language Analysis, Description and Pedagogy*. Hong Kong: Language Centre, University of Science & Technology, and Department of English. Lingnan University. In Collected Works, Vol. 4, chap. 15, 2004.

Halliday, M. A. K. and Hasan, R. (1976) *Cohesion in English*. London: Longman (English Language Series 9).

Halliday, M. A. K. and Martin, J. R. (1993) *Writing Science: literacy and discursive power*. London and Washington, DC: Falmer.

Halliday, M. A. K. and Matthiessen, C. M. I. M. (1999) *Construing Experience through Meaning: a language-based approach to cognition*. London and New York: Cassell (Open Linguistics Series).

Hamilton, J. H. and Maruhn, J. A. (1986) 'Exotic atomic nuclei', *Scientific American*. July 1986.

Hasan, R. (1973) 'Code, register and social dialect', in B. Bernstein (ed.), *Class, Codes and Control Vol. 2: applied studies towards a sociology of language*. London: Routledge & Kegan Paul (Primary Socialization, Language and Education).

Hasan, R. (1991) 'Questions as a mode of learning in everyday talk', in T. Lê and M. McCausland (eds), *Language Education: interaction and development*. Launceston: University of Tasmania.

Hasan, R. (1992) 'Rationality in everyday talk: from process to system', in J. Svartvik (ed.), *Directions in Corpus Linguistic: proceedings of Nobel Symposium 82, Stockholm, 4–8 August 1991*. Berlin and New York: Mouton de Gruyter.

Hasan, R. and Cloran, C. (1990) 'A sociolinguistic interpretation of everyday talk between mothers and children', in M. A. K. Halliday, J. Gibbons and H. Nicholas (eds), *Learning, Keeping and Using Language* Vol. 1. Amsterdam and Philadelphia, PA: John Benjamins.

Hasan, R. and Fries, P. H. (eds) (1995) *On Subject and Theme: a discourse functional perspective*. Amsterdam and Philadelphia, PA: John Benjamins.

Heath, T. (1913) *Aristarchus of Samos: The Ancient Copernicus*. Oxford: Clarendon (republished by Dover Publications 1981).

Henrici, A. (1981) 'Some notes on the systemic generation of a paradigm of the English clause', in M. A. K. Halliday and J. R. Martin (eds),

Readings in Systemic Linguistics. London: Batsford Academic (mimeo original 1966).

Hill, G. C. and Holman, J. S. (1978/83) *Chemistry in Context*. Walton-on-Thames: Nelson.

Hjelmslev, L. (1961) *Prolegomena to a Theory of Language* (Revised English edition, translated by F. J. Whitfield). Madison: University of Wisconsin Press. (Original Danish edition: *Omkring sprogteoriens grundlaeggelse*. Copenhagen: Munksgaard, 1943.)

Huddleston, R. D. (1971) *The Sentence in Written English: a syntactic study based on an analysis of scientific texts*. Cambridge: Cambridge University Press.

Huddleston, R. D., Hudson, R. A., Winter, E. O. and Henrici, A. (1968) *Sentence and Clause in Scientific English*. London: University College London, Communication Research Centre (Report of OSTI Project 'The Linguistic Properties of Scientific English').

Intermediate Science Curriculum Study (1976) *Well-being: Probing the Natural World*. Hong Kong: Martin Educational.

Johnson, A. W. and Earle, T. (1987) *The Evolution of Human Societies: From Foraging Group to Agrarian State*. Stanford, CA: Stanford University Press.

Junior Secondary Science Project (1968) *When Substances are Mixed*. Melbourne: Longman, Cheshire (2nd edn 1973).

King, P. (in press) 'Spoken and written science and engineering text', prepublication draft: English Department, University of Birmingham.

Kuhn, T. S. (1962) *The Structure of Scientific Revolutions*. Chicago: University of Chicago Press (2nd edn, 1970).

Lakoff, G. (1992) 'Metaphor and war: the metaphor system used to justify war in the Gulf' in M. Pütz (ed.), *Thirty Years of Linguistic Evolution*. Amsterdam: John Benjamins.

Lamb, S. M. (1966) Epilegomena to a theory of language. *Romance Philology* 19.

Lamb, S. M. (1999) *Pathways of the Brain: the neurocognitive basis of language*. Amsterdam & Philadelphia: John Benjamins.

Layzer, D. (1990) *Cosmogenesis: the growth of order in the universe*. New York and Oxford: Oxford University Press.

Lee, B. (1985) 'Pierce, Frege, Saussure and Whorf: the semiotic mediation of ontology', in E. Mertz and R. J. Parmentier (eds), *Semiotic mediation: socio-cultural and psychological perspectives*. Orlando: Academic Press.

Lemke, J. L. (1982) 'Talking physics', *Physics Education* 17.

Lemke, J. L. (1983) *Classroom Communication of Science*. Arlington, VA: ERIC Document System (Research in Education series, ED 222 346).

Lemke, J. L. (1984) *Semiotics and Education*. Toronto Semiotic Circle (Monographs, Working Papers and Publications 2).

Lemke, J. L. (1990a) *Talking Science: language, learning, and values*. Norwood, NJ: Ablex.

Lemke, J. L. (1990b) 'Technical discourse and technocratic ideology', in M. A. K. Halliday, J. Gibbons and H. Nicholas (eds), *Learning, Keeping and Using Language: selected papers from the Eighth World Congress of Applied Linguistics, Sydney, 16–21 August 1987*. Amsterdam: John Benjamins. Reprinted in Lemke (1995).

Lemke, J. L. (1993) 'Discourse, dynamics, and social change', *Cultural Dynamics* 6.1–2.

Lemke, J. L. (1995) *Textual Politics: discourse and social dynamics*. London and Bristol, PA: Taylor & Francis.

Léon, J., (2000) 'Traduction automatique et formalisation du langage, les tentatives du Cambridge Language Research Unit (1955–1960)', in P. Desmet, L. Jooken, P. Schmitter, P. Swiggers (eds) *The History of Linguistics and Grammatical Praxis*. Paris: Peeters 369–94.

Lucy, J. A. (1985) 'Whorf's view of the linguistic mediation of thought', in E. Mertz and R. J. Parmentier (eds), *Semiotic mediation: socio-cultural and psychological perspectives*. Orlando: Academic Press.

Lucy, J. A. and Wertsch, J. V. (1987) 'Vygotsky and Whorf: a comparative analysis', in M. Hickman (ed.) *Social and Functional Approaches to Language and Thought*. Orlando: Academic Press.

Mann, W. C. and Matthiessen, C. M. I. M. (1991) 'Functions of language in two frameworks', *Word* 42.3.

Martin, J. R. (1989) *Factual Writing: exploring and challenging social reality*. Oxford: Oxford University Press.

Martin, J. R. (1990) 'Literacy in science: learning to handle text as technology', in F. Christie (ed.), *Literacy for a Changing World*. Hawthorn, Australia: Australian Council for Educational Research. Reprinted in Halliday and Martin (1993).

Martin, J. R. (1992) *English Text: system and structure*. Philadelphia, PA and Amsterdam: John Benjamins.

Martin, J. R. (1993) 'Technology, bureaucracy and schooling: discursive resources and control', *Cultural Dynamics* 6.1–2.

Martin, J. R. and Rothery, J. (1986) *Writing Project Report 1986*. Linguistics Department, University of Sydney (Working Papers in Linguistics 4).

Martin, J. R., Wignell, P., Eggins, S. and Rothery, J. (1988) 'Secret English: discourse technology in a junior secondary school', in L. Gerot, J. Oldenburg-Torr and T. van Leeuwen (eds), *Language and Socialization: home and school* (Proceedings from the Working Conference on Language in Education, 17–21 November 1986). Macquarie University, School of English and Linguistics.

Martin, J. R. and Veel, R. (eds) (1998) *Reading Science: critical and functional perspectives on discourses of science*. London: Routledge.

Mathesius, Vilém (1928) 'On linguistic characterology with illustrations from Modern English', *The Hague, Actes du Premier Congrès International de Linguistes*. Reprinted in Josef Vachek (ed.) (1964), *A Prague School Reader in Linguistics*, Bloomington, IN: Indiana University Press.

Matthiessen, C. (1992) 'Interpreting the textual metafunction', in M. Davies and L. Ravelli (eds), *Advances in Systemic Linguistics: recent theory and practice*. London and New York: Pinter.

Matthiessen, C. (1993) 'The object of study in cognitive science in relation to its construal and enactment in language', *Cultural Dynamics* 6.1–2.

Matthiessen, C. (1995) *Lexicogrammatical Cartography: English systems*. Tokyo: International Language Sciences Publishers.

Matthiessen, C. (1998) 'Construing processes of consciousness: from the commonsense model to the uncommonsense model of cognitive science' in Martin & Veel (eds).

Matthiessen, C. (2000) 'Networks in systemic functional theory: development', in D. G. Butt and C. M. I. M. Matthiessen (eds), *The Meaning Potential of Language: mapping meaning systemically*. Macquarie University Linguistics Department (mimeo).

Matthiessen, C. (in press) 'Frequency profiles of some basic grammatical systems: an interim report', in G. Thompson (ed.), *Proceedings of ISFC 29, Liverpool 2002*.

Maxwell, J. C. (1881) *An Elementary Treatise on Electricity*. Oxford: Clarendon Press.

Medawar, P. (1984) *Pluto's Republic*. Oxford: OUP.

Michalske, T. A. and Bunker, B. C. (1987), 'The fracturing of glass', *Scientific American*. December 1987.

Newton, I. (1704) *Opticks, or a Treatise of the Reflections, Refractions, Inflections and Colours of Light*. New York: Dover Publications 1952 (London: G. Bello and Sons, 1931; based on the Fourth Edition, London 1730; originally published 1704).

Oldenburg-Torr, J. (1990) 'Learning the language and learning through language in early childhood', in M. A. K. Halliday, J. Gibbons and H. Nicholas (eds), *Learning, Keeping and Using Language* Vol. 1. Amsterdam and Philadelphia, PA: John Benjamins.

Oldenburg-Torr, J. (1997) *From Child Tongue to Mother Tongue: a case study of language development in the first two and a half years*. University of

Nottingham: Department of English Studies (Monographs in Systemic Linguistics 9).

Oldroyd, D. (1986) *The Arch of Knowledge: an introductory study of the history of philosophy and methodology of science.* Kensington, Australia: New South Wales University Press.

Osaka Port and Harbour Bureau (n.d.) (c. 1987) *Technoport Osaka: A Centennial Project of the Municipality of Osaka*: Osaka: City of Osaka Port and Harbour Bureau.

Painter, C. (1984) *Into the Mother Tongue: a case study in early language development.* London and Dover, NH: Frances Pinter (Open Linguistics Series).

Painter, C. (1989) 'Learning Language: a functional view of language development', in R. Hasan and J. R. Martin (eds), *Language Development: learning language, learning culture.* Norwood, NJ: Ablex.

Painter, C. (1993) *Learning Through Language: a case study in the development of language as a resource for learning from 2½ to 5 years.* London: Cassell.

Palmer, F. R. (ed.) (1968) *Selected Papers of J. R. Firth 1952–1959.* London: Longman (Longmans Linguistics Library).

Penrose, R. (1989) *The Emperor's New Mind: concerning computers, minds and the laws of physics.* London: Oxford University Press.

Perret, K. and Fiddes, G. (1968/77) *New Primary Maths 5.* Sydney: School Projects.

Phillips, J. (1985) *The Development of Comparisons and Contrasts in Young Children's Language.* University of Sydney, MA Honours thesis.

Priestley, J. (1767) *The History and Present State of Electricity, with Original Experiments.* London.

Prigogine, I. and Stengers, I. (1984) *Order out of Chaos: man's new dialogue with nature.* London: Heinemann.

Ravelli, L. (1985) *Metaphor, Mode and Complexity: an exploration of co-varying patterns.* Linguistics Department, University of Sydney, BA Honours thesis.

Salmon, V. (1966) 'Language planning in seventeenth century England: its context and aims', in C. E. Bazell, J. C. Catford, M. A. K. Halliday and R. H. Robins (eds), *In Memory of J. R. Firth.* London: Longman (Longmans Linguistics Library).

Salmon, V. (1979) *The Study of Language in Seventeenth Century England.* Amsterdam: John Benjamins.

Saussure, F. de (1966) *Course in general linguistics*, ed. C. Bally and A. Sechehaye. Translated by W. Baskin. New York: McGraw–Hill (original French edition: *Cours de linguistique générale*, Geneva, 1915).

Stainer, R. Y., Ingraham, J. L., Wheelis, M. and Painter, P. R. (1987)

General Microbiology (5th edn) Basingstoke and London: Macmillan Education (first published Englewood Cliffs, NJ: Prentice Hall, 1957).

Sugeno, M. (1993) 'Toward intelligent computing' (plenary paper presented to 5th International Fuzzy Systems Association World Congress, Seoul, July 1993).

Taylor, C. V. (1979) *The English of High School Textbooks*. Canberra: Australian Government Publishing Service (Education Research and Development Committee, Report 18).

Thibault, P. J. (1986) *Text, Discourse and Context: a social semiotic perspective.* Toronto: Victoria University (Toronto Semiotic Circle Monographs, Working Papers and Prepublications, 3).

Thibault, P. J. (1991) 'Grammar, technocracy and the noun: technocratic values and cognitive linguistics', in E. Ventola (ed.), *Functional and Systemic Linguistics: approaches and uses*. Berlin and New York: Mouton de Gruyter.

Thibault, P. J. (1997) *Re-reading Saussure: the dynamics of signs in social life.* London and New York: Routledge.

Trubetzkoy, N. S. (1967) *Principles of Phonology*, translated by Christiane A. M. Baltaxe. Göttingen: Vandenhoeck & Ruprecht (original German edition *Grundzüge der Phonologie*, Prague, 1939).

Vilenkin, A. (1987) "Cosmic Strings", Scientific American, December.

Wells, C. G. (1986) *The Meaning Makers: children learning language and using language to learn*. Cambridge: Cambridge University Press.

Wells, R. (1960) 'Nominal and verbal style', in T. A. Sebeok (ed.), *Style in Language*. Cambridge, MA: MIT Technology Press; New York and London: John Wiley.

White, J. (1986) 'The writing on the wall: the beginning or end of a girl's career?', *Women's Studies International Forum*, 9.5. pp. 561–74. Reprinted in Christie, F. (ed.), *Writing in Schools: reader*. Geelong, Victoria: Deakin University Press, pp. 61–72.

Whorf, B. L. (1941/56) 'The relation of habitual thought and behaviour to language' in Leslie Spier (ed.), *Language Culture and Personality: essays in memory of Edward Sapir*. Menasha, WI: Sapir Memorial Publications Fund. Reprinted in J. B. Carroll (ed.).

Whorf, B. L. (1950) 'An American Indian model of the universe', *International Journal of American Linguistics*, 16. Reprinted in Carroll (ed), 1956.

Wignell, P., Martin, J. R. and Eggins, S. (1987/93) 'The discourse of geography: ordering and explaining the experiential world', in S. Eggins et al., *Writing Project Report 1987*. Sydney: University of Sydney Linguistics Department (Working Papers in Linguistics 5). Reprinted in Halliday & Martin 1993.

INDEX

abstract, abstraction(s) xi, xvii, xix, xxi, 12,14, 17, 18–20, 27, 30–5, 38, 43, 46–8, 54, 61, 64–7, 72, 79, 87, 94–5, 111, 113, 115, 119, 121, 128, 143–4, 150–1, 154, 161, 168, 173, 180, 191, 194, 197, 212, 214, 216–7, 224

actor 57, 65, 100, 103, 146, 172, 192

adjective(s) xvi, 15, 20, 38, 40, 65, 74–7, 90, 100, 103–4, 108, 110, 173, 188, 193, 206, 212–5

adolescence xix, 25, 27, 91–2, 198

adult(s) xviii, 12, 17, 26–7, 28–30, 33, 51, 54, 93, 104, 115–6, 182, 184, 192, 199, 217–8, 224

adverb(s), adverbial 34, 40, 55, 75, 109, 110, 173, 187–8

agnate 29, 34–6, 39, 74, 84, 87, 113, 116, 131, 141–2, 147

ambiguity, ambiguous xx, 13, 30, 48, 62, 86, 93, 106, 131, 162, 169–72, 197

Arabic 94, 213

astrolabe 114, 143–4, 179, 213

attic, doric 102–4, 108, 113–6, 121–2, 128, 130–2

Bazerman, C. 180, 182, 212

biology, biological 17, 22, 26, 47, 53, 59, 97, 140, 159, 161, 176, 217–8, 222–3

Bohm, D. 129–30, 222

botany 205

brain 11, 17, 22, 51, 53, 109, 123, 208, 214

bureaucratic discourse xxi, 131, 158, 179

category, categories xii, 10–12, 14, 16, 43, 46–7, 51–2, 55–6, 63–6, 75, 78–9, 84–5, 92–4, 97, 101, 107, 109–11, 119–20, 126, 128, 132, 134, 141, 149, 153, 162, 166, 183–4, 186
  grammatical 10, 40, 56, 88, 90, 110, 188

chain 38, 61, 64, 79, 125

Chancer, G. 114–5, 123, 143–5, 147, 162, 179, 213

chemistry 39, 59, 82, 86, 140, 154, 168, 176, 185, 199, 201, 205, 215, 223

children('s), child('s) xvi-xix, 8–9, 11–22, 25–32, 37, 43, 52, 59, 80, 86, 89–93, 100, 106, 115–6, 118, 122, 124–5, 133, 158, 163, 171–3, 182–4, 197–201, 221

Chinese xvi, xviii, xxii, 22, 48–9, 65, 131, 201, 203, 208

Chomsky, N. 58, 219

classificatory 15, 204

classifier(s) 34, 38–40, 57, 60, 75, 78–9, 82, 108, 132, 141, 189–90, 192–3

clause xiii, xxiii, 58, 62–3, 71, 73–5, 77–8, 80–5, 92–5, 102–4, 109–14, 116, 119–20, 124–5, 130–1, 142, 144–52, 156–7, 164, 166–9, 171–5, 182–3, 185–98, 205, 207, 213, 216–7

complex(es) 31, 33, 35, 44, 55–6,
  76–7, 90, 103, 144, 146–7, 150,
  183, 188
  nexus 34–5, 40, 57, 73, 77, 80–4, 90,
  103, 110, 188
  type(s) 73–4, 84, 95, 111–2, 114,
  122, 128, 130, 144, 185–6, 191,
  193
commonsense xvii, 7–8, 12–5, 22,
  24–5, 27–8, 32–3, 43–8, 59, 92, 102,
  115, 118–20, 128, 160–1, 183–4,
  188–9, 204, 216, 218, 224
component(s) xiv, xviii, xx, xxii, 50,
  52, 59, 65, 69, 83, 148, 151, 156,
  175, 204, 208
computer(s), computational,
  computerized xiii, xxii-xxiv, 22, 96,
  170, 181, 224–5
congruent (lx) xvi, 14–6, 20, 22, 27–8,
  30, 32, 34, 36–40, 45–6, 48, 56–7,
  62–3, 66, 68, 71–5, 77–9, 80–5, 87,
  89–90, 92–4, 106–7, 109–18, 120–1,
  124, 127, 129, 131–3, 140, 152, 172,
  190–1, 193, 196–8
conjunction 34, 40, 52, 68, 73–5, 77,
  80, 90, 104, 108, 110, 111, 173, 188
conjunctive 40, 58, 73, 75, 85, 108
consciousness 9, 17, 26, 51, 53–4, 118,
  187
constituent 83, 109
construe xvi-xvii, xx, xxiv, 9–16, 21–
  3, 25, 31–2, 34, 36–9, 44–7, 51–8,
  61, 63, 65–6, 68–9, 71, 73, 75–7,
  79–80, 82–3, 85, 89–92, 104, 107,
  109–11, 114–5, 119–21, 124–9,
  132–4, 157–8, 182, 185, 187–8, 190,
  193–5, 198, 200, 202, 204, 208–9,
  212–9, 221, 223, 225
content xix, 7, 17, 72, 97, 123, 149,
  152–3, 168, 193, 195–6, 202, 222
  plane xv, 58, 89, 94, 210
culture(s) xix, 8–9, 12, 16, 18, 23, 94,
  103, 115, 120, 166, 209, 212

Dalton, J. 38, 162, 179
Darwin, C; Darwinism 17, 114, 129,
  162, 179
Davidse, K. 49, 101

Dawkins, R. 8, 133
declarative 70–1, 119
definitions 87, 144, 162–4, 203, 213
deictic 31, 57, 62, 77–8, 82, 124, 172,
  189–90
delicacy xii, 141
Derewianka, B. 25, 32, 91–2, 100, 115
dialect(s), dialectal 8, 12, 22, 96, 122,
  141, 202
dialogic 13, 54, 118–9, 133
dictionary 105, 195, 203, 205
discourse(s) xi, xv-xvii, xix-xxi, 8–9,
  18–9, 21, 30, 43–50, 58, 60, 62,
  67–73, 87, 89–90, 93–6, 108, 112,
  114–5, 120, 122–8, 131–4, 141–58,
  167–8, 176, 178–80, 181–5, 191–6,
  199–201, 206–7, 211–7, 223–5
  scientific xx, 18, 47, 67, 75, 89, 96,
  102, 104, 107, 123–5, 127, 148–9,
  155, 157, 160–1, 167, 174, 178,
  182, 184, 192, 199, 210, 212, 223–4
  technical xix, 33, 39–40, 131
  technocratic 131, 180
discursive(ly) 39, 45, 50, 54, 61, 69,
  71–2, 87–8, 117, 125–7, 194, 197,
  199
disjunction 22, 48, 88, 225

Edelman, G. 17, 26, 53, 92, 118
English xii-xiii, xvi-xviii, xx, 10–1, 18,
  22, 25, 28–30, 34, 38, 40, 48–9, 55,
  60–2, 64–70, 74–5, 100, 102, 104–5,
  107, 109, 114–5, 122–3, 129, 131,
  144–6, 148, 153–62, 168, 170–1,
  173–4, 176, 184–5, 187–8, 190–1,
  195, 201–3, 208, 215–8, 220–1,
  224
  scientific xxii, 58, 64, 84, 89, 112,
  114, 140–1, 143, 145, 155–6,
  158–9, 160–2, 170, 179–82, 185,
  187, 191, 201–2, 205, 213, 215,
  220
entropy 46, 128, 153
epithet 31, 40, 57, 62, 75–6, 78, 82,
  103, 108, 110, 189–90
Europe(an) 12, 15, 18, 38, 65, 94, 96,
  126, 173–4, 195, 200, 203, 213, 216,
  224

evolution(ary) xv, 8, 14, 16–7, 21, 27–8, 30, 53, 59, 67, 89, 94, 105, 114, 116–8, 121–2, 140, 155, 180–2, 192–4, 198, 208–10, 212, 215, 217, 221
expansion xvii, 33, 62–3, 123, 146, 149, 182, 190

Firth, J.R. xii, xv, 7, 219
foreground(-ed/-ing) xi, 50, 70, 122, 130–1, 148–50, 152–3, 208
function(al) xv, xxi, 8, 11, 15, 20–22, 26, 40, 43, 47–50, 53, 55–7, 61–4, 69–70, 75–6, 78–80, 82, 92–3, 95, 97, 103, 109–10, 115, 119, 125, 128, 131–3, 140–2, 146, 148, 154–5, 158, 161, 164, 174, 176, 179–80, 185, 190, 192–5, 202, 210, 216–7, 221
fuzzy 11, 74, 183, 202

Galileo 18, 59, 94, 114, 205, 216
genre(s) xx, 133, 143, 181, 212, 217
geography 162, 164
German 22, 174, 203, 213
grammar(s) xi–xvii, xix–xx, xxii–xxiii, 8–20, 22–3, 26–7, 30–2, 43–55, 58–66, 68–9, 71–3, 75, 78, 80, 83–4, 86–7, 89–90, 92–6, 102–4, 107, 109–10, 112–4, 127–30, 132–4, 143, 151, 153–6, 158, 161–2, 166–7, 172–4, 176, 179–80, 181–4, 186–92, 194–5, 197–8, 205, 207–14, 217–8, 224–5
grammatical xiii–xvii, xix–xxiii, 9–11, 31–2, 34–6, 51–2, 56–8, 68–70, 74–6, 83–4, 86–90, 102–4, 118–21, 123–27, 129–30, 158–9, 182–3, 187–8, 195–8, 205–9, 212
    analysis 176, 179, 188, 198
    category/-ies 10, 40, 56, 65–6, 79, 88, 90, 110, 188
    class(es) xvi, xxi, 15–6, 32, 38, 40, 52, 75, 103, 107, 109, 172, 185, 191
    construction(s) 46, 102, 130, 164, 202
    function(s) 40, 56, 75, 103, 109

metaphor(s) xvii, xix–xxi, 19–20, 38–40, 43, 45–7, 56, 58, 60–1, 63, 69, 75–6, 79–81, 83, 86–7, 89, 91–3, 95–6, 104, 106–11, 113–6, 120, 123, 126–7, 129, 133, 143, 147, 150, 152, 156, 158, 162, 172, 174–6, 178–9, 191–3, 197, 214–6, 220, 224–5
structure(s) xxii, 52, 65, 80, 102–3, 109, 119, 168–9, 172, 191, 196, 198, 208–9
systems(s) xiii–xiv, xxii–xxiii, 9–10, 124, 183
grammatics 49–50
Greek xvi, 22, 38, 65–7, 94, 125, 133–4, 144, 174, 212–4, 218

Hjelmslev, L. xii, xv, 54, 219
Hopi 44, 224
Huddleston, R. xxii, 112, 158
hypotaxis, hypotactic 33, 35, 73, 84, 103, 144

ideational xx, 26–7, 44, 50–1, 53–5, 66–7, 69, 87, 95, 115, 127, 131
ideology(-ical) 95, 176, 210, 212
infant(s), infancy 17, 25–6, 32, 54, 59, 86, 89–90, 106, 115, 171
instantial 39, 44, 62, 73, 87–8, 95 117, 124, 126, 192–4
intensive 58, 74, 101, 154
interface(-ing) 18, 54, 75, 94, 222
interpersonal xv, xx, 9, 26, 50–1, 54, 69, 95, 115, 119, 212
intonation 54, 70
Italian xxii, 18, 22, 49, 114, 174, 203, 205, 213, 216

jargon 161, 182, 202

language(s) xi–xxiv, 7–12, 17–23, 24–27, 29–30, 32, 38–9, 45–6, 49–54, 58–9, 61, 63–5, 88–91, 94–6, 107, 109, 113–6, 118–23, 126, 128–33, 140, 149–50, 156–62, 164, 166–8, 172–4, 176, 178–80, 181–4, 187–90, 195, 197–8, 199–214, 217–25

everyday 128, 160, 182, 188, 195, 211, 225
  human 37, 90, 94, 96, 208, 220–1
  natural 9, 23, 50, 59, 95, 109, 119, 181–2, 204, 208, 212, 218, 223
  scientific 122, 160, 179–82, 184, 195, 198, 201, 204–5, 208, 217, 224
  spoken 22, 43, 120, 168, 182–3, 225
  standard 48, 122–3, 181–2
  technical 20, 67
  written 12, 18, 27, 120–2, 168, 211, 224–5
Lemke, J. 18, 50–1, 66, 95, 118–9, 131, 180, 182, 200, 207, 217, 219
lexical xiii, xvi–xvii, xxi, 10, 36, 38, 51, 56, 58, 62–4, 70, 79, 87, 89, 102–8, 110, 123–4, 127, 149, 151, 160, 183, 191, 205–6, 212, 214, 216
  density 31, 33, 74, 157, 162, 168–9, 172, 195–6
  metaphor(s) 79, 87, 106–7, 127, 191, 214, 216
lexicogrammar, lexicogrammatical xiv–xvi, xx, 25, 51, 54–5, 58, 89–90, 93, 95, 104, 109, 119, 122, 141, 145, 150, 183, 185, 188, 201, 219, 223
linguistic xxii–xxiii, 21, 26, 104, 132, 140, 182, 202, 205, 207–8
linguistics xxii–xxiii, 92, 219–20
literacy 12, 27, 120, 199, 211
literary xi, 8, 96, 166
logical xvii, 9, 20–1, 26, 36, 43–4, 50, 67–8, 83, 92, 123, 129, 153, 157, 177–9, 185, 213
  logical-semantic 39, 58, 60, 68, 73–4, 95, 104, 111, 124, 186, 188, 191
logogenetic 88, 117, 132
logos 220

Martin, J. 25–6, 49–50, 54, 64, 66–7, 69, 72, 87–8, 95–6, 124, 126, 133, 158, 162, 164, 179–82, 198
mathematics xix, 66, 94, 119, 159, 162, 167, 174, 178, 180, 194, 216–7
Mathesius, V. 109, 122
Mathiessen, C. xii–xiv, xxiii, 29, 40, 49, 53, 69, 108, 124, 133, 183

meaning(s) xi–xvi, xviii–xxi, xxiv, 8–14, 16–8, 21, 24–9, 31, 36, 38–9, 43–4, 48, 49–56, 60–1, 64–6, 69, 87, 92–5, 105, 107, 109, 113–28, 132–4, 150, 158, 160, 164–5, 170, 182–3, 188–9, 191, 194, 198, 202, 207–8, 210–11, 214, 216, 219, 222–3, 225
  category xvi, 65–6, 107, 126
  ideational 44, 50, 69
  meaning-creating 25, 43, 49, 195, 197
  meaning-making xi, 71
  potential xiii–xv, xviii–xx, 14, 27, 33, 39, 46, 54, 60, 93, 116–7, 122, 182, 192
medieval 94, 114, 122, 144, 156, 174, 202–3, 213
meronomy 67
metaphor(s) (see also grammatical metaphor(s)) xv–xvii, 27–8, 32, 36, 43–8, 53, 55–6, 66–7, 71, 73, 75–83, 86–9, 93, 95, 107, 109–10, 113–7, 125–30, 134, 191–4, 207
metaphoric(al) xvi, xix–xx, 17, 19–20, 27–8, 32, 34, 36–7, 39–40, 43–4, 46–8, 55–6, 58, 60–1, 64, 66–7, 72–84, 86, 89, 91–4, 100, 104–18, 121, 126–7, 131–2, 134, 152, 156, 158, 191, 196, 198, 214–5, 221
morphology(-ical) 65, 102, 107, 130, 150, 183, 204–5, 207, 210, 212

network xii–xiii, xv, xviii, xx, xxii–xxiii, 183
Newton, I. xx, 18, 37, 59–60, 68, 72, 87, 94, 114, 117, 125, 145–50, 157, 162, 167, 174–5, 179–80, 205–6, 214, 216–7
nexus 31, 34–5, 40, 43, 57, 73–4, 77, 80–4, 90, 103, 110, 188
Nigel 13, 90, 92, 100
nominal 9, 21–2, 31, 33–40, 43, 52, 55–8, 61–3, 67–8, 70–1, 73–4, 76–8, 80, 82, 84–5, 89, 93, 103–4, 108–111, 114, 121, 123–6, 131, 133, 141–2, 144, 146–7, 149–54, 157, 167, 169, 171–3, 185–98, 205, 213, 216, 221, 224

nominalization(s) xvi, 32, 37, 39, 61, 66–7, 72, 78, 82, 107–8, 111, 132, 143, 148, 150–1, 157, 185, 189–90, 194, 215–6, 224

noun(s) xvi-xvii, 13–6, 19–20, 32, 35, 38, 40, 44, 55–6, 61–2, 65–6, 68, 73, 75–82, 85, 90, 94–5, 100, 103–4, 106–11, 121, 124–6, 129, 133–4, 142–4, 147, 150, 152, 157, 159, 169, 171–4, 176, 184–5, 189–90, 193, 198, 206–7, 212–7, 224

ontogenetic(ally) 30–1, 88–9, 115, 120, 132, 220

Optiks (Newton's) 37, 60, 68, 114, 125, 145, 150, 167, 179, 206

Painter, C. xvi, 25, 32, 35, 89–90, 97, 115

paradigmatic(ally) xi-xii, xviii, xxii, 63, 113, 123–4, 127, 158

passive xiii, 65, 122, 146

philosophy 51, 153, 157, 179, 203, 219, 225

phonology 17

phrase(s) 34, 40, 55, 62–3, 73–5, 77–8, 90, 104, 108–10, 114, 142, 150, 169, 173, 183, 187–8, 190, 213

physics 98, 128–9, 140, 150–1, 159, 161, 217, 222–3

plural xiv, 11–2

polarity xv, xxiii

preposition(al) 33–4, 40, 55, 74–5, 77–8, 90, 93, 104, 108–111, 142, 150, 169, 173, 187–8, 213

Priestley, J. 60, 150, 154, 162, 179

prosodic(ally) xiii, 50

protolanguage 17, 26–7, 32, 89–90, 115

rankshift(-ed, -ing) 35, 63, 73, 84–5, 114, 142

reader(s) xv, 70–2, 131, 161, 166, 170, 172, 177–9, 194, 201

reality xiv, xvii, xx, 10, 16, 21, 44, 52, 107, 125, 130, 152, 157–8, 160, 176, 183, 197, 199, 208–9, 211, 216, 218, 220, 223

realization xvi, 54, 75, 93, 107, 150, 214, 218–9, 221, 223

reasoning 20, 27, 50, 61, 67–8, 83, 88, 92, 95, 123–6, 131, 145, 149, 160–1, 174, 184, 191, 193, 195, 197

reconstrual, reconstru(-ed, -es, -ing) xvii, 13–6, 19, 39, 43, 46, 55–60, 64, 66, 82–3, 87–9, 91–6, 107, 118, 120–1, 128–9, 189–91, 198, 210, 214–5

register(s) xv, xxii, 18, 22, 39, 63, 71, 89, 94, 116, 121, 123, 132, 140–1, 158, 174, 179, 182, 205, 216–8, 224

relational 33, 43, 58, 62, 101, 103, 144, 154–5, 157, 185, 213

relator(s) 21, 36, 40, 43, 47, 58, 68, 73–9, 84–5, 90, 95, 103–4, 108, 110–11, 132, 188, 191

representational 51, 54

rheme 69–70, 72, 124, 148

rhetorical 140, 148, 153, 181, 206

rhythm 70–1

Russian 22, 174

Saussure, F. xi-xii, 218–9

science xv, xix-xxi, 13, 18–20, 43–5, 48–9, 59–60, 63, 66–8, 71–2, 87–8, 94–6, 100, 104, 107–8, 112–23, 125, 128–34, 140, 143–4, 153, 157–62, 164, 167–8, 174, 176, 178–85, 189, 194, 198–207, 210–25

sciences 20–1, 133, 140–1, 219–20
  biological 59
  natural xvii, 164
  physical 141, 217

scientific 16, 45–9, 58–61, 64–7, 72, 74–5, 88–9, 112–29, 132–4, 145–9, 152–62, 166–71, 174–98, 199–25
  discourse(s) xv, xx, 18, 47, 49, 67, 75, 89, 96, 102, 104, 107, 123–5, 127, 134, 148–9, 155, 157, 160–1, 167, 174, 178, 182, 184, 192, 199, 210, 212, 223–4
  English xxii, 58, 64, 84, 112, 114, 140–1, 145, 155–6, 158–9, 161–2, 170, 179–82, 185, 187, 191, 201–2, 205, 213, 215, 220

knowledge xx, 45, 47, 92, 95, 102, 119, 160, 181, 184, 194, 204–5, 211, 216

language(s) 122, 160, 179–82, 184, 195, 198, 201, 204–5, 208, 217, 224

text(s) xxii, 61, 109, 116, 121, 125, 132, 159, 162, 166, 181, 185, 192, 194–8, 207

theory(-ies) 38, 45–6, 51, 59, 66–7, 95, 107, 117, 123, 127, 182, 185, 192, 207–8, 212, 214, 218, 223

writing(s) xx, 48–9, 60, 74, 84, 112, 119, 153, 157, 161–2, 167–9, 171, 176, 178, 184, 195, 201

semantic xvi, 9, 11–2, 14, 27, 29, 34–6, 38–40, 43–5, 48, 51, 54–7, 62–8, 71, 74–9, 83, 85, 88, 90, 93–5, 100–1, 104, 107, 109–13, 116, 122, 124, 126–7, 131–3, 141, 152, 157, 162, 164 , 171, 176, 178, 185, 187–8, 196, 210, 213–7

category(ies) 11, 101, 107, 110

discontinuity(ies) 162, 176, 178

element 40, 76–77, 79, 83, 188

feature(s) 38, 48, 64, 66, 78, 85

figure 57, 83, 90

function(s) 75–6

junction(s) xvi, 38–40, 44, 48, 66, 78–9, 88, 94–5, 100, 107, 109, 111–2, 116, 126, 132

space 11, 14, 68, 113, 122

semantics xvi, xx, 17–9, 29, 58, 73, 75, 87, 89–90, 94, 107, 118, 120, 123, 188, 210, 218–9

semiotic xvii, xix-xxi, xxiv, 11, 14, 16–8, 22, 26, 32, 43–4, 47, 49–50, 52–4, 56, 59–61, 63, 66, 71, 73, 79, 94–6, 110, 113, 115–23, 127–33, 140, 147, 152, 156, 158, 182, 188, 194, 197, 207, 210–11, 218–24

semogenic xii, xiv-xv, 8, 10–11, 16, 25, 33, 37–9, 61, 66, 94, 113, 124, 126, 133, 194, 207, 213–4

sign 17, 54, 86, 97, 169, 218–9

social 8, 17, 25–6, 51, 53–4, 94, 119, 140, 210, 217–9, 221–2, 224

speech 17, 33, 48, 62, 70, 89, 115, 120, 129, 133, 157, 168, 172, 181, 195, 225

strat(-al, -um) xvi, xx, 17, 44, 54, 58, 75, 89, 93, 183, 219, 223

stratification xvii, 53–5, 58, 89, 118, 219

style(s) xx, 33, 36, 102, 108, 114–5, 132, 212–3, 217

Sugeno, M. xxiii, 22

syntax 183, 207

syntactic 15, 58, 162, 169

syntagmatic xii, 86, 113, 127

systemic xii-xiii, xxii-xxiii, 13, 27, 33, 39, 44, 47, 49–50, 58, 62, 68, 87–8, 95, 104, 118, 120, 126–7, 158, 192–4

taxonomy(ies) 38, 63–4, 66, 83, 93–4, 109–11, 132, 151, 164, 166, 193, 205, 216

taxonomic 38, 63, 66, 83, 94, 166, 205

technical xv-xvii, 9, 19–20, 32–3, 37–40, 43–4, 46, 60–1, 64, 70, 72, 87–9, 94–5, 115–8, 120–1, 123, 126–8, 143–4, 150–1, 160–4, 179, 184–6, 191–5, 198, 204–7, 214–7, 219, 224

concept(s) 88, 107, 117, 126, 164, 191, 205

discourse xix, 33, 39, 40, 131

knowledge xix, 19, 27–9, 32, 43, 48–9, 94, 116, 127

taxonomy(ies) 60, 95, 147, 153, 162, 164, 193, 204, 216

terminology 39, 67, 162, 166, 184, 205, 217

terms xix, 19, 38, 44, 61, 87–8, 94, 115, 147, 150, 161–3, 184, 193, 201, 205–6, 212, 214–5

technology xv, xxi, xxiii, 18, 22, 63, 95, 121, 124, 128, 156, 176, 212–3, 216, 221, 225

technological 16, 21, 67, 121, 144, 153, 210, 221, 224

tenor 140, 194

tense xiv, xxii, 40, 62, 75, 108, 122, 124, 208

terminology 39, 65, 67, 162, 166, 184, 205, 217
theme 39, 44, 69–73, 87, 91, 95, 122, 124–5, 142, 146, 148–51, 153, 166, 193–4
thematic 44, 69–70, 122, 125, 127, 133, 142, 148, 151–2
Thibault, P. xii, 95, 119
translation xxii, 93, 181, 208, 213

unpack(-ed, -ing) 24, 28–30, 32, 36–40, 44–8, 73, 79, 81, 87–8, 92–3, 104, 116, 118, 127–8

variation xv, 31, 33, 36, 74, 106, 109, 113, 140, 149, 166, 168, 187, 202, 208–9, 218, 221

verb(s) xvi, 13–6, 20, 32–3, 35–6, 38, 40, 43–4, 55, 61, 65–6, 75–9, 85, 90, 95–6, 100, 103–10, 117, 126, 129–30, 132–3, 149, 152, 154–5, 157, 170–3, 174–6, 184–6, 191, 193, 212–5, 224
vocabulary 10, 63, 104, 116, 122, 130, 160–2, 172–3, 176, 183–5, 205, 207–8

Wharf, B.L. 44, 92, 209, 216, 219, 224
Wignell, P. 26, 64, 158, 162, 164, 179–80
writing xvii, xix-xxi, 12, 14, 19, 22, 29, 32–3, 60, 74, 84, 104, 112, 114–5, 119–21, 147, 150, 153, 157, 160–2, 166–9, 171, 174, 176, 178, 184, 195, 199, 201, 203–4, 214, 225
  scientific xx, 60, 74, 84, 112, 119, 153, 157, 161–2, 167–9, 171, 176, 178, 184, 195, 201